MW01438077

Rhetoric, Politics and Society

Series editors
Alan Finlayson
University of East Anglia
Norfolk, UK

James Martin
Goldsmiths, University of London
London, UK

Kendall Phillips
Syracuse University
Syracuse, NY, USA

Rhetoric lies at the intersection of a variety of disciplinary approaches and methods, drawing upon the study of language, history, culture and philosophy to understand the persuasive aspects of communication in all its modes: spoken, written, argued, depicted and performed. This series presents the best international research in rhetoric that develops and exemplifies the multifaceted and cross-disciplinary exploration of practices of persuasion and communication. It seeks to publish texts that openly explore and expand rhetorical knowledge and enquiry, be it in the form of historical scholarship, theoretical analysis or contemporary cultural and political critique. The editors welcome proposals for monographs that explore contemporary rhetorical forms, rhetorical theories and thinkers, and rhetorical themes inside and across disciplinary boundaries. For informal enquiries, questions, as well as submitting proposals, please contact the editors: Alan Finlayson: a.finlayson@uea.ac.uk James Martin: j.martin@gold.ac.uk Kendall Phillips: kphillip@syr.edu

More information about this series at
http://www.palgrave.com/series/14497

Giuseppe Ballacci

Political Theory between Philosophy and Rhetoric

Politics as Transcendence and Contingency

palgrave
macmillan

Giuseppe Ballacci
University of Minho
Braga, Portugal

Rhetoric, Politics and Society
ISBN 978-1-349-95292-2   ISBN 978-1-349-95293-9 (eBook)
https://doi.org/10.1057/978-1-349-95293-9

Library of Congress Control Number: 2017959840

© The Editor(s) (if applicable) and The Author(s) 2018
The author(s) has/have asserted their right(s) to be identified as the author(s) of this work in accordance with the Copyright, Designs and Patents Act 1988.
This work is subject to copyright. All rights are solely and exclusively licensed by the Publisher, whether the whole or part of the material is concerned, specifically the rights of translation, reprinting, reuse of illustrations, recitation, broadcasting, reproduction on microfilms or in any other physical way, and transmission or information storage and retrieval, electronic adaptation, computer software, or by similar or dissimilar methodology now known or hereafter developed.
The use of general descriptive names, registered names, trademarks, service marks, etc. in this publication does not imply, even in the absence of a specific statement, that such names are exempt from the relevant protective laws and regulations and therefore free for general use.
The publisher, the authors and the editors are safe to assume that the advice and information in this book are believed to be true and accurate at the date of publication. Neither the publisher nor the authors or the editors give a warranty, express or implied, with respect to the material contained herein or for any errors or omissions that may have been made. The publisher remains neutral with regard to jurisdictional claims in published maps and institutional affiliations.

Cover illustration: Qweek

Printed on acid-free paper

This Palgrave Macmillan imprint is published by Springer Nature
The registered company is Macmillan Publishers Ltd.
The registered company address is: The Campus, 4 Crinan Street, London, N1 9XW, United Kingdom

ACKNOWLEDGMENTS

This book has been written over a long period of time. In this period, I have incurred many debts of gratitude. The book grew out of a PhD dissertation, completed in 2010 at Universidad Autónoma de Madrid. My first gratitude thus goes to my two supervisors: Rafael del Águila, who unfortunately passed away some months before completing my PhD, and Elena Garcia Guitián. I am much indebted to both of them for their support and contribution to my research. I would like also to thank Javier Roiz of Universidad Complutense de Madrid, who is responsible for my first contact with many of the ideas and thinkers I deal with in this book. The thesis was converted into a book while I was a Postdoctoral Research Fellow at the Centre for Humanistic Studies of the University of Minho. I would like to thank all my colleagues there and in particular those of the Political Theory Group, which in the meantime has been transformed into a new independent research centre affiliated to the University of Minho: the Centre for Ethics, Politics and Society. I received precious comments and advice from: João Rosas, David Álvarez, Alexandra Abranches, Roberto Merrill, José Colen, and Pedro Martins. As a PhD student I benefited from a four-year grant from the Comunidad Autónoma de Madrid and as Postdoctoral Research Fellow from a six-year grant from the Portuguese Foundation of Science and Technology (both co-funded by the European Social Fund). These grants also sponsored periods of research abroad that have been very important for the development of the book. In particular I would like to thank Claudia Baracchi, who I met when I was a visiting PhD student at the New School for Social Research, and Linda Zerilli, who I met at the University of Chicago in the course of the period I spent there as visiting researcher. In addition I need to thank a number of colleagues for their encouragement and help during the process of writing, as well as for the conversations we had that contributed to clarify, develop, or problematize my position on many ideas I discuss in the book. Among them are: Alessandro Ferrara, Justine Lacroix, Jean-Yves Pranchere, Thomas Bern, Louis Carré, Antoon Braeckman, Paula Diehl, Mihaela Mihai, and Mathias Thaler. At Palgrave Macmillan, Imogen Gordon Clark has delivered important support during the preparation of the manuscript and has been very patient with my delays and hesitations. Furthermore, I have to express my gratitude to Palgrave Macmillan's anonymous reviewer, who wrote very positive comments and suggestions on the original book proposal. My deepest gratitude however goes to James Martin, one of the editors of the series in which this book is included. Beyond supporting this project from the beginning, he has read the whole manuscript and offered excellent advice, comments, and critical remarks. A different kind of gratitude goes finally to the people who are closest to me: my parents and my partner Raquel. My PhD dissertation was dedicated to them, and I also want to dedicate this book to them. It is one of the inconveniences of rhetoric to make formulas, which are used countless of times, appear a bit hollow. But I have to say that without their love, support, and understanding, writing this book would have been much more difficult.

Chapter 3 is based on material published in 2015 with the title "Reassessing the Rhetoric Revival in Political Theory: Cicero, Eloquence, and the Best Form of Life" in *Redescriptions: Political Thought, Conceptual History and Feminist Theory*, vol. 18(2). Chapter 5 was published in a slightly different form in 2017 as "Richard Rorty's Unfulfilled Humanism and the Public/Private Divide", *The Review of Politics*, vol. 79(3). A version of Chapter 6 was published with the title "Actualizing Democratic Citizenship: Arendt and Classical Rhetoric on Judgment and Persuasion" in P. Kitromilides (ed.), *Athenian Legacies. European Debates on Citizenship* (Florence: Leo S. Olschki, 2014). I am grateful to the publishers for permission to reuse these works.

Lisbon, July 2017

Contents

1 Introduction 1

Part I 11

2 Between Philosophy and Rhetoric: Plato and Aristotle 13

3 The Union of Philosophy and Rhetoric: Cicero and Quintilian 51

Part II 85

4 Politics as Transcendence: Leo Strauss 87

5 Politics as Contingency: Richard Rorty 119

6 Politics as Transcendence and Contingency: Hannah Arendt 149

7 Afterword 183

Bibliography 187

Index 207

CHAPTER 1

Introduction

According to the ancient tradition of rhetoric, one of the most important moments in the composition of a discourse is that of *inventio*: the discovery of the argumentative premises from which to start developing the discourse. The search for these premises was considered to be a creative and ingenious process of looking over usual arguments, or common places (also known in rhetoric as "topics of invention", from the Greek *topoi*, which means places), in order to locate the resources to construct one's own discourse. Ingenuity and creativity were considered necessary skills in this process, because only through them can we find unexpected and unusual connections between apparently distant questions and develop new arguments. In ancient rhetoric this process was systematized into a method known as *ars topica*. Rhetoricians believed that this art has to be accompanied by another—*ars critica*—which submits to critical analysis the arguments found in order to check their logical consistency. Giambattista Vico, one of last exponents of the long tradition of rhetoric, explained that these two arts should go together, because without one the other would have been crippled. *Ars topica*, as he said, "finds and amasses" while *ars critica* "divides and removes."[1] Nevertheless for him the former had a certain priority, since as he wrote in the *Scienza Nuova* it is:

© The Author(s) 2018
G. Ballacci, *Political Theory between Philosophy and Rhetoric*, Rhetoric, Politics and Society,
https://Doi.org/10.1057/978-1-349-95293-9_1

an art of regulating well the primary operation of our mind by noting the commonplaces that must all be run over in order to know all there is in a thing that one desires to know well, that is, completely.[2]

Vico stressed in particular the creative aspect of *ars topica*. For him this art has the great merit of making minds inventive and providing discourse the breadth and fecundity typical of a cultivated intellect. A discourse developed through *ars topica*, Vico said, is one that gives the impression of not having left anything relevant out of it.[3]

Looking at the debate in contemporary democratic deliberation and legitimacy, it seems that some of those involved have made a good use of *ars topica*, recovering central insights of that tradition of which this art is a part: rhetoric. Indeed, in the last two decades, an increasing number of theorists have turned to the ancient tradition of rhetoric to find arguments to overcome the hyper-rationalist paradigms of public deliberation. They have recovered ancient rhetoric (mainly Aristotle's version of rhetoric), in order to find support for developing a better account of democratic deliberation: less biased in evaluating the role of extra-rational mechanisms of communication and judgment, and more attentive to the different forms they take according to their aims and contexts. It is a new and growing trend that has been labelled by one of its exponents, Bryan Garsten, a "rhetoric revival in political theory."[4] In effect, as Garsten himself recognizes, the rhetoric revival in political theory is much broader than that observed in the debate on deliberative democracy. It is a trend that has to be located in a much more general cultural and philosophical context, going back to the first part of the twentieth century, which saw the primacy of the category of truth questioned and, simultaneously, the linguistic character of reality vindicated. This new context has clearly been vital to the development of a renewed sensibility for the rhetorical aspects of society and culture and thus permits rhetoric, with its exceedingly long tradition, (re)emerge from the depths of discredit to which it descended with the consolidation of the rationalist and positivist principles of modernity.[5]

Today there is a vast panoply of ways that rhetorical categories and concepts are employed and studied in different areas of the social sciences and humanities. And a great variety of references to rhetoric is also visible in the domain of political science or, more specifically, of political theory, which is the domain in which this book is located. For instance, scholars such as Quentin Skinner and Maurizio Viroli, in their attempt to revive the republican tradition, have also recovered rhetoric as the central component of that tradition.[6] Skinner, furthermore, has combined Austin and Wittgenstein's views on language as a kind of action with the insights of ancient rhetoric to elaborate a new methodology for the history of ideas. Here ideas are seen not only as abstract descriptions or appraisals of some state of affairs, but also as instruments and tools to be employed strategically in an ideological and political debate.[7] A poststructuralist thinker such as Ernesto Laclau has come to explain the ontological structure of society in terms of a rhetorical, or more specifically tropological, process of transposing meanings.[8] Rhetoric has also been proposed by other theorists as the basis to a new conceptual framework for the study of politics, which gives prominence to its ideological, linguistic, and strategic dimensions.[9] Or there have been theorists who have employed insights from ancient rhetoric to inquiry into the nature of judgment and practical reason in politics[10]; or to assess populism by drawing parallelisms between it and ancient demagoguery.[11] Finally, this new rhetorical sensibility has inspired a number of works on rhetoric and the history of political thought.[12]

This cursory overview demonstrates that today rhetoric is amply used and recognized in the domain of political science and political theory. Nevertheless, I think that a creative exercise of *ars topica* in relation to the arguments and insights provided by the tradition of ancient rhetoric is certainly still possible. In this book I propose an exercise of that kind by exploring the significance for political theory of rhetoric from the perspective of its debate with philosophy. My aim is to bring to the fore how that debate gave expression to a tension which lies at the very core of politics: that between the contingency in which politics occurs and the transcendence toward which it strives. The relation between these two dimensions of politics is tense but necessary, and in it rhetoric can play the crucial role of a mediating force. The quarrel between philosophy and rhetoric is a central episode not only in the history of the two disciplines, but more in general for the development of western culture. Stanley Fish, for instance, has written that "the history of Western thought could be written as the history of this quarrel." For him we can see there a sort of original confrontation between two opposite ways of thinking: a "foundational thought" and a "rhetorical one." This confrontation engendered a series of dichotomies—"inner/outer, deep/surface, essential/peripheral, reason/passion, things/words, realities/illusions, fact/opinion, neutral/partisan"—that according to him have marked the development of our culture ever since.[13] Fish is referring here to two opposing positions that can be identified respectively with Plato and the sophists. It is one of the aims of this book, however, to show that the relation between philosophy and rhetoric can be, if never completely unproblematic, less binary and more collaborative. In order to do this, I will leave aside the position of the sophists and concentrate on three other great interpreters of the rhetorical tradition: Aristotle, and above all Cicero and Quintilian. Each of them can be said to take a middle ground between Plato and the sophists, to the extent that each defended rhetoric but at the same time didn't repudiate the 'pole' of philosophy. Beyond them, however, I will need to engage with Plato's attack on rhetoric. It is that attack, in effect, that came to constitute the framework in which the relation between philosophy and rhetoric was generally assessed after him.

My analysis of Plato and Aristotle's conceptions of rhetoric will be presented in Chap. 2, while that of Cicero and Quintilian will be found in Chap. 3. Chapter 2 starts with a brief historical reconstruction of the quarrel between philosophy and rhetoric in ancient Greece. After that I take in consideration, first, Plato's famous critique of rhetoric and, then, move on to Aristotle to discuss his theory of rhetoric as the first systematization of the art of speaking. Plato's critique of rhetoric testifies to the relevance of the pole of transcendence in politics. It is an attack made in the name of an ethical and political necessity to transcend conventions by pursuing absolute knowledge. Aristotle's theory of rhetoric, on the other hand, offers the first systematic defence of the art by way of a revaluation of contingency as the specific realm of human affairs. In his view rhetoric represents one of the most important forms of the kind of reason proper to this realm: practical reason. Chapter 2 might be considered an introductory chapter. Its main function in the general argument of the book is to demonstrate how the dimensions of transcendence and contingency correspond to philosophy and rhetoric. In Chap. 3 I move to Cicero's ideal of the perfect orator and the 'formative' process, as it is described in Quintilian's *Institutio oratoria*. The figure of the perfect orator is for Cicero the incarnation of his ideal combination of philosophy and rhetoric or, to use his words, of wisdom and eloquence. This chapter is the most important to the argument of the book, since it is dedicated to one of the most compelling attempts to combine, through rhetoric, the transcendent and contingent dimensions of politics. In Cicero's view rhetoric assumes a central role because it is considered the skill to make theoretical knowledge bear on practice and practical experience bear on theory, thereby creating an adequate communicative interaction between the two realms.

The ideal associated with the figure of the perfect orator is one of the founding elements of humanism and in it rhetoric came to assume arguably the highest status it has ever attained. As a formative model, its aim is the creation of a broad, enlarged individual, in which the two poles in the quarrel between philosophy and rhetoric—reason and emotions, theory and practice, impartiality and partisanship, etc.—are made to coexist. It is an idea that shows at the same time that the question of rhetoric goes far beyond the theme of public deliberation, bringing to the fore an existential dimension: the question of the best form of life. For Cicero the best form of life is the combination of the *vita activa* and the *vita contemplativa*, which can be reached only through, and in, perfect eloquence. The process to acquiring this ability is for him one of both self-cultivation, achieved through the pursuit of an encyclopedic wisdom, and civic education. As I will argue, in this way the figure of the perfect orator helps us re-think the relation between the 'existential' and the 'political' by conceiving the human good in terms of 'communicative' virtues.

The first two chapters constitute the first part of the book. In the second part I will move to modern political theory. Here the question discussed in the first part will be deepened by engaging with three influential twentieth-century theorists: Leo Strauss, Richard Rorty, and Hannah Arendt. This operation may seem questionable at first sight. First of all, because of the temporal gap that exists between these thinkers and ancient rhetoric. Second, because neither Strauss, nor Rorty, nor Arendt has ever really discussed at length rhetoric as a tradition of political thinking. Nevertheless what I hope to demonstrate is that a dialectical relationship between the transcendent and contingent sides of politics, with rhetoric operating as a mediating force, can be found playing a central role in their political theories. Strauss, Rorty, and Arendt in effect provide quite different understandings of the ideas of transcendence, contingency, and of their relationship, and hence also of rhetoric as a mediating force. But, in a sense, they all testify to the relevance of that tension within politics between the contingency in which it occurs and the impulse to transcend what is given (what is given could be false opinions, as in Strauss, or one's own self-image, as in Rorty, or the mute mechanical repetitions of nature, as in Arendt). Furthermore all of them believe that rhetoric—here broadly understood as the capacity to master communication—is essential to mediate that tension. In this sense recovering the ancient quarrel between philosophy and rhetoric can be considered an exercise of *ars topica* in that it helps to recover an argumentative scheme, or a general principle, to interpret politics by engaging influential theorists from a different perspective.[14]

Discussing Strauss, Rorty, and Arendt allows me to extend and refine the questions that emerged in the first part of the book. At the same time, it also allows me to throw new light on their works and thus explain why the themes raised by ancient rhetoric are still relevant today. In this regard, we have to keep in mind that for each of these thinkers ancient thought was an important point of reference. This is true to some extent even for the least classically minded among them, Rorty, who explicitly came to define his position on the, for him, central topic of the relation between the private and the public as 'anti-Platonic' (something I discuss at length in Chap. 5). Now, clearly the fact that none of these twentieth-century thinkers has thoroughly engaged with the tradition of ancient rhetoric means that my discussion will necessarily require an important level of interpretation and extrapolation. But my reading is based on a careful, synoptic analysis of the major works of Strauss, Rorty, and Arendt. Through it I demonstrate how each of their political theories can be seen as to foreground the importance in politics of the relation between contingent and transcendent dimensions, and of the role of rhetoric in mediating them.

Chapter 4 is dedicated to Leo Strauss. Recovering a Platonic and Socratic perspective, Strauss conceived philosophy as a process that, starting from the opinions of the citizens (the contingent realm), strives to transcend them in search of truth. The political tension generated by this process of continuous questioning and striving for transcendence creates the necessity for philosophy to employ a particular rhetorical technique—the 'art of writing between the line'—in order to justify and protect its role. Nevertheless, because according to Strauss the whole process is exclusively led by the pole of transcendence (philosophy)—contra Aristotle, Cicero, and Quintilian—rhetoric can only acquire an instrumental role. It is because of this prevailing instrumental dimension, I argue in the end, that Strauss's conception of rhetoric is prone to anti-democratic uses. In Chap. 5 I explore Richard Rorty's thought, by comparing his position on the relation between the private and the public with the rhetorical-humanistic tradition of Cicero, Quintilian, and Vico. Both Rorty and those thinkers share the idea that the mastery of communication skills—what Rorty called 'the art of redescription—is key to the emancipation both of the individual and the community. But differently from that tradition, for Rorty the two transcendent endeavours cannot be reconciled. This incapacity to conjoin the private and the public, I contend, is rooted in a radical understanding of contingency that produces contradictions not only with that tradition but also with basic aspects of his own project. In Chap. 6 I move to Hannah Arendt. As I show, among the three modern theorists analysed in the book, she is the one most akin to the rhetorical-humanistic tradition. Indeed Arendt's political theory provides the most balanced account of the relation between transcendence and contingency. The former dimension is expressed in the idea she shares with Cicero that politics is the main form humans have to endow the world with meaning and thus to transcend what is given by nature. The dimension of contingency, instead, is clear in her idea that the conditions of plurality and natality are two essential features of the political realm. It is from such an account, which she opposed to the one traditionally given by philosophy, that she derived the rhetorical conclusion that persuasion and judgment are the two basic political capacities. Like Cicero, for Arendt politics entails a striving for distinction, an endeavour that for her cannot but be expressed through judgment and persuasion. In this sense, then, she can be said to reconcile the deliberative and agonistic dimensions of politics.

Bryan Garsten, in his important book *Saving Persuasion*, has convincingly argued that at the root of modern liberalism lies a deep-seated suspicion of rhetoric. This, in turn, is based on a strong scepticism concerning the capacity of citizens to judge and not to fall victim to the incendiary oratory of religious and political demagogues. From this analysis, Garsten defends an enlarged conception of deliberation centred upon rhetorical persuasion, but at the same time that respects the principle of moral autonomy.[15] This same direction has been followed by other theorists of public deliberation, thereby giving birth to the contemporary 'rhetoric revival' in political theory. With this book I offer my own contribution to that revival. I hope to show that the significance for contemporary political theory of what Roland Barthes has once defined as the ancient "empire of rhetoric"—an empire, "broader and more tenacious ... than any other political imperium"—goes far beyond the theme of deliberation.[16] But this book is not only about rhetoric and political theory. It is also about transcendence and contingency in politics. More precisely it is a study of how these two dimensions interact, how this interaction can be mediated, and how this interaction shapes political activity. Contingency is today a dimension generally recognized as central to politics.[17] Reading Strauss, Rorty, and Arendt through the perspective of the relation between rhetoric and philosophy helps us to see why this dimension has to be understood together with an ongoing attempt to transcend and resignify what is given. For them it is this striving for transcendence that endows politics with an intrinsic value, which makes it different from the mere struggle of (pre-given) interests.

Notes

1. My translation. Giambattista Vico, "Seconda Risposta," in *Opere*, ed. Fausto Nicolini (Milan and Naples: Riccardo Ricciardi, 1953), 358.
2. Giambattista Vico, *The New Science of Giambattista Vico*, trans. Thomas Goddard Bergin and Max Harold Fisch (Ithaca: Cornell University Press, 1948), 149 par. 497.
3. Giambattista Vico, "Autobiografia," in *Opere*, ed. Fausto Nicolini (Milan and Naples: Riccardo Ricciardi Editore, 1953), 17; Giambattista Vico, "Prinicipi Di Scienza Nuova," in *Opere*, ed. Fausto Nicolini (Milan and Naples: Riccardo Ricciardi Editore, 1953), par. 498.
4. Bryan Garsten, "The Rhetoric Revival in Political Theory," *Annual Review of Political Science* 14 (2011). See also: Iris Marion Young, *Inclusion and Democracy* (Oxford and New York: Oxford University Press, 2000), 65–70; Danielle S. Allen, *Talking to Strangers: Anxieties of Citizenship since Brown V. Board of Education* (Chicago: University of Chicago Press, 2004); Benedetto Fontana, Cary J. Nederman, and Gary Remer, eds., *Talking Democracy: Historical Perspectives on Rhetoric and Democracy* (University Park: Pennsylvania State University Press, 2004); Bernard Yack, "Rhetoric and Public Reasoning: An Aristotelian Understanding of Political Deliberation," *Political Theory* 34 (2006); Bryan Garsten, *Saving Persuasion: A Defense of Rhetoric and Judgment* (Cambridge, MA: Harvard University Press, 2006); Arash Abizadeh, "On the Philosophy/Rhetoric Binaries: Or, Is Habermasian Discourse Motivationally Impotent?," *Philosophy and Social Criticism* 33 (2007); Simone Chambers, "Rhetoric and the Public Sphere: Has Deliberative Democracy Abandoned Mass Democracy? ," *Political Theory* 37 (2009); John S. Dryzek, "Rhetoric in Democracy: A Systemic Appreciation," *Political Theory* 38 (2010); Giuseppe Ballacci, "Reassessing the Rhetoric Revival in Political Theory: Cicero, Eloquence, and the Best Form of Life," *Redescriptions: Political Thought, Conceptual History and Feminist Theory* 18 (2015).
5. Garsten highlights two interrelated philosophical developments that converge to create a philosophic context in which a new rhetorical sensibility could rise in the humanities: on the one hand, the combination of Nietzschean and Heideggerian post-foundationalism and the linguistic turn in its analytical and poststructuralist versions; on the other, the revival

of ancient prudential thinking instigated by Heidegger and developed by figures such as Oakeshott, Strauss, Arendt, and Gadamer. Garsten, "The Rhetoric Revival in Political Theory," 161–2. On the cultural background of the current rhetoric revival in political theory, see also: Daniel J. Kapust, *Republicanism, Rhetoric, and Roman Political Thought: Sallust, Livy, and Tacitus* (New York: Cambridge University Press, 2011), 13–21. For a wider analysis of the resurgence of rhetoric in the twentieth century see, e.g., James Arnt Aune, "Coping with Modernity Strategies of 20th-Century Rhetorical Theory," in *The Sage Handbook of Rhetorical Studies*, ed. Rosa A. Eberly, Andrea Lunsford, and Kirt H. Wilson (London: SAGE, 2009); Dilip P. Gaonkar, "The Revival of Rhetoric, the New Rhetoric, and the Rhetorical Turn: Some Distinctions," *Informal Logic* 15 (1993).
6. Skinner in particular has turned more and more to the study of ancient and Renaissance rhetoric: Quentin Skinner, *Reason and Rhetoric in the Philosophy of Hobbes* (Cambridge: Cambridge University Press, 1996); Quentin Skinner, *The Foundations of Modern Political Thought: Vol. 1. The Renaissance* (Cambridge and New York: Cambridge University Press, 1978); Maurizio Viroli, *Republicanism* (New York: Hill and Wang, 2002).
7. For instance: Quentin Skinner, *Visions of Politics, Vol. 1: Regarding Method* (Cambridge: Cambridge University Press, 2002). On the role of rhetoric in Skinner see: Kari Palonen, *Quentin Skinner: History, Politics, Rhetoric* (Cambridge and Malden, MA: Polity Press, 2003).
8. For instance: Ernesto Laclau, *The Rhetorical Foundations of Society* (London: Verso, 2014).
9. For instance: Alan Finlayson and James Martin, "'It Ain't What You Say...': British Political Studies and the Analysis of Speech and Rhetoric," *British Politics* 3 (2008); Alan Finlayson, "Rhetoric and the Political Theory of Ideologies," *Political Studies* 60 (2012); James Martin, *Politics and Rhetoric: A Critical Introduction* (London: Routledge, 2014).
10. For instance: Garsten, *Saving Persuasion*; Eugene Garver, *Aristotle's Rhetoric: An Art of Character* (Chicago and London: University of Chicago Press, 1994); Victoria McGeer and Philip Pettit, "Sticky Judgment and the Role of Rhetoric," in *Political Judgement: Essays for John Dunn*, ed. Richard Bourke and Raymond Geuss (Cambridge: Cambridge University Press, 2009).
11. Nadia Urbinati, *Democracy Disfigured: Opinion, Truth, and the People* (Cambridge, MA: Harvard University Press, 2014).
12. Just to mention some interesting works on theorists of different epochs: Kapust, *Republicanism, Rhetoric, and Roman Political Thought*; Skinner, *Reason and Rhetoric in the Philosophy of Hobbes*; Paddy Bullard, *Edmund Burke and the Art of Rhetoric* (Cambridge: Cambridge University Press, 2011).

13. Stanley Fish, *Doing What Comes Naturally: Change, Rhetoric, and the Practice of Theory in Literary and Legal Studies* (Durham, NC and London: Duke University Press, 1989), 474, 484.
14. On *ars topica* as the art of finding 'argument schemes', see: Sara Rubinelli, *Ars Topica: The Classical Technique of Constructing Arguments from Aristotle to Cicero* (New York: Springer, 2009).
15. Garsten, *Saving Persuasion*, Ch. 6.
16. My translation. Roland Barthes, *L'aventure sémiologique* (Paris: Éd. du Seuil, 1985), 88.
17. See for instance: Kari Palonen, "Contingency in Political Theory," *Redescriptions: Political Thought, Conceptual History and Feminist Theory* 3 (1999); Ian Shapiro and Sonu Bedi, eds., *Political Contingency: Studying the Unexpected, the Accidental, and the Unforeseen* (New York: New York University Press, 2007).

PART I

CHAPTER 2

Between Philosophy and Rhetoric: Plato and Aristotle

2.1 Introduction: Philosophy Against Rhetoric?

Plato is a crucial figure in western culture not only because of his unparalleled influence in shaping the conception of philosophy for the following centuries, but also because he has fundamentally contributed to determine our conception of rhetoric as well. He is rightly considered the most influential critic rhetoric has ever had. And, more than probably any other philosopher, he has set the tone for how rhetoric has traditionally been seen, not only in relation to philosophy but also more in general to society. Elements of Plato's view on rhetoric can be found in the positions of many major philosophers: from Hobbes, Descartes, Locke, Kant, Hegel, up to Rawls and Habermas.[1] In a nutshell his position, as famously expressed in the *Gorgias*, is that rhetoric should be condemned, morally and politically, since it is prone to become an instrument of demagogical manipulation. In effect, in another dialogue, the *Phaedrus*, Plato defended a more positive view attributing to rhetoric a positive function in society as an instrument of persuasion, even if under the strict guidance of philosophy. But it is his negative judgment which has contributed in a crucial way to set up a strict hierarchical dichotomy between philosophy and rhetoric, which has become somehow authoritative. It is a dichotomy that identifies the former with "devotion to truth, intellectual honesty, depth of perception, consistency, and sincerity" and the latter with "verbal dexterity, empty pomposity, triviality, moral ambivalence, and a desire to achieve self-interest by any means."[2] According to this view the opposition between philosophy and rhetoric is radical: it involves a basic disagreement about two opposite visions: that is, two existential, moral, and political theories. On the one hand there is, to use Richard Lanham's fortunate expressions, the position of the *homo serious* who postulates that humans have a central and irreducible self, and that live in a physical reality, which, being independent from them and functioning as a referent for them, has to be discovered in its essence and then represented and communicated clearly and faithfully. On the other, there is that of the *homo rhetoricus*, which sees reality as something public, like a stage, and as something that can be manipulated as needed rather than as something that can be discovered. Accordingly, for the *homo rhetoricus* the self is a contingent entity, which assumes different forms depending on the circumstances and which can commit to different system of values.[3]

This book provides a quite different idea of the relation between philosophy and rhetoric (and therefore politics) more in line with the thought of the politician, rhetorician, and philosopher, Cicero, who has shown why such relation can and should be more one of interdependence and complementarity than of irreconcilability. In the last decades various scholars of rhetoric, with a much more positive idea of this art than Plato's, have attempted to reassess it outside the terms imposed by his bifurcated view. It is the predominance in our culture of this bifurcated view that has prevented a deeper comprehension of rhetoric, obscuring the dialogical and constructive interactions between two disciplines and practices that have struggled, but also influenced each other along the centuries.[4] It is certainly true, for instance, that Plato employed the terms 'rhetoric', 'sophistry', or 'myth', also as a dialectical counterpoint to forge and legitimize his idea of 'philosophy' by projecting on them defects that the latter was supposed to avoid.[5] His was a period in which such words had still to find a stable meaning and were subject to semantic dispute. And Plato clearly participated in such dispute. In this sense, it has been argued that possibly it was the same Plato to coin the word *rhetorike* for polemical purposes, in order to differentiate his art of *logos* from that practiced by the sophists, which he understood as the systematic attempt to manipulate language with the aim of persuading.[6]

The period between the fifth and fourth centuries saw in Athens a momentous political and cultural battle to substitute the old educational ideal of Homeric poetry, by opposing figures such as Plato and his idea of philosophy, on the one hand, with Isocrates and other sophists who held (different) ideas of the art of discourse, on the other. The fact that the former used particularly polemical tones against the other side can be explained certainly with this more contingent and practical motive: the aim of forging a new cultural hegemony. Nevertheless, neither this circumstance, nor the fact of stressing the interconnection among the two parts, can be used to deny that among philosophy and rhetoric there are substantial key differences. Plato's attack against rhetoric hits a critical note, as is confirmed by the fact that the history of this art, seen from the perspective of those who defend it, could be told also as an ongoing attempt to try to respond to such criticism.[7] The depth of his criticism, however, shows how relevant the question of political communication, and therefore rhetoric, was for him. And in this respect, it is certainly correct, as it has been suggested, to consider him "a rhetorical theorist of the first order."[8]

In the background of the development of the democratic regime between the fifth and fourth centuries, rhetoric, as the practice of speaking and arguing in public and then as the systematization of such practice into a discipline, came to assume a particularly relevant role in Greece.[9] The promotion and teaching of such art is generally attributed to the sophists. They were known for teaching techniques useful for achieving influence in politics. For them rhetoric was the art of speaking persuasively and that was the core of their teaching. Even if today classicists are increasingly revealing the specificities and distinctions between different sophists, it is not inaccurate to attribute to them in general an instrumental conception of rhetoric, which stresses above all its power to manipulate the will of the audience, mainly through the employment of extra-rational means, to obtain persuasion. In this view, then, what really counts in rhetoric is its effect.[10] Among them, Isocrates is considered a central figure and to some extent also an important exception. He is the one who was able to bring together and further develop "the various trends and influences of Greek sophistic."[11] Certainly Isocrates attributed a great value to the art of speaking in public and didn't disregard its power as an instrument of persuasion. But his vision is different in crucial aspects from the instrumental view generally associated with the sophists: for him the art of speaking was not only as a simple technique for persuasion but, moreover, a crucial element of civilization. In this sense, he agreed with Plato in condemning the art of speaking as it was taught by the other sophists, that is, as a morally neutral technique of persuasion. Indeed, he didn't even refer to his art of speech with the term rhetoric (*rhetorike*). Rather he preferred to employ the same word Plato used—*philosophia*—to designate what he considered to be a comprehensive cultural, ethical, and political general programme and an associated educative practice (*paideia*), which pivoted around a conception of practical wisdom based on the use of *logos*, or civic discourse, with ethical ends.[12]

The idea of philosophy advocated by Isocrates, however, was very different from that of Plato. Isocrates attempted to create a new ethical and cultural standard centred on the primacy of political life, but at the same time without the mundane and prosaic character of the sophists.[13] Criticizing the pretention to obtain absolute knowledge, which he attributed to Socrates and considered an attitude of detachment from more urgent political objectives, Isocrates defended the necessity to cultivate the studies necessary to practical life. In this context, he attributed to the art of speaking a central role: it is from *logos* that civilization arises and maintains itself; it is thanks to *logos* that human beings can raise their spirit and aspire to reach high ethical ends.[14] We can say then that Isocrates represents one of the first important examples of someone who tried to inhabit the "no man's land between rhetoric and philosophy—too philosophic for the politician, and too aware of the immediate and the changing for the philosopher."[15] And as a consequence of his challenge to the dichotomical opposition between rhetoric (and more generally politics) and philosophy, he is also one of the first to have suffered the fate of being considered an unremarkable representative of both. But the role of Isocrates in the history of rhetoric and more in general of western culture is important precisely because of his attempt to strike a middle way between the position of Plato and that of the sophists. As Werner Jaeger wrote in his regard:

> the new rhetoric had to find an ideal which could be ethically interpreted and which at the same time could be translated into practical political action. This ideal was a new moral code for Greece. It gave rhetoric an inexhaustible theme; in it the ultimate topic of all higher education seemed to have been discovered once and for all.[16]

This 'ultimate topic' mentioned by Jaeger is the subject around which the rhetorical-humanistic tradition will develop in the following centuries. Isocrates indeed is rightly regarded as a proto-humanist, whose influence has extended in different epochs through figures such Cicero, Quintilian, Plutarch, and then the humanists of the Renaissance.[17] His broad conception of the art of speaking is essential to understand the relevance of rhetoric in Athens and the conception of citizenship to which it was associated. Rhetoric was not only an instrument for persuasion. It was the core of a cultural, political, and pedagogical ideal that aspired to a committed and virtuous form of citizenship. The capacity of citizens to live together through the practice of argued discussion was supposed to provide the basis to society.[18] Such a conception of citizenship will be later expanded by Cicero's republican political theory and by his combination of rhetoric and philosophy, on which I will focus in Chap. 3.

Before coming to Cicero, however, it is necessary to analyse the position of Plato and Aristotle on rhetoric and, in particular, on the relation between rhetoric and philosophy. Plato's position is fundamental in that it provides the paradigmatic form of the critique that would be directed against rhetoric for most of the rest of its history by philosophers. His attack on rhetoric is emblematic of a wider suspicion he had of politics (and that, according to Arendt, is shared by the majority of philosophers). It is a suspicion of its contingent dimension and a vindication of a dimension that, as we will see better in the following chapters, we can designate as transcendent. Aristotle instead is important for the argument of this book, because his account of rhetoric is the first systematic philosophical defence of this art as a form of practical reason, a manifestation of *phronesis*. It is a defence that openly vindicates the dimension of contingency as the proper dimension for politics and rhetoric. This understanding of rhetoric can be found not only in Cicero and in later rhetoricians, but will be the point of reference for the much of the recovery of rhetoric in the twentieth century.

2.2 Plato's Paradigmatic Critique of Rhetoric on Behalf of Philosophy

Plato's reflections on the practice and meaning of rhetoric concern questions that are at the very core of his philosophy, having to do with the relation between truth and how it is represented in language, on the one hand, and justice and the good on the other. But, at the same time, as I have mentioned, these reflections are developed in the background of a very specific historical situation, which means that they are not devoid of more practical and political finalities. In attacking rhetoric, and above all the sophists, Plato was making a philosophical argument and at the same time defending his ideas within the political and cultural arena of Athens.[19] At the more general level, Plato's attack on the rhetoric practiced and taught by the sophists is a confrontation between two ideas of discourse, or *logos*, and the political and ethical effects they produce in the city. Plato opposes the rhetoric of the sophists to Socratic dialectic.[20] The latter represents for him the paradigmatic form of philosophical and scientific discourse and the model for his own conceptions of dialectic. In his early studies on Platonic dialectic, Hans-Georg Gadamer explained that the Socratic dialogue, as it is rendered by Plato, is the first example of scientific discourse; a discourse that aspires "to arrive at a really secure stance toward the things" through a stylized methodology, the *elenchus*, made of succession of short questions and answers aimed at drawing out the underlying presumptions of unexamined opinions to show their logical inconsistencies.[21] But the goal that moves to investigate through this form of dialogue into the "question of *what* something is", as Gadamer remarked, is moral and political rather than epistemological: Plato is concerned with the risk inherent in a *logos* incapable of saying what it really means, in the a-critical acceptance of one's own opinions and those more prevalent in a community, and finally in the possibility that someone could take advantages of such situation.[22] If words are means to represent things, then that implies that words have an independent life from what they represent and therefore that there is always "something inessential about them." The risk of being misled into taking "that which is inessential for something essential" is what for Plato we need to prevent.[23]

For Plato the weakness of the *logos* posits a serious moral and political threat. This is because *logos* is the essential means for human beings to access the world and as a consequence the essential means they have to construct a community. Socrates' questioning started precisely from the opinions of his fellow citizens on themes of crucial importance for the community—the essence of justice, virtue, and the good—in order to transcend them and penetrate into "the depths in which human obligation has its foundation", avoiding thus the risk of arbitrariness. "It is among Plato's keenest and most marvellous insights," wrote Gadamer, "that this danger has its source in the weakness of the *logoi*, the weakness which the new *paideia* in the age of sophism exploits."[24] Since human beings gain access to the world through *logos*, Plato believed that to different *logoi* correspond different existential attitudes. In particular he opposed the *ethos* of the philosopher to that of the sophist: if the former is moved always by the love for wisdom and the search for true justice, the sophist is moved by the desire to excel and gain ascendency on the others (*phthonos*).[25] Moved by the desire to, as Plato famously put it, "never condescending to what lies near at hand",[26] the philosopher tries to establish with his interlocutors a process of dialectical interchange aimed at making "the facts of the matter visible in their being."[27] This is a process in which those who participate have to commit with no other intentions than that of finding the truth and thus with an attitude of openness to debate and disputation. On the other hand, the sophist uses discourse to fulfil his desire to mundane glory and power, with the consequence that his interlocutors would not be partners in the common search of truth but, rather, objectives to be conquered. The paradigmatic form the discourse of the sophist takes, for Plato, is the kind of negative rhetoric he described in the *Gorgias*.[28]

Plato's position on rhetoric is strictly related to his general philosophic outlook and in particular to his political philosophy. In its most developed version, it is formulated in the *Gorgias*, a dialogue that deals with the nature of rhetoric and its role within the community. In this dialogue his position on rhetoric takes the form of a harsh attack against it. Three characters appear successively in dialogue with Socrates, all of them well versed with the art of rhetoric: first, the prominent teacher of rhetoric, Gorgias, then his pupil, Polus, and finally the ambitious politician, Callicles. Socrates's intention is to inquire into the nature of rhetoric, examining through his dialectical method one of its most renowned experts: Gorgias. The conversation takes place during the troubled period of the Peloponnesian war and the death of Pericles. In such a politically turbulent period, the sophists exerted a powerful influence that was considered a threat by Plato and in need of scrutiny. On the other hand, philosophy itself needed to legitimate its position in the city. If the critical activity of the philosopher, with its disruptive effects on the conventions and common opinions, led inevitably to reaction from the city (as tragically testified by Socrates' condemnation to death), then rhetoric was not only a threat but also a useful instrument for the philosopher to defend himself.[29] These two different order of reasons brought Plato to turn his attention to rhetoric.

In the *Phaedrus* the question related to rhetoric with which Plato dealt concerns essentially its positive role in helping to legitimize philosophy's status within the city. In the *Gorgias*, instead, the theme is the serious political threat that rhetoric represents. The *Gorgias* starts with the words "battle and war"[30] and this indeed it what seems to occur within it: the *mise en scène* of a confrontation between philosophy and rhetoric on the question of which among them deserve the role of new spiritual guide to educate its future political leaders.[31] In questioning the famous rhetorician

Gorgias, Plato tried to show the epistemological and moral inconsistencies of rhetoric which could be exploited by an unscrupulous politician; someone like Callicles, who later on will join the dialogue. It is in the first lines that Socrates puts the decisive questions to Gorgias: Who are you? Which is the art you are considered an expert of? And what is the object of this art?[32] In putting these questions Socrates wants to reveal the contradictions of an alleged art that, on the one hand, its advocates claim to be concerned with the most important things, able to bring freedom to mankind and give to those who master it the dominion of the city; but, on the other, that is described by those who practice and teach it as a mere ability to persuade through speeches.[33] It is the impossibility to make coexist the substantive and merely instrumental dimensions of rhetoric that Plato's Socrates wants to expose by interrogating Gorgias. The contradiction here is between something that is associated with some of the highest things but that, at the same time, is elusively defined as an art of discourse, without a specific object beyond persuasion. In such a contradiction lies, for Plato, the moral and political threat of rhetoric.[34] If rhetoric were really concerned with the most important things, then it would need to develop a knowledge about them. Without such knowledge it cannot be anything more than an instrument; and, as such, it is something equally at disposal for just and unjust purposes. The first responses of Gorgias doesn't deny this argument. Rhetoric, he admits doesn't need real knowledge since its audience is made of ignorant people. It is indeed an instrument whose only goal is to make arguments persuasive at the level of beliefs without instructing, and as such which can be used either rightly or wrongly.[35]

It is on this attachment to the realm of opinions (*doxai*), which Socrates opposes to the realm of knowledge, that he builds his compelling attack against rhetoric. It is an attack constructed on a series of connected dichotomies, which he will gradually introduce in the dialogue—knowledge/opinion, instruction/persuasion, language/content, appearance/essence, emotions/reason, many/few—and which ends up creating an absolute opposition between rhetoric and philosophy.[36] Rhetoric doesn't have a knowledge of the topics it speaks about, but it can be more convincing than an expert because it knows how to speak to the unknowledgeable crowd. The rhetor only needs to make appear to those who don't know that he knows better than those who really know. This is why for Socrates rhetoric is a phantom of politics and justice. It claims to speak about justice, but without having any substantive knowledge of it, it can only persuade through flattery, by pandering and manipulating the desires and emotions of the audience, without being able to teach anything. If real politics should aim to improve the soul of the citizens, rhetoric can only satisfy their bodies. Socrates can thus conclude that rhetoric, in comparison with politics, has the same relation to justice that culinary skills do to medicine or cosmetics to gymnastics in relation to the body: like culinary skills and cosmetics, it is not an authentic art (*techne*) but a mere knack. It is unable to articulate its methods and principles. And instead of providing what is really just, it can only simulate it, inducing pleasure and gratification in its audience through flattery.[37]

This is the political and moral deficiency that Plato imputed to rhetoric: that it doesn't promote a critical and inquiring attitude in its auditors, but rather favours a passive perseverance in their prejudices that ends up making them slaves. In this way rhetoric produces injustice by strengthening dogmatism and favouring the exercise of power for the sake of power.[38] Thus rhetoric was dangerous for Plato for similar reasons he thought a particular kind of poetry can be.[39] Because mimetic poetry tries to seduce its audience by exciting those most reassuring passions, compassion and laughter (through respectively tragedy and comedy), its result is to strengthen the strongest source of conventionalism: the love for oneself.[40] Plato's attack on (mimetic) poetry in the *Republic* can be explained as an attack on an art he believes can become a formidable obstacle to the process of questioning necessary for justice; because "the poets," as Nietzsche wrote, "are always the valets of some morality."[41] This kind of conventionalism that easily blends with hypocrisy is a defining feature of Plato's account of the tyrannical city, where not only the tyrant but also the citizens pretend. Authority is not respected because it is believed to truly embody justice; but only for reasons of personal interest that cannot be publicly declared.[42]

Rhetoric, however, is more a threat than poetry because it can be a much more powerful instrument at the disposal of cunning and unscrupulous demagogues. Such a possibility is made patent not by Gorgias but by the other two characters who take part in the dialogue: Polus and, above all, Callicles.[43] Their interventions make clear how rhetoric contributes to injustice and becomes an instrument of tyranny. It is Polus who explicitly reveals the link between rhetoric and tyranny—a link only hinted in Gorgias's intervention—when without consideration he extols the possibility by means of rhetoric to easily obtain power; and once obtained, to commit injustice without incurring in any punishment.[44] Polus is the paradigm of the unreflective citizen, who takes for granted the conventions of the city and makes justice coincide with what is generally held.[45] But the real enemy of Socrates is Callicles, who doesn't represent hypocrisy and superficiality but outspoken immoralism. Callicles' intervention has been famously defined as "the most eloquent statement of the immoralist's case in European literature."[46] In opposition to Socrates's doctrine that committing injustice is worse than suffering it, Callicles advances an equally shocking thesis (one that Nietzsche will recover centuries later): that committing injustice is wrong not according to nature (*physis*) but only according to conventions (*nomoi*), which have been instituted by the common effort of the weakest only to subjugate those who are stronger than them.[47] He defends the idea that those who are stronger should seek to satisfy their own, larger appetites and desires without restraint and to do this by becoming experts in all that is required to have power in public life, including rhetoric. This search for power is worthy of the respect of gentlemen, he says, not Socrates's devotion to philosophy (an occupation that is acceptable only for the young). In a sinister presage of Socrates' trial and condemnation, Callicles admonishes Socrates by saying that he would be helpless to defend himself in front of a jury, in case someone should drag him there, and he will end up being put to death.[48]

These comments then make clear that the dispute around the nature of rhetoric is related also to another theme: the question about the best form of life, the dispute between the life devoted to philosophy, personified by Socrates, and that devoted to politics and rhetoric personified by Callicles.[49] Beyond the harsh tones and the caricaturized traits with which Callicles is described, we can perceive differences between him and Socrates that are not only ethical and political but also existential. Socrates, the philosopher, is moved by the love for *sophia*; Callicles, the politician, by the love for the *demos*. Callicles is in search of political power and thus he needs to adapt himself to the regime in which he lives, that is, to a democracy and thus to the *demos*. He needs to appear similar to the *demos* to show that he accepts its wisdom in order to be able to flatter it and conquer its will. But those who aspire to political power need not only to appear similar to the *demos*. They also need to learn to imitate those already powerful, to avoid becoming their victims. On the other hand, we have the philosopher, who is in search of wisdom and who would address the city only to indicate what is really best for it rather than what is pleasant. This is what Socrates regards as the true political art. An art that improves the citizens and, like a doctor with his patients, that sometimes can also compel them to do things they don't desire, but which are good for them.[50] In all Athens,

Socrates declares not without a certain irony, he is the only one to practice such art.[51]

The *Gorgias* has traditionally been read as the paradigmatic attack on behalf of philosophy against the moral and epistemological inconsistency of rhetoric. In this respect, to defend the value of rhetoric some scholars have complained that Plato gives a caricatured version of this art so as to carry out more effectively his attack against what he sees as a dangerous enemy. Rhetoric was for him a political enemy, since it was a practice of doing politics through arguments, indissolubly connected with the democracy of Athens, towards which, as we know, Plato nurtured no sympathies. And it was also a cultural and existential enemy, since it represented a practical alternative to the philosophic mode of life.[52] Nevertheless the *Gorgias* provides also a plastic representation of the inherent risks of the art of speaking and, by contrast, of the benefits of philosophy. Rhetoric is condemned essentially because it is incapable of detaching itself from the contingencies of political life and transcending them, as philosophy does, in order to find what is really just and good beyond the here and now.

On the other hand, behind this apparent simplicity in the contrast between philosophy and rhetoric, the *Gorgias* also offers hints that suggest a more complex relation between them and thus between transcendence and contingency in politics. The dialogue ends up without really giving the impression of making a conclusive and truly persuasive argument for philosophy. Socrates is not really able to convince any of his interlocutors about his positions: neither Gorgias, who despite his interest in Socrates's ideas doesn't resume the conversation with him after being rebutted at the beginning of the dialogue; nor Polus, who doesn't seem to grasp the real relevance of the questions debated; and even less Callicles, who indeed abandons the dialogue upset and leaves Socrates to talk alone.[53] Against those who underline the failure of Socrates, however, it is always possible to argue that the aim of Plato was to show the moral inconsistency of those who interact with Socrates. The particularly bitter character of the *Gorgias* can be explained in this way. Plato's dialogues assume different forms depending on the characters of the persons intervening in them: their tone can be more aggressive and polemical, when the interlocutors don't have the capacity to philosophize or represent a moral threat (Thrasymachus in the *Republic* or Callicles in the *Gorgias*, for instance), or more instructive and philosophically engaging in the opposite case (Glaucon and Adeimantus in the *Republic*, or Phaedrus in the *Phaedrus*, for instance).

But beyond this there is another possible explanation that helps explain not only Socrates's inability to convince his interlocutors but also why some of his arguments seem not very convincing at all, being based on very caricaturized and extreme representations of the other position. A number of studies have explained the caricaturized and extreme representations of the other positions in the *Gorgias*, by arguing that Plato not only wanted to make a strong critique of rhetoric but, at the same time, show Socrates's inability to fully defend his position. In this way Plato was at the same time suggesting that philosophy cannot dispense altogether with rhetoric. In this sense more than offering a neat opposition between philosophy and rhetoric, the *Gorgias* seems to evoke the difficulty involved by a situation characterized by an opposition "between a dialectic that alters no one's convictions and a rhetoric that is effective but knows neither how it is effective nor what it effects."[54] Indeed in the dialogue Socrates himself mentions "a noble rhetoric"—a rhetoric that, however, as he specifies, has never existed—which is practiced by a noble man who has justice, temperance, and virtue, in view of what is best for the city.[55] Such a rhetoric can be a very important ally for philosophy. Indeed it can help not only in justifying to the city the necessity of philosophy, but also in making the city accept the bitter medicines that, as a doctor, the philosopher needs to prescribe.[56]

The noble rhetoric mentioned in the *Gorgias* was developed in more detail by Plato in the *Phaedrus*. In this dialogue Socrates returns to the question of rhetoric but without the polemical attitude he had earlier. The dialogue occurs in a much more friendly atmosphere, with Socrates engaging with the young and perceptive Phaedrus, someone who clearly has the moral and intellectual capacities to become a philosopher. Plato's account of rhetoric here is much more positive. Rhetoric is not reduced to a flattering discourse motivated by political reasons but referred to as a general art of discourse; an art whose goal is that to influence with words.[57] Rhetoric then reacquires its status of an art (*techne*): one aimed specifically at persuading. It is an art that here Plato seemed to consider necessary in those cases, as Socrates says, even if one knows the truth but is unable to produce persuasion by it alone. For that he needs to know the art of persuasion; which has to be based however on authentic, philosophical, knowledge.[58] Such knowledge is necessary for two reasons. In order to know the truth about something it is necessary to use one of the most important techniques of rhetoric: the art of disputation, which consists in offering two different arguments, one on each side of an issue. But to use the art of disputation, in turn, we need to distinguish the topics on which there is more probability to disagree—like discourses on justice and the good for instance—from those about which there is less probability, and to move slowly through similarities from one thing to another showing why they are similar.[59] This in turn requires knowledge on those topics. But there is another, more important reason. In the dialogue Socrates defines rhetoric as the art of leading the souls through persuasion. If this is so, then, it would need knowledge also on the nature of the souls, and specifically of the different kinds of souls that exist and of the reasons why a particular soul is necessarily persuaded by a particular kind of discourse.[60] That is the specific kind of knowledge on which the rhetorician should become expert.

It is a sort of 'philosophical' rhetoric then that Plato developed in the *Phaedrus*, which can count on the support of philosophy and of the dialectic method of collecting and dividing to find the proper arrangement of the content of the speech.[61] Such a reformed rhetoric, because is under the guidance of philosophy and thus in line with justice, can employ its more conventional techniques. These techniques are those compiled by the handbooks: like the proper ordering of the parts of the discourse to make it clear and lively like "a living organism;" or the use of images or other rhetorical figures to stimulate the emotions of the audience; or even the use of deception.[62] Despite its philosophical character, this reformed rhetoric maintains its privileged relation with the realm of practical affairs and its special ability to deal with contingency. Particularly telling in this respect is the importance Socrates concedes to *kairos*—a very important concept in rhetoric—underlining that the speaker should be able to recognize the proper moment to speak and to know how to apply all these techniques to what the circumstances, the 'here and now', require.[63] The recognition of the importance of *kairos* is an important concession Plato made to contingency, because the same idea contradicts his attempt to build "a rhetorical methodology within a foundational epistemology, since any time is the 'right time' when one possesses the truth."[64]

In conclusion, we can say that, overall, rhetoric assumes an important role in the philosophy of Plato, even if a strictly subordinate and instrumental one. He recognized that its techniques are a useful and even sometimes necessary instrument in order to help the philosopher lead the souls of his audience towards the truth: not only the souls of the lay citizens, but also of those few individuals, who have the talent for philosophizing yet who need to be seduced to undertake the difficult path towards philosophy.

A philosophically informed rhetoric should be, for Plato, a technique founded on knowledge, able to explain how persuasion occurs and how, in particular, different kinds of discourse affect different characters.[65] Once anchored in philosophical knowledge, then, Plato recovered many of the characteristic traits of the rhetorical art—which were judged negatively in the *Gorgias* because of the polemical and critical scope of the dialogue— such as its special link with the *kairos* and the realm of opinions and the verisimilar; the fact that its object is the art of speaking in general; or its capacity to move the emotions through stylistic devices such as myths, similes, erotic language, humour, personification, and other tropes.[66] In particular, the anchorage to philosophy guarantees that even some morally ambiguous rhetorical practices—the manipulation of the emotions, for instance, or the practice of arguing on both sides of the same question— can be used by the philosopher because such use is for just reasons. Plato's famous theory of the noble lie can also be explained in this way.[67]

More generally, it is well known that Plato, despite his critique of rhetoric, made considerable use in his works of many rhetorical and stylistic devices to convey things that rational argumentation alone cannot convey. His preference for the dialogical forms, with all its dramatic elements such as the modulation of tone according to the audience, or his recourse to the myths in crucial moments of his dialogues, testify his rhetorical sensibility.[68] We should remember in this respect that Plato's whole philosophy has been interpreted as more than a philosophical system, but as a symbolical representation of the philosophical way of life.[69] This means that the striving toward the transcendent that this way of life embodies is conceived as an endeavour which inevitably has to adapt to and unfold among a flux of contingent circumstances. Nevertheless, the fact that the philosophical search assumes an absolute hierarchical position in comparison to this adaptation to the contingent (that is, to political and practical concerns) implies that we cannot go beyond an instrumental view of rhetoric and therefore that the relation between the two poles will be always asymmetrical and hierarchical. In Chap. 4, in discussing Strauss's similar conception of rhetoric, I will indicate some political implications of this outlook.

2.3 Aristotle's Full Revaluation of Rhetoric

If Plato is remembered in the history of rhetoric as its first and most compelling critic, Aristotle is regarded as the first to have proposed a systematic account of the art.[70] His work on rhetoric has been extremely influential along the centuries. In particular, it has covered a pivotal role in the recovery of rhetoric in the twentieth century: both within philosophy, with figures such as Chaïm Perelman and Hans-Georg Gadamer, and in its own right, as an independent discipline, with the so-called 'new rhetoric' in the field of literary studies promoted by Kenneth Burke and others.[71] The recovery promoted by Perelman and Gadamer of Aristotle's *Rhetoric* is especially important for the perspective of this book. According to their interpretation, for Aristotle the art of speaking corresponds to the art of judging and deliberating in the realm of contingency—the realm where things happen not by necessity—and constitutes a very important element of his practical philosophy.[72] In this sense, the role of Aristotle in the history of rhetoric is crucial not only because he contributed to emend the under-theorized approach common in the rhetorical handbooks of his time, but also because he gave a full revaluation of rhetoric as a substantive activity, whose value cannot be reduced to that of an instrument. It is to this Aristotelian understanding of rhetoric that in recent years, a group of theorists of democracy—the theorists of the current 'rhetoric revival' in political theory—have turned to rediscuss public deliberation beyond the strictures of rationalism.

As we have just seen, Plato attacked rhetoric because he thought that, without the support of knowledge both on justice and the good and on its method and principles, it can become a dangerous instrument for demagogues and despots. This is the problem that Aristotle attempted to solve. At the same time, Aristotle was concerned with the reductive version of rhetoric—rhetoric as a set of predefined devices and techniques that could be learned and employed according to one's own purposes—promoted by many of the rhetoricians of his time. In the opening lines of the *Rhetoric*, Aristotle complained of the fact that those who write manuals on the art of persuasion completely neglect what for him is essential: the proof of persuasion (*pistis*) and the form this proof takes, the rhetorical syllogism (*enthymeme*), which constitutes for him the "body of persuasion."[73] Centring rhetoric on the enthymeme and the *pistis*—which was for Aristotle the only artistic part of rhetoric and as such the only part that can be systematized—implied defending an idea of this art as an argumentative practice in which its methods (such as the use of the emotions, or the display of the character to persuade) cannot be considered completely separately from the subject-matter under discussion. For Aristotle, however, rhetoric assumed a substantive character not only because of its argumentative nature but also because it is an argumentative art for the ethical and political domain. Aristotle firmly established rhetoric in this domain; in the expression of Pierre Aubenque, the domain of the "ontology of contingency."[74] This is the realm of ontological indeterminacy, where things don't happen by necessity, leaving the space for human freedom to express itself through actions whose effects are ultimately uncertain. It is the realm in which ethics and politics can develop. Rhetoric is an art to argue and deliberate in this realm and as such it is a manifestation of practical reason. This is, in very general terms, the biggest difference between Aristotle's view of rhetoric and that of Plato. In the words of William Grimaldi:

> Plato put this art at the exclusive disposition of the speculative intellect... Aristotle, on the other hand, recognized the whole area of contingent reality...Herein man is faced not with absolutes but rather with facts, problems, situations, questions, which admit of probable knowledge and probable truth and call for deliberation before assent. It is the area in which the intelligent and prudential course of action which is most conformable to the concrete reality and truth is determined in a given instance by the specific circumstances which appear most valid. Analyzing the rhetorical art at this level Aristotle in terms of his own philosophy could never divorce intellect from the emotions or the appetitive element in man.[75]

As a first approximation, then, we can say that according to Aristotle rhetoric has to do with a capacity to make judgment and argue on things about which is possible to debate: things that "seem to be capable of admitting two possibilities", since they are "for the most part capable of being other than they are."[76] Rhetorical reasoning provides arguments on this kind of thing by starting from premises that are themselves also verisimilar rather than absolute. The validity of its arguments therefore cannot but remain in the field of the verisimilar. We see why we are moving clearly in what Aristotle understood as the realm of ethics and politics; where the precision and absoluteness of mathematics are not to be expected.[77] In this realm things maintain an intrinsic dimension of unpredictability and thus of liberty, since they are the combination of accidental circumstances and of different deliberations taken by a plurality of individuals who differ in character, emotional involvement, beliefs, and so on. If, for Aristotle, rhetoric was a general art of argumentation, then, we can see why for him it was mainly an art for the *polis*, a civic art. As such it is a kind of art that is not reserved for the specialists but is available to all.

This important point is raised by Aristotle at the very beginning of his work when he states that rhetoric—similarly to its counterpart (*antistrophos*) dialectic—is not concerned with any particular object and doesn't belong to any particular science. To a certain extent, he says, it is a capacity that every human being can develop naturally. At the same time, however, Aristotle immediately adds that practicing successfully this capacity is not a question of mere chance but, rather, depends also on experience. This is why the way in which rhetoric operates can be systematized and thus why it can be transformed into an art (*techne*).[78] The particular goal of that art is, according to Aristotle's definition, "to see the available means of persuasion" in each particular case. This, specifies Aristotle, is the "function of no other art."[79] The aim of rhetoric, its *telos*, is to find the available means of persuasion on a variety of different topics. These topics, however, will be generally handled without the direct support of specialist knowledge. The rhetor does not need to develop an in-depth knowledge of the subjects about which he will speak. His specific expertise is rather on the mechanisms of discourse themselves. Indeed Aristotle argues that the more an argument becomes specific and technical, approaching the first principles of that specific topic, the more it moves away from rhetoric and comes closer to the science of that topic.[80]

A key feature of rhetoric is thus precisely the fact of being not a specialist kind of discourse. Although the rhetorician can use the knowledge of experts, normally his material come from the *endoxa*—the generally accepted opinions of the community. A rhetorical speech is addressed to an audience of ordinary citizens, people able to deliberate, but who cannot normally count on a broad education and a sophisticated capacity to judge. Therefore, because rhetoric teaches us to construct the discourse by taking into consideration the audience, then an important requirement for a rhetorical discourse is to avoid a technical and complex language.[81] This is the first level of Aristotle's response to Plato's critique of rhetoric. For him the limitations among which rhetoric operates—limitations in the capacity of the audience to judge and limitations in the knowledge on which the speaker can count—were not reasons for debasing it to a mere (and dangerous) knack. On the contrary, they were basic conditions of the realm in which rhetoric operates—the realm of 'contingency'—and as such have to be understood in order to deal properly with them. The *Rhetoric* is Aristotle's attempt to provide such systematic appreciation in order to produce an art that, by combining and merging with practical reason, can help to move in this contingent realm.[82] The main features of rhetorical discourse—its being based on a verisimilar syllogism (the *enthymeme*), the fact that it persuades through rational (*logos*) and extra-rational means (*ethos* and *pathos*), and the fact that it moulds itself according to its audience—derive from the fact that rhetoric is an art of the contingent. This implies that, as we'll see more in detail later, it is an art that can be systematized but only to a certain extent. Rhetoric's nature is something in between an art and a virtue. It can be formalized but it requires also to be embodied in one's *ethos* through practice.

It is this double dimension that produces the paradoxical and inevitably ambiguous nature of rhetoric and the reason why also in Aristotle's positive view of it we still find elements that make it morally suspicious. One question—if not the main one—which faces scholars of the *Rhetoric* is if it is possible, and if so, how, for Aristotle to have coexist a rhetoric understood as a technique and as a civic and moral virtue.[83] Because, on the one hand, for him rhetoric was clearly an art for the public sphere with a political and ethical value. Rhetoric is "an offshoot of Dialectic and of the science of Ethics, which may be reasonably called Politics,"[84] and all the three genres of rhetoric he distinguishes—deliberative, forensic, and epideictic—have to do, broadly speaking, with political affairs.[85] On the other, it is also clear that, as a technique, something that can be systematized and reduced to a set of norms, it can be considered morally neutral: an instrument to be employed in one way or another.[86] In this respect, the problem lies not only in the fact that, as we have just seen, rhetoric operates with opinions, rather than truth, and persuades only a specific audience (usually made of ordinary people, with all the limitations that this implies), rather than a universal one. The problem is also that rhetoric is morally neutral because it is a discursive capacity, and as such something to some extent autonomous from its contents. Its *telos* is to find the available means of persuasion. It can argue on both sides of the same question. It can employ what is really persuasive, but also what appears to be such.

Reconciling the instrumental and substantive nature of rhetoric is not an easy task. That explains why Aristotle's treatment of rhetoric maintains a certain ambiguity. On more than one occasion he seems to suggest that the speaker can take advantage of the ambiguities and flexibility of the verisimilar in order to defend his case, independently from the soundness and truthfulness of his argument. Such allowances, however, are counterbalanced not only by some moralistic counterpoints made by Aristotle,[87] but also by an optimistic epistemological hypothesis he assumed, which postulates that the truth is by nature more persuasive than its contrary and that the capacity to find the truth and that is held to be true are the same. Moreover, it is clear that Aristotle's view about the relation between opinion and truth is much less dichotomous than that of Plato. So the dependence of rhetoric on generally accepted opinions rather than knowledge is not as problematic as it is in Plato, since it doesn't imply that its arguments are necessarily far from truth.[88] But these considerations are not enough to dispel all the doubts about the moral ambiguity of rhetoric we still find in Aristotle's account.[89]

The crucial step to dissolve such ambiguity is to focus on the dependence of rhetoric on politics. Political science was for Aristotle the most authoritative among the sciences since it is the science that prescribes what must be done in view of the ultimate ends of the *polis*. Political science is the architectonic science: it encompasses all the other sciences and decides on how they should be taught and on their role in the community.[90] Because of its technical character, rhetoric doesn't have in itself the standards for the rightness of its outcomes. They have to be provided by something external: political science.[91] In a sense, rhetoric was for Aristotle an art and, as such, something that can be used both for negative and positive purposes. Under the supervision of political science, however, it can find a direction and thus contribute positively to the well-being of the city. Of course, we need to specify in what form such a contribution consists. In this respect, considering the fact the rhetoric works with opinions, the central question to respond in this regard will be: "can the good orator lift the rhetorical exercise above the level of a mechanical or uncritical popular morality?"[92] Rhetoric employs arguments whose premises come from commonly accepted opinions. And common opinions, with their substratum of particularistic attachments, emotional load, and self-interested or simply indolent deficit of reflectivity, can easily bring unreflective conventionalism or even straightforward bigotry as Plato denounced. This is the material the demagogue manipulates to carry out his strategies. So to what extent must an art of rhetoric contribute to the pursuit of a just community, according to the ultimate ends provided by the science of politics, or become an instrument of demagoguery?

Aristotle thought that rhetoric is an art that helps in arguing and persuading over political and ethical questions and, as such, it is an important element of practical reason. For him it was a basic element of citizenship, since citizenship has to do with the practice of deliberating and deciding in common about the most advantageous and just course of action for the community.[93] But such deliberation is always, to use Bryan Garsten's expression, "situated" and "partial."[94] That is, deliberation about the common good cannot avoid taking into consideration the particular interest. This is because political community is not only, for Aristotle, an organization for the sake of the good life, the honourable and the just, but also in a more realistic interpretation, for the sake of mutual advantage. Even if these two dimensions cannot find a definitive and perfect compromise, they need to be reconciled.[95] The function of rhetoric is to mediate between the abstract generality of political and ethical principles and the concrete particularity of specific cases and individuals, through judgments formulated in verisimilar discourses, which combine rational, emotional and ethical elements, and which aim at persuading.

Because of the nature of human affairs, for Aristotle, political and ethical principles are intrinsically imprecise and debatable[96]; even more so when they are taken in their popular form (*endoxa*), as in the case of the debate that occurs in the public sphere. These principles are brought to bear on specific cases, in which a plurality of points of view, interests, and desires, interact and often clash, inevitably creating a situation in which it is necessary to judge and deliberate in order to conciliate the general and the particular. This is why rhetoric was so important for Aristotle: because it is a form of judgment of particularities that appeals not only to reason but also to emotions and ethical considerations.[97] This is also why the question of rhetoric clearly fits into the more general question, central in Aristotle's philosophy, of the relation between ultimate principles and their contingent materialization, and thus of the role of judgment and practical reason.[98] Rhetoric's political relevance lies in the fact that it is the only way to convince without appealing either to violence or to 'necessary' truths but, rather, through verisimilar arguments that leave actual choice to the audience that is addressed.[99]

But we still need to specify the political role of rhetoric for Aristotle. In particular, we need to see how rhetoric can mediate between the particular and the general, though judgments about particulars that call upon the emotions and the character. In the first part we saw how Aristotle defends rhetoric's position in the state by underlining its argumentative nature, linking it to dialectic, and emphasizing the proximity between truth and the verisimilar. This is the part concerning *logos*. Now we must focus on *pathos* and *ethos*. In general terms, for Aristotle the passions are what allows a connection between a general rule and a particular case and hence permits us to move from thought to action. It is through the experience of an emotion that we can feel a general and abstract principle as something real and tangible and thus find the motivation to move from a simple belief to action. Differently from rational truth, which only needs to be recognized and contemplated, rhetorical persuasion requires convincing people not only to change their mind but also to act accordingly. For that reason it also needs to appeal to their particular attachments, identities, and affects, since appealing to rational arguments alone is insufficient to create such motivation.[100] Nevertheless Aristotle accepted the arousing of the passions only under a crucial condition: that it is made together with reason, that is, that the passions that are aroused are relevant to the matter under discussion and not used in a merely instrumental way. He believed that this function and this condition was best fulfilled by one of the three genres of rhetoric he distinguished: the deliberative (the other two being the forensic and the epideictic). This is why, as Garsten suggests, Aristotle in opposition to the general opinion of his time, considered deliberative rather than forensic rhetoric the most important: because it is only in the former that we can see at work that kind of 'situated judgment' and 'deliberative partiality' which for Aristotle was key to the political process of the *polis*.[101]

Garsten and other theorists of the contemporary 'rhetoric revival' have recovered Aristotle's *Rhetoric* precisely for the insights it can offer on public deliberations; those that can help us go beyond the strictures of contemporary rationalist understandings of deliberation. While the rationalist paradigm of deliberation is concerned with the possibility that rhetoric's extra-rational appeals distort the capacity of citizens to reason impartially, Aristotle found the idea that rhetoric's "appeals to peoples' partial and passionate points of view could often be a good means of drawing out their capacity for judgment and so drawing them into deliberation."[102] Indeed, according to Garsten, Aristotle believed that rhetoric can improve deliberation because for him citizens judge better when they have to deliberate about questions that concern them directly and thus that have also an affective value for them.[103] This is because in these cases, they can judge from their own values and ends, but at the same time maintain an openness towards others' arguments. Such openness rests not only on moral reasons but also on realist ones: first, because the citizens have a stake in the decisions to be taken and thus are interested in finding the best arguments and, second, because they are also concerned with their public reputation and thus compelled to employ arguments that can be accepted in public.

On the other hand, Aristotle believed that partiality can become dangerous when it doesn't contribute to the deliberative process. That happens, for instance, when we try to arouse emotions that are not related with the matter under discussion and thus for other purposes than that of promoting the deliberative process. This is what often happens for Aristotle in the courts, when the jurors are called to judge on questions on which they don't have a direct stake. In those cases, it is more likely that the arousing of emotions is made by the speaker in a mere instrumental way, with the only aim of persuading the audience by "warping" their judgment, as Aristotle said.[104] On the other hand, when we have to deliberate about questions that affect our own interests, the emotions aroused are more likely directly concerned with the matter at hand and therefore to be intertwined with the argument we are making, rather than external.[105] This explains why Aristotle criticized the handbooks of rhetoric of his time for dealing almost exclusively with "matters external to subjects"—that is, with how to arouse the emotions—and completely disregarding what makes of rhetoric an argumentative art: the proofs (*pisteis*) and in particular the *enthymeme*, the rhetorical syllogism which constitutes the 'body' of the proof.[106]

Aristotle, then, didn't create an opposition between reason and the emotions. For him, emotions are grounded in beliefs. Even though they are not completely explicable by them, such grounding in beliefs provides a certain cognitive content and thus makes them susceptible of being modified though argument.[107] On the other hand, the emotions play a crucial role in the way in which we form our beliefs, because as he said, "the judgements we deliver are not the same when we are influenced by joy or sorrow, love or hate."[108] Indeed, one way to understand the emotions for Aristotle is as "those things through which, by undergoing change, people come to differ in their judgments."[109] This is why the emotions can take part in the deliberative process. It is also why for Aristotle it was crucial for the orator to acquire an expertise in dealing with them. Rhetorical discourse has to do with specific and concrete questions, which have certainly also a political and ethical value, but which are not abstract as dialectical arguments. Arousing some particular emotions in the audience is then necessary to bring the audience, not only to share certain arguments in general, but also to take a specific decision about a course of action. In this sense, it was considered by Aristotle a rhetorical proof, since it is a necessary condition for a rhetorical argument to be fully persuasive, moving us from argument to action.

There is also a further reason, however, why the capacity to connect with the emotions was important for Aristotle. Because rhetorical arguments have to do with ethical and political questions, the motivations and purposes of the speaker cannot be a matter of indifference. What is necessary is that the orator is capable of putting the audience into a certain emotional state, displaying a benevolent and friendly attitude towards them to manifest a concern with their situation. This attitude of goodwill (*eunoia*) is one of the three qualities Aristotle listed as necessary for the *ethos*—for him, the most important source of persuasion—to be persuasive.[110] It is a further way in which rhetoric can, through the arousing of the emotions, exercise its mediating role from the particular to the general. As mentioned before, Aristotle' position is in a sense realistic, since it assumes that the aim of a political community is to promote not only the virtuous life, but also mutual advantage. That implies, among other things, that he didn't consider impartiality and detachment as the key condition for public deliberation as is generally assumed by contemporary theorists of democracy. On the contrary, for Aristotle, a politician who fails to show that he is concerned with the particular interests of the audience he is addressing will inevitably fail to gain its support whatever the merit of his argument in terms of justice.[111] This connection with the particular is considered by Aristotle an essential part of how political persuasion works.

If all these ways show how a *certain* level of partiality and attachment is indispensable for political deliberation, we can still ask how we are to establish the limit. Because, of course, responsiveness to the particular, taken at its most extreme manifestation, becomes synonymous with flattery and thus demagoguery. We have also to consider in this respect the further circumstance that for Aristotle the specific aim to which deliberative rhetoric (as we have said, the most important genre for him) is directed is the advantageous, not the noble. Finally, there is the fact that the way that Aristotle discussed *phronesis* in the *Rhetoric* seems to be closer to a merely calculative, morally neutral capacity, than to something in connection with moral virtues, as happens in the *Ethics*.[112] Differently from ethical treatises where the individual endowed with *phronesis* deliberates about what is advantageous for himself but always in the broader horizon of the good life, bringing him to consider the general interest, in the more realist *Rhetoric* such broader horizon recedes into the background so that the advantageous and the noble may find themselves more openly in tension.[113] In this sense, it is clear that Aristotle didn't make *phronesis* and rhetoric completely coincide; even though he listed *phronesis* as one of the features of the *ethos* necessary to make of it a rhetorical proof.[114] The former is a virtue of the intellect, whilst the latter is an art; even if it is an art that can become part of *ethos*. But the point is that the *Rhetoric* is concerned with analysing the mechanisms of persuasion and this implies that the realist dimension of the political process becomes more prominent, in comparison to the *Ethics* or the *Politics*. To show that a course of action is advantageous it is necessary to convince the audience to accept it. Nevertheless, that doesn't mean sacrificing justice for expedience since Aristotle believed that the advantageous is necessary in politics, as it establishes the conditions for its flourishing.[115] The orator deliberates and tries to persuade on political questions and these questions, more or less directly, are always relevant to the well-being of the community.[116] If the relation between the particular and the general in the political realm is necessary because of the reasons we have seen, then such a relation has to be found through the interactions between particular points of view in deliberation. Rhetoric in this sense is for Aristotle the privileged art through which such deliberation should occur. Under the guidance of political science, rhetoric acquires an important role in the city. In order to correctly perform that role, Aristotle believed it is necessary to study and systematize rhetoric. Transforming rhetoric into an art allows us to understand how it works and how to use it for the good of the community, avoiding its use as an instrument of demagoguery. This is the aim of the *Rhetoric*.[117]

Nevertheless, for Aristotle it is not only the supervision of politics and its artistic status that make rhetoric safe and useful for the community. There is a further crucial element: the long process of practice through which the principles of rhetoric become so embedded in the practical reasoning of an orator as to become incorporated into his own *ethos*. This is how for Aristotle rhetoric can develop into a civic virtue. To understand such an essential aspect it is important to keep in mind that according to his definition rhetoric is not the art of persuading but rather the art of finding the available means of persuasion. That is, Aristotle shifted the focus from the result of persuasion to the moment of finding the means through which persuasion is attempted. The normativity of rhetoric is crucially related to this aspect. Rhetoric can persuade using three means, rational and extra-rational: *logos, ethos,* and *pathos*. The way in which the proportion and relation between these three means of persuasion is calculated, in every specific circumstance, is crucial to assess how rhetoric has been employed. To a certain extent such assessment is independent from whether it has achieved, or not, persuasion. If rhetoric was for Aristotle an argumentative art, than it is essential that the rational and extra-rational means it uses to persuade are intermingled and rightly calibrated in a way to form a good argument that the audience can in part or completely accept (or reject).[118] Here persuasion occurs because, as Garver says, the form of the argument—the enthymeme—is passed from the speaker to the audience.[119] It is this aspect that makes of rhetoric a virtue.

The way in which the orator chooses the means of persuasion has to do with his *ethos* because rhetorical deliberation, as a manifestation of *phronesis*, concerns the means rather than the ends, but always in the teleological perspective of the good life. Because politics was essentially for Aristotle the practice of deliberating in common about the good life, rhetoric—as the form of this deliberation—cannot be just an instrument to an end; rather it is also the medium in which such ends are constituted.[120] The quality of rhetoric then is essential to assess the quality of the whole political process, including its ultimate ends. Now, the orator, in order to convince his audience, should employ not only *logos* but also *pathos* and *ethos*. He needs to understand the specificities of audience, in particular its emotions and character. These elements will limit the form of the argument he can develop. At the same time, he should be able to integrate the extra-rational elements with the rational ones, *pathos* and *ethos* with *logos*, creating thus an argument that is directed toward the common good, being at the same time receptive of any particularities. But in forming (and delivering) this argument the orator is simultaneously showing his own character, his *ethos*. In showing what kind of sources of persuasion he chooses (what kind of emotion he decides to arouse and how, for instance) and the form in which he moulds them into an argument, he reveals his own emotive responsiveness, his capacities to distinguish the circumstances, to weigh the probabilities, his logical capacity to argue, his disposition towards the audience and his intentions (if he aims to mere persuasion or to persuade according in view of the common good).[121] In this sense he should display an *ethos* that, differently from that of the demagogue, is able to persuade because it is "evidence of *phronesis* and character" and, as such, something that engenders trust in its audience.[122] The *ethos* of the speaker was indeed considered by Aristotle to be the most important source of persuasion because ethical and political deliberations cannot completely eliminate all the uncertainties.[123] The audience cannot rely only on the argument, because rhetorical deliberation develops merely verisimilar arguments. For this reason the audience needs to form its judgment also by assessing the ethical qualities of the speaker (that is, his capacity to reason rhetorically) displayed in the argument. It is in this sense then that we can say that rhetoric for Aristotle could overcome its merely technical dimension and become a civic virtue and thus part of one's character.

It is this substantive version of rhetoric that Aristotle redeemed as an essential art of the *polis*. It is an art whose function concerns the mediation between the particular and the general. Rhetorical deliberation is a way to find an equilibrium between them, between private and particular interests and beliefs and a more general view of the public good. Or from a different perspective, it is a way to concretize abstract and transcendent principles within the contingent reality of political life. But a definitive point of equilibrium can never be found. The particularisms of a political community cannot be fully reconciled among themselves and never fully harmonized with the general principles. This means that the rhetorical activity of mediation can never be conclusive.

Notes

1. On this see e.g., Samuel Ijsseling, *Rhetoric and Philosophy in Conflict: An Historical Survey* (The Hague: Martinus Nijhoff, 1976), 84–6; Renato Barilli, *Rhetoric* (Minneapolis: University of Minnesota Press, 1989), 6; Brian Vickers, *In Defence of Rhetoric* (Oxford: Clarendon Press, 1988), 83–4.
2. George Kennedy, *A New History of Classical Rhetoric* (Princeton, NJ: Princeton University Press, 1994), 9.
3. Richard A. Lanham, *The Motives of Eloquence: Literary Rhetoric in the Renaissance* (New Haven: Yale University Press, 1976), 1.
4. On the relation between philosophy and rhetoric see e.g., Ijsseling, *Rhetoric and Philosophy in Conflict*, 1–18; Vickers, *In Defence of Rhetoric*, i–viii, 83–4, 212; Kennedy, *A New History of Classical Rhetoric*, 6–9; David M. Timmerman and Edward Schiappa, *Classical Greek Rhetorical Theory and the Disciplining of Discourse* (New York: Cambridge University Press, 2010), Ch. 3.
5. Andrea W. Nightingale, *Genres in Dialogue: Plato and the Construct of Philosophy* (Cambridge: Cambridge University Press, 1995), 14; Kathryn A. Morgan, *Myth and Philosophy from the Pre-Socratics to Plato* (Cambridge and New York: Cambridge University Press, 2000), 1–2, 33.
6. Thomas Cole, *The Origins of Rhetoric in Ancient Greece* (Baltimore: Johns Hopkins University Press, 1999), 2, etc.; Edward Schiappa, *The Beginnings of Rhetorical Theory in Classical Greece* (New Haven, CT. and London: Yale University Press, 1999), 14–19.
7. James Kastely, "In Defense of Plato's Gorgias," *PMLA* 106 (1991): 96.
8. Harvey Yunis, *Taming Democracy: Models of Political Rhetoric in Classical Athens* (Ithaca and London: Cornell University Press, 1996), 17.

9. The literature on the history of rhetoric is of course extremely vast. On its origins in particular, see for instance: Vickers, *In Defence of Rhetoric*, 1–11; Kennedy, *A New History of Classical Rhetoric*, Chs. 1, 2, 3; Michel Meyer, *Histoire de la rhétorique des Grecs à nos jours* (Paris: Librairie générale française, 1999), 19–25; Yunis, *Taming Democracy*, 1–15.

10. E.g. Gorgias, *Encomium of Helen*, trans. D. M. Macdowell (Bristol: Bristol Classical Press, 1982), 8; Barbara Cassin, *L'effet sophistique* (Paris: Gallimard, 1995), 66–99. In the last twenty years or more, there has been a significant upsurge of interest in the sophists. This interest has developed in two directions. On the one hand, an increasing number of theorists have tried to rehabilitate the image of sophists such as Protagoras, or Gorgias, with the argument that they were the first to disclose the power of language to create reality, as an instrument for democratic emancipation, and to posit an alternative to Plato's foundationalist and authoritarian philosophy. On the other, there are other scholars who have come to the conclusion that it is untenable the same idea that it is possible to associate to the sophists in general a distinctive philosophical conception and a distinctive conception of rhetoric. Cf.: G. B. Kerferd, *The Sophistic Movement* (Cambridge: Cambridge University Press, 1981); John Poulakos, *Sophistical Rhetoric in Classical Greece* (Columbia, SC: University of South Carolina, 1995); Christopher L. Johnstone, "Sophistical Wisdom: Politikê Aretê and 'Logosophia'," *Philosophy and Rhetoric* 39 (2006); Schiappa, *The Beginnings of Rhetorical Theory in Classical Greece*.

11. George Kennedy, *Classical Rhetoric and Its Christian and Secular Tradition from Ancient to Modern Times* (Chapel Hill: University of North Carolina Press, 1980), 31.

12. Timmerman and Schiappa, *Classical Greek Rhetorical Theory and the Disciplining of Discourse*, 54 and Ch. 3; John Poulakos, "Rhetoric and Civic Education: From the Sophists to Isocrates," in *Isocrates and Civic Education*, ed. Takis Poulakos and David J. Depew (Austin: University of Texas Press, 2004), 69–74.

13. E.g. Isocrates, "Against the Sophists," in *Isocrates II*, trans. George Norlin (London: William Heinemann, 1929), 20.

14. Isocrates, "Antidosis," in *Isocrates II*, trans. George Norlin (London: William Heinemann, 1929), 50, 84–5, 253–8, 70–1, 85; Isocrates, "Helen," in *Isocrates III*, trans. Larue Van Hook (London: William Heinemann, 1945), 1, 5.

15. Allan D. Bloom, "The Political Philosophy of Isocrates" (PhD Dissertation, University of Chicago, 1955), 3. Plato himself regarded Isocrates as someone between a philosopher and a politician. Plato's opinion of Isocrates however was not completely negative, since he didn't

consider him totally devoid of philosophical talent. What he criticized was his idea of philosophy, which he considered deficient as it denies the necessity to investigate into the foundations of moral and political principles and contents itself with endorsing the conventional norms of the city. Terence H. Irwin, "Plato: The Intellectual Background," in *The Cambridge Companion to Plato*, ed. Richard Kraut (Cambridge: Cambridge University Press, 1992), 67; Plato, *Phaedrus*, trans. Christopher Rowe (Warminster: Aris and Phillips, 1986), 279a–b; Plato, *Euthydemus*, trans. Rosamond Kent Sprague (Indianapolis: Bobbs-Merrill, 1985), 305b–06c.

16. Werner Jaeger, *Paideia: The Ideals of Greek Culture. Vol. 3: The Conflict of Cultural Ideas in the Age of Plato* (Oxford: Basil Blackwell, 1945), 53.
17. Ibid., 46–7; Paul O. Kristeller, *Renaissance Thought and Its Sources*, ed. Michael Mooney (New York: Columbia University Press, 1979), 218.
18. On Isocrates's political, pedagogical, and cultural conception see in particular: Takis Poulakos and David J. Depew, eds., *Isocrates and Civic Education* (Austin: University of Texas Press, 2004). Cf. Yunis, *Taming Democracy*, 28.
19. This point has been made more recently by: Danielle S. Allen, *Why Plato Wrote* (Malden, MA: Wiley-Blackwell, 2010).
20. I have to clarify here that even if Plato normally associated rhetoric with the art of speaking of the sophists, he didn't conflate them. Indeed his view of rhetoric was not completely negative, as it was instead his view on the art of speaking of the sophists. See e.g., Plato, *Gorgias*, trans. Donald J. Zeyl (Indianapolis: Hackett, 1987), 465c.
21. Hans-Georg Gadamer, *Plato's Dialectical Ethics: Phenomenological Interpretations Relating to the "Philebus"* (New Haven: Yale University Press, 1991), 20.
22. Hans-Georg Gadamer, *Dialogue and Dialectic: Eight Hermeneutical Studies on Plato* (New Haven: Yale University Press, 1980), 118, 22–3.
23. Ibid., 114. See also: Martin Heidegger, *Plato's Sophist* (Bloomington, IN: Indiana University Press, 1997), 16ff.
24. Gadamer, *Dialogue and Dialectic*, 116.
25. Gadamer, *Plato's Dialectical Ethics*, 3–4, 33–51. Cf. Marina McCoy, *Plato on the Rhetoric of Philosophers and Sophists* (Cambridge and New York: Cambridge University Press, 2008).
26. Plato, *The Theaetetus of Plato*, trans. Jane Levett (Indianapolis: Hackett, 1990), 174a.
27. Gadamer, *Plato's Dialectical Ethics*, 46.
28. So we can say that at the most general level Socrates and Plato's "deepest criticism of rhetoric is that it is a perversion of our relation to the power of speech." Joe Sachs, "Introduction," in *Plato: Gorgias, and Aristotle: Rhetoric*, trans. Joe Sachs (Newburyport, MA: Focus, 2009).

29. Devin Stauffer, *The Unity of Plato's Gorgias: Rhetoric, Justice, and the Philosophic Life* (Cambridge: Cambridge University Press, 2006), 38, 166; Yunis, *Taming Democracy*, 157–60; Alessandra Fussi, "Why Is the Gorgias So Bitter?," *Philosophy and Rhetoric* 33 (2000). In the *Republic* the positive function attributed to rhetoric is broader, because it concerns also the possibility to persuade the city to be governed by the philosophers. In this dialogue, the key character in this respect is Thrasymachus, because Socrates thinks that his rhetorical ability can be useful for such purpose. Leo Strauss, *The City and Man* (Chicago: Rand McNally & Company, 1964), 23–4.
30. Plato, *Gorgias*, 447a.
31. Eric Voegelin, *Order and History, Volume III: Plato and Aristotle*, ed. Dante Germino (Columbia: University of Columbia Press, 2000), 78ff.
32. Plato, *Gorgias*, 449a–d.
33. Ibid., 452d–53a.
34. Stauffer, *The Unity of Plato's Gorgias*, 32. Regarding the vagueness of the object of the art of discourse employed and taught by the sophists, according to Plato, Heidegger has written: "It precisely refuses to deal substantially with that regarding which it is supposed teach others how to speak. It is a know-how that is not oriented toward any substantive content but instead aims at a purely extrinsic, or, as we say, 'technical', procedure." Heidegger, *Plato's Sophist*, 215.
35. Plato, *Gorgias*, 454e–55a, 456d, 457a–b, 459a–d.
36. Cf. Bruce McComiskey, "Disassembling Plato's Critique of Rhetoric in the Gorgias (447a–466a)," *Rhetoric Review* 10 (1992).
37. Plato, *Gorgias*, 462c, 463d, 464c–65d, etc.
38. Similarly in the *Philebus* Plato attributed to Gorgias the opinion that "the art of persuasion makes everything its slave not by force but by willing submission," evoking again the parallel between rhetoric and tyranny. Plato cited in: Yunis, *Taming Democracy*, 120.
39. In the *Gorgias* music and poetry are explicitly associated to rhetoric by Socrates, as practices that produce only pleasure without any concern for the public good. Poetry is also defined a form of public speaking. Plato, *Gorgias*, 501a–02d.
40. Allan D. Bloom, "Interpretative Essay," in *The Republic of Plato*, trans. Allan D. Bloom (New York: Basic Books, 1991), 434.
41. Nietzsche cited in Leo Strauss, "Plato," in *History of Political Philosophy*, ed. Leo Strauss and Joseph Cropsey (Chicago: Rand McNally, 1963), 66; Plato, *The Republic of Plato*, trans. Allan D. Bloom (New York: Basic Books, 1991), 386a ff., 398c ff., 602c–06d. Cf. Strauss, "Plato," 66–7; Leo Strauss, "The Problem of Socrates: Five Lectures," in *The Rebirth of Classical Political Rationalism: An Introduction to the Thought of Leo Strauss*, ed. Thomas L. Pangle (Chicago: University of Chicago Press, 1989), 177–83; Gadamer, *Plato's Dialectical Ethics*, 63.

42. Roger Boesche, *Theories of Tyranny: From Plato to Arendt* (University Park: Pennsylvania State University Press, 1996), 44–5.
43. As some commentators have suggested, if Socrates's tone with Gorgias is polite and even respectful, with Polus he becomes condescending, and with Callicles patently aggressive. Gorgias is, among Socrates's three interlocutors, the one who is more open to justice and thus also a potential point of reference to develop the kind of positive rhetoric Plato will defend in the *Phaedrus*. Fussi, "Why Is the Gorgias So Bitter?," 55; Stauffer, *The Unity of Plato's Gorgias*, 37–8.
44. Plato, *Gorgias*, 466c.
45. Ibid., 473e. Eric Voegelin has written that Polus represents "the type of man who will piously praise the rule of law and condemn the tyrant and who fervently envies the tyrant and would love nothing better than to be one himself. In a decadent society he is the representative of the great reservoir of common men who paralyze every effort at order and supply mass-connivance in the rise of the tyrant." Voegelin, *Order and History, Volume III: Plato and Aristotle*, 80. In this respect we can recall Polus's comments on the tyrant of Macedonia, Archelaus, whom he considers an example of an unjust but happy person. Plato, *Gorgias*, 469d–71d.
46. Paul Shorey cited in Stauffer, *The Unity of Plato's Gorgias*, 3.
47. Plato, *Gorgias*, 483b–d, 492a–c.
48. Ibid., 484d–86b, cf. 521d–22a. Plato, "Apology," in *Plato: Complete Works*, trans. G. M. A. Grube and ed. John M. Cooper (Indianapolis: Hackett, 1997), 28b–d.
49. Plato, *Gorgias*, 500c, see also 487e–88a.
50. Ibid., 502e–03a, 512e–13e, 515a, 517b–c, 521a–d.
51. Ibid., 521d. This declaration contrasts with the admission of political ineptitude made by Socrates earlier in the dialogue (474a).
52. See for instance: Vickers, *In Defence of Rhetoric*, 83ff.; McComiskey, "Disassembling Plato's Critique of Rhetoric in the Gorgias (447a–466a)." Cf. Ijsseling, *Rhetoric and Philosophy in Conflict*, Ch. 2; Barilli, *Rhetoric*, 6–9; Kennedy, *A New History of Classical Rhetoric*, 35–9.
53. Socrates shows at least that his interlocutors do not know how to defend their positions and demonstrate that his opinions are wrong. Plato, *Gorgias*, 509a, 527a–b.
54. Seth Benardete, *The Rhetoric of Morality and Philosophy: Plato's Gorgias and Phaedrus* (Chicago and London: University of Chicago, 1991), 13.
55. Plato, *Gorgias*, 503a–04e.
56. Cf. Kastely, "In Defense of Plato's Gorgias"; Fussi, "Why Is the Gorgias So Bitter?," 39; Stauffer, *The Unity of Plato's Gorgias*; McCoy, *Plato on the Rhetoric of Philosophers and Sophists*, 86.

57. Plato, *Phaedrus*, 261a–b. Against the traditional reading that sets the *Gorgias* in contrast with the *Phaedrus*, some scholars have argued that there is no real difference among these two dialogues in relation to Plato's approach to rhetoric. The difference for them is contingent, it depends on the character of Socrates's interlocutors. In the former dialogue, the corrupt or deficient moral character of his interlocutors means that they can employ rhetoric in a dangerous way, while in the latter, the situation is the opposite. McCoy, *Plato on the Rhetoric of Philosophers and Sophists*, 189.
58. Plato, *Phaedrus*, 260d.
59. Ibid., 261c–63c.
60. Ibid., 266c–74b.
61. Ibid., 265d–e.
62. Ibid., 264c, 266d ff. According to Murray the *Phaedrus* doesn't offer a simple re-evaluation of rhetoric in comparison to the *Gorgias*, but rather a new theory of rhetoric. This new rhetoric, because it is under the supervision of philosophy, can employ also morally questionable instruments as deception. James S. Murray, "Disputation, Deception, and Dialectic: Plato on the True Rhetoric (Phaedrus 261–6)," *Philosophy and Rhetoric* 21 (1988). Cf. with note 57.
63. Plato, *Phaedrus*, 272a–b.
64. McComiskey, "Disassembling Plato's Critique of Rhetoric in the Gorgias (447a–466a)," 206.
65. Plato, *Phaedrus*, 271a, 277b.
66. McCoy, *Plato on the Rhetoric of Philosophers and Sophists*, 193.
67. Plato, *The Republic of Plato*, 389b–c, 414b–15d.
68. The literature on this dimension of Plato's philosophy is vast. For a recent treatment see: McCoy, *Plato on the Rhetoric of Philosophers and Sophists*, 15.
69. Eric Voegelin, "Reason: The Classic Experience (1974)," in *Pubblished Essays, 1966–1985*, ed. Ellis Sandoz (Baton Rouge and London: Louisiana State University Press, 1990); Voegelin, *Order and History, Volume III, Plato and Aristotle*; John Sallis, *Being and Logos: Reading the Platonic Dialogues* (Bloomington: Indiana University Press, 1996); Strauss, *The City and Man*.
70. See for instance: Kennedy, *A New History of Classical Rhetoric*, 53; Eugene Garver, *Aristotle's Rhetoric: An Art of Character* (Chicago and London: University of Chicago Press, 1994), 87. On the systematicity of Aristotle's *Rhetoric*, however, there is an ample debate spurring from the fact that this treatise (which is a collection of notes from his courses, edited at different times) suffers from some conceptual inaccuracies and a certain disunity in the structure. In the last decades an increasing number

of scholars have countered this view on the *Rhetoric* stressing instead its coherence, both in terms of the work in itself—as a theory of rhetoric based on the creation of proofs through inference—and in light of Aristotle's *corpus* as a whole, in particular in relation to his political and ethical works. For the former argument see: William M. A. Grimaldi, *Aristotle, Rhetoric I: A Commentary* (New York: Fordham University Press, 1980); Chaïm Perelman and Lucie Olbrechts-Tyteca, *Traité de l'argumentation. La nouvelle rhétorique* (Brussels: Editions de l'Université de Bruxelles, 1988); Alan G. Gross, "The Conceptual Unity of Aristotle's Rhetoric," *Philosophy and Rhetoric* 34 (2001). And for the latter: Amâelie Rorty, ed., *Essays on Aristotle's Rhetoric* (Berkeley and London: University of California Press, 1996).

71. According to Alan Gross and Arthus Walzer "all subsequent rhetorical theory is but a series of responses to issues raised by" Aristotle's *Rhetoric*. Alan G. Gross and Arthur E. Walzer, "Preface," in *Rereading Aristotle's Rhetoric*, ed. Alan G. Gross and Arthur E. Walzer (Carbondale: Southern Illinois University Press, 2000), ix. The influence of this work in the tradition of rhetoric however has not been constant along the centuries. If in ancient times the *Rhetoric* was generally considered a point of reference, in the Middle Age its study was restricted to scholastic philosophers, since professional rhetors privileged the works of Cicero or Quintilian. See: William W. Fortenbaugh and David C. Mirhady, eds., *Peripatetic Rhetoric after Aristotle* (New Brunswick, NJ: Transaction Publishers, 1994); George A. Kennedy, "Prooemion," in *Aristotle: On Rhetoric: A Theory of Civic Discourse*, trans. George A. Kennedy (New York and Oxford: Oxford University Press, 1991).

72. The recovery of Aristotle's view of rhetoric as a manifestation of *phronesis* can be included in the more general revival of Aristotle's practical philosophy that occurred in the second half of the twentieth century. This revival was instigated by Heidegger's influential lectures in Marburg between 1924 and 1925 on Aristotle's *Ethics* and *Rhetoric*, in which he explored the pre-theoretical, practical grounds of philosophy, as a way of life in the *polis* through speech and dialogue. Heidegger, *Plato's Sophist*; Martin Heidegger, *Basic Concepts of Aristotelian Philosophy* (Bloomington: Indiana University Press, 2009). These early explorations of Heidegger in ancient practical philosophy, with their emphasis on language and hermeneutics, played an important role in shaping the future research of figures such as Gadamer, Strauss, or Arendt (who attended those courses). See: Daniel M. Gross and Ansgar Kemmann, eds., *Heidegger and Rhetoric* (Albany, NY: SUNY, 2005); Garver, *Aristotle's Rhetoric*, 3–12; Bryan Garsten, "The Rhetoric Revival in Political Theory," *Annual Review of Political Science* 14 (2011): 162.

73. Aristotle, *On Rhetoric: A Theory of Civic Discourse*, trans. George A. Kennedy (New York and Oxford: Oxford University Press, 1991), 1355a. Cf. Plato, *Phaedrus*, 269b–d.
74. Pierre Aubenque, *La prudence chez Aristote* (Paris: Presses universitaires de France, 1963), 65.
75. William M. A. Grimaldi, "Rhetoric and the Philosophy of Aristotle," *The Classical Journal* 53 (1958): 372.
76. Aristotle, *On Rhetoric*, 1357a.
77. Aristotle, *The Nicomachean Ethics*, trans. Hippocrates G. Apostle (Dordrecht and Boston: Reidel, 1980), 1094b, 1098a.
78. Aristotle, *On Rhetoric*, 1354a.
79. Ibid., 1355b.
80. Ibid., 1358a, cf. 1359b.
81. E.g. ibid., 1354a, 1357a, 1404a. See also: Aristotle, *The Nicomachean Ethics*, 1179b.
82. Cf. Garver, *Aristotle's Rhetoric*, 40; Bryan Garsten, *Saving Persuasion: A Defense of Rhetoric and Judgment* (Cambridge, MA: Harvard University Press, 2006), 129. As Martha Nussbaum has explained, in ancient Greek thought and particularly in Plato's philosophy, *techne* is set in opposition to contingency (*tuche*) and conceived as a way to control it. She writes: "[t]echne...is deliberate application of human intelligence to some part of the world, yielding some control over *tuche*; it is concerned with the management of need and with prediction and control concerning future contingencies. The person who lives by *techne* does not come to each new experience without foresight or resource. He possess some sort of systematic grasp...that will take him to the new situation well prepared, removed from blind dependence on what happens." Martha Nussbaum, *The Fragility of Goodness: Luck and Ethics in Greek Tragedy and Philosophy* (Cambridge: Cambridge University Press, 2001), 95.
83. Probably the most sophisticated analysis of this crucial question in Aristotle's *Rhetoric* is the following: Garver, *Aristotle's Rhetoric*.
84. Aristotle, *On Rhetoric*, 1356a. Cf. Aristotle, *The Nicomachean Ethics*, 1094b.
85. Aristotle, *On Rhetoric*, 1358b.
86. Before the *Rhetoric* began to be recovered as an important philosophical work by the pioneering analysis of Gadamer and Perelman, the prevailing opinion was that this work doesn't provide much more than a handbook of rhetorical techniques with a merely practical content. For instance: W. D. Ross, *Aristotle* (London: Methuen & Co., 1923), 289–90. For a more contemporary position in the same line, see: Kennedy, *A New History of Classical Rhetoric*, 55–6. In the last years, however, a number of studies have been published that emphasize the importance of the

Rhetoric within the philosophy of Aristotle. See e.g., Garver, *Aristotle's Rhetoric*; Stephen Halliwell, "Popular Morality, Philosophical Ethics, and the Rhetoric," in *Aristotle's Rhetoric: Philosophical Essays*, ed. David J. Furley and Alexander Nehamas (Princeton: Princeton University Press, 1994); T. H. Irwin, "Ethics in the *Rhetoric* and in the Ethics," in *Essays on Aristotle's Rhetoric*, ed. Amâelie Rorty (Berkeley and London: University of California Press, 1996). See also the less recent: William M. A. Grimaldi, *Studies in the Philosophy of Aristotle's Rhetoric* (Wiesbaden: Franz Steiner Verlag, 1972). See supra note 70.

87. For instance, in one occasion Aristotle suggests that in a trial the speaker can take advantage of the ambiguities of the law to defend his case. On the other hand, he underlines that the technique to argue on both sides shouldn't be used to persuade to take the wrong decision, but only to discover when an opponent is using an fallacious argument. Aristotle, *On Rhetoric*, 1375a–b.

88. Stephen Halliwell explains that the fact that rhetoric relies on opinions, rather than on truth, is not morally problematic for Aristotle because for him: first, the opinions on justice of the multitude and the few wise are not systematically divergent; second, in some cases the multitude can even be a better judge than the few wise; finally, the beliefs of the latter are included in popular morality (*endoxa* is not simple common sense, but the most authoritative commonly held opinions). Halliwell, "Popular Morality, Philosophical Ethics, and the Rhetoric," 214.

89. Robert Wardy for instance has cast doubts on the epistemological optimism Aristotle expresses on the capacity of truth to be stronger than its contrary and hence on the capacity of Aristotle to conciliate morality with the rhetoric as a neutral instrument. For Wardy, if assuming such natural presupposition of truth is problematic in the case of dialectical argumentation (where truth results from a struggle between opposite arguments), in the rhetoric it is much more so, since rhetoric has to do with extrarational elements. After all, Wardy asks, if truth is naturally stronger than its contrary, as argued by Aristotle, why would we need rhetoric to persuade in the first place? Robert Wardy, "Might Is the Truth and It Shall Prevail?," in *Essays on Aristotle's Rhetoric*, ed. Amâelie Rorty (Berkeley and London: University of California Press, 1996).

90. Aristotle, *The Nicomachean Ethics*, 1094a, 152b. See also: Aristotle, *Politics*, trans. C. D. C. Reeve (with introduction and notes) (Indianapolis: Hackett, 1998), 1282b.

91. Cf. Arash Abizadeh, "The Passions of the Wise: 'Phronêsis', Rhetoric, and Aristotle's Passionate Practical Deliberation," *The Review of Metaphysics* 56 (2002): 277.

92. Stephen Halliwell, "The Challenge of Rhetoric to Political and Ethical Theory in Aristotle," in *Essays on Aristotle's Rhetoric*, ed. Amâelie Rorty (Berkeley and London: University of California Press, 1996), 179.
93. E.g., Aristotle, *Politics*, 1252b–53a, 1275a.
94. Garsten, *Saving Persuasion*, Ch. 4.
95. A more realistic interpretation of Aristotle's view of politics and deliberation, in which rhetoric 'partiality' plays an important mediating role has been proposed by: Bernard Yack, "Rhetoric and Public Reasoning: An Aristotelian Understanding of Political Deliberation," *Political Theory* 34 (2006). See also: Bernard Yack, *The Problems of a Political Animal: Community, Justice, and Conflict in Aristotelian Political Thought* (Berkeley: University of California Press, 1993), Ch. 3.
96. E.g. Aristotle, *The Nicomachean Ethics*, 1094a–b.
97. Aristotle, *On Rhetoric*, 1377b, cf. 1391b.
98. Given the centrality of rhetoric in the Aristotelian conception of practical reason, Garver notes, it is surprising that thinkers who have been so engaged in the recovery of this aspect of his philosophy, as Hannah Arendt or Alasdair MacIntyre, have neglected the *Rhetoric*. For Garver this text constitutes a crucial moment in the "history of prudence." Garver, *Aristotle's Rhetoric*, 5.
99. The words with which Perelman and Olbrechts-Tyteca conclude their famous *Traité de l'argumentation* remark the crucial link between rhetoric, understood as a form of reasoning, and freedom: "only the existence of an argumentation, that is neither binding, nor arbitrary, gives meaning to human freedom." My translation. Perelman and Olbrechts-Tyteca, *Traité de l'argumentation*, 682. Cf. Danielle S. Allen, *Talking to Strangers: Anxieties of Citizenship since Brown V. Board of Education* (Chicago: University of Chicago Press, 2004), 141; Garsten, *Saving Persuasion*, 4–10.
100. The motivating capacity of rhetoric is one of its aspects that has been more emphasized by the theorists of the 'rhetoric revival'. Garsten, "The Rhetoric Revival in Political Theory"; John S. Dryzek, "Rhetoric in Democracy: A Systemic Appreciation," *Political Theory* 38 (2010); Iris Marion Young, *Inclusion and Democracy* (Oxford and New York: Oxford University Press, 2000), 65–70.
101. Garsten, *Saving Persuasion*, Ch. 3. Cf. Mary P. Nichols, "Aristotle's Defense of Rhetoric," *The Journal of Politics* 49 (1987): 663.
102. Garsten, *Saving Persuasion*, 13.
103. Ibid., 6.
104. Aristotle, *On Rhetoric*, 1355a.
105. Garsten, *Saving Persuasion*, 119–28.

106. Aristotle, *On Rhetoric*, 1354a. In relation to the arousing of the emotions, some scholars have seen a contradiction in the *Rhetoric* between the critical remark Aristotle makes in the first book, when he says that "is wrong to warp the jury by leading them into anger or envy or pity" and the rest of the treatise (in particular the second book), where he approves the emotions as a rhetorical proof. Ibid., 1356a. This contradiction is one of the elements that have been indicated to corroborate the idea that the *Rhetoric* is not a unique work, but the result of a later edition of different and incoherent texts. However other scholars have sustained that what Aristotle is really arguing against is a prejudicial arousing of the emotions, one that is made independently from argument and the matter at hand. Cf. Grimaldi, *Studies in the Philosophy of Aristotle's Rhetoric*, 44; Robert Wardy, *The Birth of Rhetoric: Gorgias, Plato, and Their Successors* (London and New York: Routledge, 1996), 112–13; Jamie Dow, *Passions and Persuasion in Aristotle's Rhetoric* (Oxford: Oxford University Press, 2015), Ch. 7.

107. One way to understand what means for Aristotle that the emotions have a cognitive dimension is to see them as "representational states in which the subject takes things to be the way they are represented." Dow, *Passions and Persuasion in Aristotle's Rhetoric*, 1.

108. Aristotle, *On Rhetoric*, 1356a.

109. Ibid., 1378a. That for Aristotle the emotions are connected to beliefs can be seen, for instance, in the definition he gives of 'anger' (*orge*): "desire, accompanied by distress, for conspicuous retaliation because of a conspicuous slight that was directed, without justification, against oneself or those near to one." 'Fear' (*phobos*), to cite another example, is defined by him as "a sort of pain or agitation derived from the imagination (*phantasia*) of a future descriptive or painful evil;" and pity (*eleos*) as "a certain pain at an apparently destructive or painful evil happening to one who does not deserve it." Ibid., 1378a, 82a, 85b. These examples show that for Aristotle the emotions are not deprived of a rational content, since they are based on perceptions and judgments of value. On the emotions in Aristotle, see: Martha Nussbaum, "Aristotle on Emotions and Rational Persuasion," in *Essays on Aristotle's Rhetoric*, ed. Amâelie Rorty (Berkeley and London: University of California Press, 1996); Dow, *Passions and Persuasion in Aristotle's Rhetoric*, Ch. 8–10; Larry Arnhart, *Aristotle on Political Reasoning: A Commentary on the Rhetoric* (DeKalb: Northern Illinois University Press, 1981), 113–15; William W. Fortenbaugh, *Aristotle on Emotion: A Contribution to Philosophical Psychology, Rhetoric, Poetics, Politics and Ethics* (London: Duckworth, 2002); Nichols, "Aristotle's Defense of Rhetoric," 664.

110. Aristotle, *On Rhetoric*, 1378a.

111. Yack, "Rhetoric and Public Reasoning: An Aristotelian Understanding of Political Deliberation."
112. Aristotle, *On Rhetoric*, 1417a23–27.
113. Cf. Aristotle, *The Nicomachean Ethics*, 1140a, 1144a–45a; Aristotle, *On Rhetoric*, 1366b36–67a61, 1390a1.
114. On the relation between *phronesis* and rhetoric, see: Garver, *Aristotle's Rhetoric*, Chs. 5 and 6.
115. Halliwell, "Popular Morality, Philosophical Ethics, and the Rhetoric," 186. Cf. Aristotle, *On Rhetoric*, 1365b25, 1375b3; Aristotle, *Politics*, 1278b21–23; Aristotle, *The Nicomachean Ethics*, 1160a8–25.
116. Aristotle, *On Rhetoric*, 1359a30–63b.
117. The *Rhetoric* thus can be read also as Aristotle's attempt to convince the rulers of the utility of the art of rhetoric for the *polis* through the explanation of how it can enhance public deliberation. Garver, *Aristotle's Rhetoric*, 25, 245. Garsten, *Saving Persuasion*, 117; Dow, *Passions and Persuasion in Aristotle's Rhetoric*, Ch. 3.
118. According to Garver, rhetoric is a *praxis* and a civic virtue because it prioritizes what he calls its 'guiding ends', over its 'given' ones (or also, its 'internal' over its 'external' ends). The former are standards of judgment that are internal to the practice itself—rhetoric as an argumentative art—while the latter are related to the external aim of persuasion. Garver, *Aristotle's Rhetoric*, 33–5 and *passim*.
119. Ibid., 32.
120. Cf. Ronald Beiner, *Political Judgment* (Chicago: University of Chicago Press, 1983), 94–95.
121. In particular, Aristotle specifies that to win the trust of the audience and thus be persuasive, the *ethos* of the speaker should display: *phronesis*, *arete* (virtue), and *eunoia* (goodwill). This is the first and more relevant sense in which according to Aristotle the *ethos* can persuade. Aristotle, *On Rhetoric*, 1356a4–13, 1366a8–16, 1377b20–24, 1378a6–15. Aristotle refers also to a second important sense in which the *ethos* can persuade: when the speaker persuades because his discourse takes in consideration the *ethos* of the audience (its tastes, moods, beliefs, etc.). Ibid., 1365b21–28, 1388b31–89a2. On this topic see: Abizadeh, "The Passions of the Wise: 'Phronêsis', Rhetoric, and Aristotle's Passionate Practical Deliberation," 288; Wardy, "Might Is the Truth and It Shall Prevail?," 63; Garver, *Aristotle's Rhetoric*, Ch. 5. Before Aristotle, however, it was Plato to suggest that the *ethos* is a source of persuasion. Plato, *Phaedrus*, 269d–74a.
122. Garver, *Aristotle's Rhetoric*, 147.
123. The higher the level of uncertainty, the more important becomes for Aristotle the *ethos* as a source of persuasion. It is important also to under-

line that for him the trust generated in the audience by the *ethos* of the speaker should be the result of a judgment on the speech itself and not on any previous notions the audience may have of him. Aristotle, *On Rhetoric*, 1356a4. Cf. Aristotle, *The Nicomachean Ethics*, 1112b. On the relevance of rhetoric as a way to engender trust in societies characterized by historically deep rooted cleavages see: Allen, *Talking to Strangers*. Cf. Aristotle, *On Rhetoric*, 1356a13.

CHAPTER 3

The Union of Philosophy and Rhetoric: Cicero and Quintilian

3.1 Introduction: Bringing Philosophy and Rhetoric Together

With a common concern about the possibility that rhetoric could become an instrument for demagoguery, Plato and Aristotle arrived at two different conclusions about the relevance and scope of this art. The former underlined above all the risks rhetoric represents for the city (in the *Gorgias*) and eventually allowed its presence only after its submission to philosophy (in the *Phaedrus*); the latter, instead, vindicated its great value for the city, as an art for dealing with contingency in politics, through a practice of public deliberation aimed at the good of the community. Such difference clearly reflects the broader divergence Plato and Aristotle exhibit on the question of the relation between the ideal and the contingent, theory and practice. Nevertheless despite their differences, Plato and Aristotle also shared a crucial element: both were philosophers and believed that the *bios theoretikos,* or the *vita contemplativa*—that is, a life devoted to the contemplation of the first principles governing the cosmos—is the best form of life.[1] In this sense, they are emblematic representatives of a position generally shared by ancient philosophy and based in the belief that, in the words of Arendt, natural things, or "things that are by themselves whatever they are," are ontologically superior to "things which owe their existence to man."[2] Philosophers, Arendt explained, held

© The Author(s) 2018
G. Ballacci, *Political Theory between Philosophy and Rhetoric*, Rhetoric, Politics and Society,
https://doi.org/10.1057/978-1-349-95293-9_3

that humans can aspire to contemplate (*theorein*) these natural, eternal things only in a state of absolute quiet (*skholia*); and therefore, they saw action as something intrinsically inferior to theoretical contemplation.[3]

In this chapter, by contrast, I will focus on the contribution of thinkers such as Cicero, Quintilian, and some of their followers in Renaissance Humanism up until Giambattista Vico, who shared the idea the *vita activa* is the most important one; but at the same time who claimed that wisdom is an indispensable element. They believed that wisdom is important not only for the well-being of the individual, but also to avoid debasing politics to an all too mundane continuous search for compromises, or even worse a naked struggle for power. In other words, even if they proclaimed the superiority of the *vita activa* they considered the *vita contemplativa* a very noble and necessary endeavour. Indeed in all these thinkers the relation between these two forms of life and the difficult attempt to combine them is a central topic. As I will show in the following pages, it is mainly because of that that rhetoric came to assume for them an absolute central position in their conceptions. Isocrates, as we have seen, can be considered one of the first exponents of such a tradition of thinking. But Cicero represents without doubt the most significant example of this tradition: not only because the question of the relation between the *vita contemplativa* and the *vita activa* and how to combine them runs through many of his writings, but also because he tried to combine them in his own life. How to inhabit that 'no man's land' between politics (and rhetoric) and philosophy, raised in the first chapter in relation to Isocrates, became the primary goal for Cicero. Part of the criticisms that he has attracted along the centuries for his supposedly superficiality, lack of originality, and excessive eclecticism—by thinkers such as Plutarch, Montaigne, Nietzsche, Hegel, Croce, or Heidegger—can be explained to some extent by an underlying assumption of an intrinsic incompatibility between philosophy and politics.[4] Cicero's thought instead is marked by a continuous exploration of the possibilities (and of the obstacles) to combine these two poles. And it is precisely in eloquence that he individuated the key factor to operate such a combination. This is the main reason why it is to Cicero that we owe the most ambitious conception of rhetoric in the tradition of this art: the concrete manifestation of an encyclopaedic wisdom that, in its capacity to actualize and accomplish itself in political action through communication, reaches its perfection—what the humanist Coluccio Salutati will call a *summa consummataque sapientia*.[5] The art of rhetoric, which Cicero called 'eloquence' (or also 'oratory'), became for him the supreme *ars civilis* and one of the highest virtues, combining a practical capacity to persuade and a theoretical openness toward the ultimate ends of justice.[6] Cicero's conception of the necessary union between rhetoric and philosophy (or, as he said, *eloquentia* and *sapientia*) is thus central to his project to bridging the gap between philosophy and politics, theory and practice. And it this conception that, as it has been written, "is first and foremost what makes Cicero Ciceronian."[7]

The Ciceronian conception of rhetoric found a great defender in Quintilian. Despite the fact that he has often been considered more a compiler of other points of view rather than an original thinker, the breadth and comprehensive scope of his idea of rhetoric in the *Institutio oratoria* has made George Kennedy define that work "the finest statement of ancient rhetorical theory."[8] Among the various authors who influenced him, Cicero has to be considered undoubtedly the most important.[9] Writing a century later than Cicero, Quintilian attempted to recover the lofty political and spiritual value Cicero attributed to rhetoric but in a period in which the Roman Republic and the birth of the Empire meant that the possibilities to practice rhetoric as a form of political action were strongly reduced. Nonetheless that change didn't prevent Quintilian developing a very ambitious account of rhetoric, in line with the model developed by Cicero. But its political value was made less apparent through a shift of focus from the immediate role of rhetoric in the city toward its pedagogical value. For both authors the mastery of eloquence requires a long formative process, which is conceived as a necessary condition to enter the public arena. But it is Quintilian who provided the most accomplished account of such a process. In the new context of the Empire, he made even more patent what is already clearly visible in Cicero: the existential value intrinsic to this conception of rhetoric, or in other words, the fact that eloquence is not only a political practice but also a process of self-creation.[10]

The unparalleled scope of rhetoric exemplified by Cicero and Quintilian thus has to do with the fact that for them it was not only a political art, the supreme *ars civilis*, but also an existential accomplishment. For both, eloquence was key to an ideal that is at the same time political and related to a view of human perfection. Such an ideal is embodied by the figure of the *orator perfectus*, a figure that in combining these two dimensions offers the paradigmatic representation of both the virtuous *vir civilis* and the wise individual. It is a figure that, through eloquence, combines theory and practice, philosophy (and, more generally, 'wisdom') and politics. In the public performance of public speech on political matters we find the highest representation of the orator's civic function, since it is mainly through discourse that he actualizes his wisdom and justice. At the same time, it is through and in such acts that the orator displays the ethical qualities he has developed through the process of self-creation necessary to becoming a good orator and politician. If rhetoric attained such high status in ancient culture—as, Nietzsche once wrote, "the education of the ancient man customarily culminates in rhetoric: it is the highest spiritual activity of the well-educated political man"[11]—it is because it was not only a republican art, as we can see in the Aristotle, but also the core of an educational programme and an ambitious program of self-fashioning and self-improvement.

Cicero and Quintilian's conceptions of rhetoric are at the core of the tradition of thinking that started with Isocrates and that will be recovered by humanists such as Brunetto Latini, Francesco Petrarca, Coluccio Salutati, Leonardo Bruni, Lorenzo Valla, and later on by Giambattista Vico. It is a tradition that offers an alternative understanding of the question of the relation between theory and practice—*vita comtemplativa* and *vita activa*, self-constitution and political commitment—to the Platonic-philosophic position that stresses the tension between these pairs.[12] Rhetoric is for all those authors central in providing the ground for such an alternative. In this chapter I explore this alternative, focusing in particular on Cicero's ideal of the union between rhetoric and philosophy as it is incarnated in the figure of the *orator perfectus* and on the rhetorical formative process Quintilian delineated in the *Institutio oratoria*. In this sense, the analysis I develop here is crucial to the whole argument of the book since it provides the best example of how the transcendent and contingent dimensions of politics are related and how rhetoric is key in mediating such relation.

3.2 Cicero: Eloquence as a Political, Ethical, and Existential Ideal

Cicero's renowned eclecticism and capacity to absorb from very different sources can be seen also in the way he arrived at his view of rhetoric. In his position we can clearly detect the spirit of Isocrates' conception, some significant Aristotelian insights, and the weight of the tradition of the Roman orator. All these different influences were merged and expanded by Cicero to create a comprehensive view of rhetoric that posits the meaning of rhetorical art far beyond that of a mere technique of persuasion, making it the core of a political, ethical, and existential ideal that combines the theoretical and practical ways of life, in a superior form whose concrete manifestation is given by eloquence itself.[13] But rhetoric couldn't achieve the unparalleled scope Cicero gave it if he hadn't also taken in consideration Plato's critique. Because it is in attempting to render compatible the defence of the primacy of political life with the importance Plato grants to philosophy, that Cicero came to see rhetoric as the point of encounter between these two activities. In this respect, we can say that Cicero represents certainly the most ambitious attempt to bring the long battle between rhetoric and philosophy, or in his words between *eloquentia* and *sapientia*, to an end.

The role of eloquence in Cicero's political theory cannot be overstated: it is the pivot around which his thinking revolves. Similarly to Aristotle and Isocrates, who locate the basis of human political nature in *logos*, Cicero saw politics essentially as an activity developed through the medium of language. From here he drew the idea of the centrality of eloquence for politics, since if "society finds its primordial ordering principle in the human interaction of speech" then "the proper regulation of speech...is the original and essential virtue of civil life."[14] But Cicero's went further than Aristotle and Isocrates as he tried to embrace in his conception of rhetoric Plato's position on the necessity to provide a philosophically informed background to rhetoric and politics. The radical implications of Cicero's view on this matter emerge precisely from the perspective of the difficult relationship between philosophy, politics, and rhetoric; a topic which covers a central place in all his rhetorical writings.[15] Cicero's awareness of the relevance of this question can be traced back to his earliest work in *De inventione*. In a famous passage, after raising the question of under what conditions eloquence can be useful, he concluded there that "wisdom without eloquence does too little for the good of the states" and "eloquence without wisdom is generally highly disadvantageous and is never helpful."[16] If eloquence needs the moral guidance of philosophy in order to avoid becoming a mere instrument of power, wisdom would be completely helpless without the capacity of eloquence to animate and spread its principles throughout the community. Wisdom would become an inarticulate knowledge, unable to communicate with the city and thus to act, and closed-up in a self-referential and arrogant posture. It is the combination of eloquence and wisdom that opens the way to a civilized life. In a passage of the *De inventione* that will be cited innumerable times by the Renaissance humanists,[17] Cicero evoked the creation of civilization out of a primordial state of nature, when wise and eloquent men, through a wisdom that is not "mute and voiceless" since it combines reason and eloquence, persuaded "wild savages" to abandon their solitary and brutish life and join together in a political community.[18] For him, even if it belongs to the natural disposition of human beings to live in community, such disposition cannot be fulfilled without the power of eloquence to transform it into an action.[19] As Cicero will write later in the *De officiis*, thought (*cogitatio*) is directed towards the search for truth, but it is appetite (*appetitus*) that prompts action.[20] Then it is eloquence, with its capacity to stimulate the extra-rational, that is a necessary complement of wisdom to fulfil human potentiality.

This same position will be re-proposed in a much more articulated way in his mature dialogue *De oratore*.[21] There, through the character of Crassus, his mouthpiece in the dialogue, Cicero passionately called for an end to the long quarrel between philosophy and rhetoric and defended their necessary combination.[22] Through a quasi-mythical reconstruction of an unspecified past epoch, Crassus explains the creation of the separation between philosophers and rhetors, from their original unity when "knowledge of the most important things as well as practical involvement in them was, as a whole, called 'philosophy'." The separation according to Crassus was the consequence of Socrates's fatal splitting apart of *cor* and *lingua*, the inner world of meaning and its external manifestation in speech. It was Socrates's idea that "the knowledge of forming wise opinions and of speaking with distinction" were two separate endeavours that, for Crassus, initiated the quarrel between philosophers and rhetors and made the former indifferent and aloof from political affairs and the latter narrow-minded and all-too mundane.[23] In a direct response to the Platonic critique of rhetoric, Cicero thus pulled the whole domain of philosophy—which includes questions "about justice, about moral duty, about establishing and governing communities, actually about the whole conduct of life, and…even about the explanation of nature"—back into the realm of oratory, from whence, according to him, it was usurped by the philosophers.[24] Not only philosophy however is claimed as a necessary support for oratory. What is defended in *De oratore* is the idea that the orator should embrace the "entire study and knowledge of everything…relevant to human conduct, to human life, to virtue, and to the state" because, being involved in politics, this constitutes the material with which he is concerned.[25] An encyclopedic sort of knowledge, with a strong emphasis on the literature, philosophy, law, and history, is what the orator is required to master in order to comply with his role.[26] Without this foundation, Cicero makes Crassus conclude (repeating Socrates's position in the *Gorgias* almost verbatim) rhetoric could run the risk of becoming "weapons into the hands of madmen."[27]

Cicero's conception of eloquence, and in particular his combination of eloquence and wisdom, has to be understood in the broader perspective of the political, ethical, and existential problem of the relation between politics and philosophy, *vita activa* and *vita contemplativa*, and self-cultivation and political commitment. The question of how to combine the poles of these dichotomies in a higher combination represents the main pivot around which Cicero's thought turns and the idea that eloquence constitutes the main catalyst for such a combination is one of his most important contributions. This is a question that unfolds on different levels. First of all, it is related to the question, raised by Aristotle, of the kind of background knowledge that is required to speak about political matters in a pertinent way. In the *De oratore* Cicero explains the necessity for the orator/politician to study philosophy, because every particular question (*hypothesis*) with which he has to deal in his political activity inevitably implies a more general question (*thesis*), which is studied by philosophers. The general knowledge provided by philosophy is therefore a necessary support for the orator/politician to argue on the great variety of questions involved in public affairs.[28] Nevertheless, again as it was for Aristotle, Cicero's orator/politician does not need to become a fully-fledged philosopher, or an expert in the particular question he is talking about. He is, rather, a very knowledgeable and cultivated person whose main ability is that of speaking eloquently about the most important things to the majority of the people, rather than to a few experts, and thus to put his discourses into practice[29]; a person who is committed first and foremost, not to the search for truth and theoretical knowledge, but rather to the good of his community.[30] Cicero, however, clearly recognizes that the theoretical life is something important, not only from an epistemological point of view, but also for deeper ethical and political reasons. The arguments that the orator/politician offers in the public debate should certainly be oriented to the value of truthfulness and thus informed by solid knowledge. But knowledge is important not only for itself but also because its cultivation, and especially the cultivation of philosophy, permits the development of a critical attitude. It is this striving to transcend the unquestioned conventions that is the necessary counterweight to the familiarity with common opinions and ordinary ways of thinking the orator/politician needs in order to carry on his activity.[31] In this sense, philosophy is necessary both because among his tasks the orator/politician has to instruct the audience and because philosophy teaches us to think autonomously, to find the detachment necessary to follow a vision of the good, independently from practical and strategic considerations.

It is by incorporating philosophy then that for Cicero rhetoric can avoid becoming merely instrumental and contribute to raising politics to a higher status.[32] Cicero tried himself to accomplish such a combination in his own life, not only as he says by drawing inspiration and guidance for his political speeches and action from philosophy, but also through his ambitious project to create a Roman tradition of philosophy.[33] This was a project through which he hoped to continue giving his contribution to public life, once, with the crisis of the Republic, the circumstances for direct participation were more favourable.[34] The weight of philosophy and politics in Cicero's life also changed according to the circumstances. But the idea of their combination is always present in him. So, even when the possibilities for doing politics started to wane with the consolidation of Caesar's power and philosophy became for Cicero the most important occupation, he will continue to claim that a perfect philosophy is that which is "able to discuss the most momentous questions copiously and elegantly."[35] That is, philosophy has to be political and thus rhetorical.

The way that philosophy nurtures eloquence and expands the horizon of the orator/politician has been explained in a very interesting study by Ingo Gildenhard. He has shown how in many of Cicero's speeches we find a complex mediation between rhetorical exigencies to mould argument and style according to the specific features of the audience and the capacity of philosophy to "expand and redefine the conventional conceptual framework" and help to "think outside the box."[36] Beyond providing a set of theoretically informed notions and categories, and conceptual clarity, philosophy intervenes in the construction of the argument providing a more critical and ideal normative perspective on the topic at hand.[37] The two dimensions at work in Cicero's speech—philosophy and rhetoric—however don't operate independently. They mutually interact and modify each other in a complex set of relations, negotiations, and tensions. The normative and conceptual creativity provided by philosophy needs to interact with the rhetorical necessity to be attentive to the specificity of the audience (its values, interests, background, etc.), and more in general to the practical necessity to consider what is at stake politically (including the more prosaic political ambitions of Cicero). Philosophical creativity then is allowed to enter a political discourse only after a meticulous process of rhetorical adaptations and elaboration; and, in particular, after passing through the same technique Plato recommends, that of *dissimulatio*, in order to disguise the most unconventional ideas. As Gildenhard explains, such philosophical creativity in Cicero's speech can be found in three main areas: the idea of human nature, society, and the divine. A good example in this respect is the conception of law that Cicero applies in some of his speeches. This is a conception in which he includes not only the formal respect of the procedures—positive law—but also, in line with Stoic philosophy, the more idealistic meaning that defines law as what is right according to nature, that is, natural law. Cicero referred to this broader concept of law on several occasions, for instance when he countered measures adopted by the members of the Senate by arguing not against their procedural incorrectness, but rather against their injustice.[38]

Philosophy clearly contributes to endowing Cicero's speeches with a strong normative accent. This philosophically informed normativity sometimes assumes the vehement moralistic and uncompromising tone so characteristic of Cicero's oratory. On other occasions, what we see is that more concrete practical and political exigencies outweigh the immediate respect for abstract principles of justice, so that Cicero's oratory acquires the form of a prudent and sober arguing, under which a careful calculation tries to balance the ethics of responsibility with that of conviction (to use Weber's expression). In both cases, it is practical reason, of which rhetoric is part, that decides how to mediate philosophy with the context. We can see how this happens in the oration *Pro Murena*, for instance. In the context of a difficult political situation in which the conviction of his client—the consul Murena—on a charge of corruption could leave the state in a delicate situation (it was the turbulent epoch of Catiline's conspiracy), Cicero employed his eloquence to attack personally his opponents—the prosecutors, Cato the Younger and Sulpicius—rather than their arguments. What he aimed to show is how the prosecutors' too strict attachment to abstract ideas in accusing Murena (Stoic principles in the case of Cato and the ideal of the law in that of Sulpicius) could put the republican constitution and Rome itself at risk. This oration shows how rhetoric entails the exercise of a practical reason that contextualizes ethical and political principles through an engagement with the concrete situation.[39]

We can also see the interaction between philosophy and politics through the mediation of rhetoric from the other side: looking at how Cicero's philosophic writings are moulded and shaped by rhetorical considerations. The philosophical writings of the 40s are an interesting case in this respect. As I mentioned earlier, in that period Cicero turned to philosophy with the idea that in this way he could continue to offer his contribution to Rome, establishing a discipline that instructs on great ethical and political questions. Such a political, ethical, cultural, and also existential project however was in need of a public justification. Cicero not only had to justify his choice to abandon politics and devote himself to the study of philosophy, but he had also to defend his project to an audience that was traditionally hostile toward a discipline it associated with the foreign and suspect culture of the Greeks. In order to do that he had to employ his rhetorical abilities.[40] So in the preface to the *Paradoxa stoicorum*, for instance, Cicero cites the example of Cato the Younger, an orator who, as mentioned above, often made use in his speech of difficult philosophical ideas to sustain his arguments. In *De oratore* Cicero had asserted that the most serious error an orator could commit is "to shrink away from the common mode of speech, and from the custom derived from communal sensibility." But here, in order to defend the utility of philosophy, Cicero mentions the example of this famous orator who uses successfully uncommon philosophical arguments, through a rhetorical form that makes it adapt to the public forum.[41] Cicero underlines that the reasons for Cato's success lie in his ability to make such arguments more acceptable—more verisimilar and approvable—for his audience. But then Cicero adds that he himself has made use of philosophy in his own discourses and that he has been even more successful than Cato. He gives to reasons to explain why he has been even more successful: first, because differently from the Stoicism of Cato—whose views are very distant from common sense—his philosophical school (the scepticism of the Academia) holds views much more in common with popular values; and second because his philosophical school makes of the capacity to argue with verisimilar arguments its core. What Cicero is stressing here is that, although using philosophy in public speech is good (a philosophical argument), it is more useful and effective if such views are not too much far from common feeling (a rhetorical argument).[42]

More generally, we can say that the aspiration to "bring politics and philosophy, together in a harmonious whole"[43] in Cicero's philosophical works can be seen in the same idea that animates his project to create a

Roman philosophy: the idea of wanting to combine Greek philosophical principles with Roman *exempla* taken from the past, so as to make such principles more vivid and concrete. The capacity of rhetorically elaborating *exempla* to make abstract principles more vivid and understandable is indeed a basic principle of rhetoric itself.[44] And it played a very important role in shaping the whole philosophical enterprise of Cicero.

The combination of philosophy and rhetoric is for Cicero not only a political goal; it has also a more ethical dimension since, for him, such combination constitutes also a form of virtue. Practising eloquence means practising a public art; it means to abide by the primary duty to dedicate oneself to political life and contribute to the destiny of one's own community.[45] In Cicero's critique of those philosophers who neglect the art of rhetoric, there is also a clear ethical posture. Their detachment from the public sphere is described with a tone of censure, as when Crassus in *De oratore* talks about those philosophers debating among themselves in "holes and corners", spending their time in "idle" ways, and speaking in a "thin and bloodless" language.[46] After Cicero, Quintilian will use much harsher words against the philosophers who neglect eloquence and politics in his *Institutio oratoria*. Unconditional champion of the motto *ut vivat, etiam quemque dicere*—the traditional Roman belief that speaking well and acting well are interconnected[47]—Quintilian upturned Plato's accusation of deceptiveness against rhetoric, writing that "philosophy may be counterfeited, but eloquence never."[48] He admitted that "many of the old philosophers inculcated the most excellent principles and practised what they preached;" but in his own time, long after philosophy and rhetoric had been separated:

> the philosopher has too often been the mask for the worst vices. For their attempt has not been to win the name of philosopher by virtue and the earnest search for wisdom; instead they have sought to disguise the depravity of their characters by the assumption of a stern and austere mien accompanied by the wearing of a garb differing from that of their fellow men.[49]

Quintilian told how philosophers without eloquence (weaker intellects, he called them) claimed the exclusive right to teach morals and civil laws. They arrogated for themselves the title of *studiosi sapientiae*—a distinction that "neither the greatest generals nor the most famous statesmen and administrators have ever dared to claim for themselves, for they preferred the performance to the promise of great deeds"—displaying an attitude of conceited detachment from the public affairs. They hid behind a "stern and sever mien", an "affected contempt" and attitude of "moral superiority", the "depravity of their characters."[50]

Quintilian's animosity against philosophy can certainly be imputed to some extent to his desire to ingratiate himself with the despotic Emperor Domitian,[51] who expulsed philosophers from Rome. But, beyond this practical motive, there is certainly also the idea that to neglect the *ars bene dicendi* is tantamount to an arrogant attitude of indifference toward the beliefs and problems of the community, so that the detachment from the public sphere, its language and norms, is interpreted as a form of haughty solipsism, an evident sign of moral corruption.[52] For both Quintilian and Cicero, the practice of eloquence was indissoluble from the existential search for an ethical life, since eloquence is what allows the abstract principles reached in *foro interno* to materialize through action and be assessed by the scrutiny of one's fellow citizens. The study of the abstract principles of philosophy needs to be accompanied and complemented by the practice of eloquence. Only through eloquence can these principle be communicated to the community, materialized into action, and transformed according to what practice teaches. Only through eloquence can philosophy find the stimulus and direction toward which to develop. In this respect, we can say that the necessary correspondence between eloquence and ethical behaviour is but a manifestation of a broader idea—central in this rhetorical-humanistic tradition—that makes of the correspondence between *res* and *verba*, content and form, a fundamental value. As Ernesto Grassi has defended, it is one of the most distinctive elements of the tradition that goes from Cicero and Quintilian up to the Italian humanists such as Petrarca, Bruni, Valla, and later Vico to put in question the priority given by philosophy to the epistemological problem of knowing the essence of being (*res*) and claim that it cannot be dissociated with that of language (*verba*). In Grassi's reading according to this tradition the former question can never be understood without taking in consideration how knowledge is communicated and materialized into the various domains of human activity.[53] That is, the capacity to create meaning, acquire knowledge, and to communicate it cannot be separated. The ethical purse of justice cannot be dissociated from the effort to communicate it through eloquence. This is why all those authors believed that eloquence cannot exist without ethics, and ethics without eloquence.[54] For all them eloquence meant first of all to be able to interact and engage with the others through communication. It is an antidote against the tendency to self-certainty and self-rightness that philosophic reflection is so inclined to engender.

The indissoluble correspondence between ethical character and the capacity to speech is of course connected with the question of the best form of life, the diatribe between the *vita contemplativa* and the *vita activa*. This is a very relevant topic in ancient thought, and particularly in Cicero. It concerns the existential choice of what kind of life is better to live for the individual. But at the same time it also has a political-ethical meaning since such a choice bears upon the relation between the individual, the community, and the idea of the good. In Cicero's writing this question comes up over and over again. In particular it appears at the very beginning of two of his three most political works (together with *De legibus*): *De re publica*, dedicated to the best form of the state, and *De oratore*, which can be read as a dialogue about the formation of a statesman.[55] Cicero's response to this question is provided by his figure of the perfect orator: the one who incarnates at the same time the best statesman and the best individual; who, through the practice of eloquence, materializes the ideal combination of philosophy (and wisdom in general) and politics, theory and practice.[56]

In representing this figure Cicero defined an ideal being: an individual who has devoted his life to what he considers the highest duty, the call of politics, but who at the same time has found in philosophy a fundamental guide, not only for him as individual, but also as politician and member of a community. Through the description of this figure Cicero tried to show how in practice the *vita activa* and the *vita contemplativa* could be reconciled, and how through the process of becoming eloquent the best form of life for the individual comes to coincide with what is best for the community, inasmuch as that the cultivation of individual excellence and the pursuit of the common good of the community become two intertwined ends. This is what Crassus reveals in a key passage of *De oratore* when he declares that "the wise control of the complete orator is that which chiefly upholds not only his own dignity, but the safety of countless individuals and of the entire State" so that it is in his "power to become a glory to [himself], a source of service to [his] friends, and profitable members of the Republic."[57] All the characters we find in Cicero's rhetorical writings are indeed politicians who, even if they cannot be said to have realized the ideal of the perfect orator, are nevertheless great orators who employ their art for the good of their community and who in the exercise of their art also show their greatness as individuals.[58]

The originality of this ideal lies precisely in this double dimension: in the fact of making the existential cultivation of the self and the political search for the common good coincide in the creation of a 'communicative' ideal of personhood.[59] By describing the meaning of life in terms of a quality such as 'the ability to communicate', instead of in terms of adherence to truth, Cicero offered a different view of the relationship between philosophy and politics than that, ultimately incompatible, given by Plato and generally accepted by the bulk of the philosophical tradition. The figure of the perfect orator had for Cicero a function not far from that of the Platonic ideas. It is an ideal character, "an eternally absent figure," which serves as a model.[60] But differently from the Platonic ideas it is a model that, the same time, maintains an essentially practical character.[61] Eloquence is an ideal that acquires its full meaning only through practice. The process of becoming eloquent is understood by Cicero as an extremely demanding process of self-creation[62]—whose basic ingredients are education, practice, and natural talent—in order to enter into the public sphere. Through such process the artistic competences should come to integrate so deeply with the person of the orator to the point of disappearing into him. These considerations about the nature of Cicero's perfect orator can be extended also to Quintilian, who inherited this ideal and gave to that figure a more concrete dimension, providing an extraordinary account of the formative process perfect eloquence requires. It is to Quintilian that I will turn now.[63]

3.3 Quintilian's *Institutio oratoria* and the Rhetorical Formation of the Self

The *Institutio oratoria* is a canonical text in the history of rhetoric and more generally in western culture because of the contribution it made to the formation of the humanistic pedagogical ideal.[64] Similarly to Aristotle and Cicero, Quintilian saw eloquence more as a *praxis* and a way of life than a technique that can be reduced to a set of clear-cut rules.[65] Underlining the idea of eloquence as a praxis, Quintilian rejected the reduction of eloquence to the mere goal of persuasion, arguing that persuasion can be obtained equally by adulators, seducers, or prostitutes, but only the eloquent speaks well, that is, according to justice. What really counted for him is not the art and its principles but, rather as he said, the artist: he who is able to embody its principles in practice.[66] Like Cicero,

Quintilian envisaged an extraordinarily challenging formative process for those who want to undertake the path to eloquence, centred on the study of broad and multidisciplinary curriculum, with a particular emphasis on liberal disciplines such as history, moral philosophy, literature, and of course rhetoric.[67] As we have seen, the breadth and depth of this formative process correspond to the magnitude of responsibility that weighs on the shoulder of the orator/politician—that of governing a State according to justice—and the power his eloquence could exert.[68] The orator, as a politician, has to move in a vast space: that between the intricate web of the contingencies political actions creates and the ideal ends that should inspire his actions.

Compared to philosophical *paideia*, however, in Quintilian's rhetorical formative model it is the significance of the contingent dimension that emerges. In the philosophical paideia, the formative process is understood essentially as a process of strengthening reason to the detriment of the emotive and instinctive parts of the soul, in order to ascend from mere contingent opinions and attachments toward transcendent truths by way of the dialectical method of inquiry. It is the difficult search, as Gadamer has put it, for a precarious equilibrium between two opposite tendencies: the vitalist and combative will to power, on the one hand, and the rational and pacific love for justice and truth, on the other.[69] In Quintilian's rhetorical model instead education is understood as process, equally difficult, of forming not just a philosopher but, at the same time, a good person and a good citizen capable of living in justice among his fellows. More than for the strict rule of the rational over the extra-rational, this goal calls for a polyphonic and pluralist order: the "cultivation of what is specifically and purely human in all spheres of life" and the development "of the harmonious human being."[70]

In more concrete terms, the purpose of encouraging plurality and polyphony in *foro interno* corresponds to the breadth of the educational curriculum and the varieties of experience the individual is asked to undergo. The rhetorical formative process aims at the creation of a comprehensive human being. For Quintilian education should amalgamate the natural qualities of the person strictly through practice to become one indistinguishable thing.[71] That is why, as he recommended, the process of self-creation needs to start from childhood—which is for him absolutely the most important phase[72]—and accompany him during all the phases of his life.[73] Quintilian stressed the great influence the formation of this period bears on the rest of the life of the person. Education for him was not like a progressive accumulation of information, in which what has been acquired in the past is indifferent for what can be learned in the future. On the contrary, what we can learn in a specific moment depends in a fundamental way on what we have learned before, since education has deep effects on character, which accumulate and consolidate along the years in a long process of sedimentation.[74]

A fundamental premise of the pedagogical ideal defended by Quintilian (and the same is valid for Cicero as well) is the idea of human nature as something that can be moulded thoroughly, if only gradually, through education and practice.[75] As mentioned before, the extraordinary scope of this process of self-creation corresponds to the great extension of the world in which the orator/politician should move and the variety of situations he will have to face.[76] As Quintilian emphatically wrote, how could the speaker recommend a particular policy decision if he does not know what is convenient to do? How could he plead in the courts if he ignores what justice is? How may he invoke courage if he does not know the nature of this virtue?[77] This is of course the same point that Plato made in the *Gorgias*, but here the question is broader. Quintilian (and Cicero) did not put emphasis only on the acquisition of theoretical knowledge but, rather, on the way in which this is internalized and embodied. The highly idealistic traits that characterize the figure of the perfect orator are thus counterbalanced by a continuous emphasis on its practical and embodied dimension.

We can see what this means by focusing on one of the main virtues the orator is required to develop according to Quintilian: the capacity to stir the emotions in the listeners. This capacity—one of the three sources of persuasion according to Aristotle—acquired in the Roman tradition of rhetoric an unparalleled importance, becoming almost the core of rhetoric.[78] For Quintilian such an ability was not only the most important power oratory offers, it is also the most difficult to develop.[79] In order to avoid the accusation of immorality, he specified that this power should be employed in all its strength only in those cases where there are no other means "for securing the victory of truth, justice and the public interest."[80] But the reason why his position on the emotions cannot be reduced to an instrumental one is deeper. Quintilian argued that the difference between the Greek terms *ethos* and *pathos* is a difference in degree of the same phenomenon: the former refers to the most intense and fleeting passions, while the latter to the more gentle and stable ones that arise from the moral character of the speaker.[81] An important feature of *ethos*, he added, is that the "chief merit in its expression lies in making it seem that all that we say derives directly from the nature of the facts and persons concerned and in the revelation of the character."[82] The capacity to arouse emotions certainly requires technical skill. The style, for instance, should be carefully chosen by taking into consideration the situation and the audience[83]; the use of *tropoi* is fundamental to enhance the suggestive power of language, to make it more vivid and move the emotions of the audience; so is important the capacity to redescribe a particular fact, highlighting one aspect of it over another in order to change the moral appreciation we make of it (the technique of *paradiastole*).[84] As a musician the speaker should be able to modulate the intensity of his discourse, "enhancing or attenuating the force of the words", through *amplificatio* (or its contrary *minutio*), and choosing the right words and delivering them in the right way.[85] But such technical and performative ability is not enough. What is required is also a deeper process of learning through experience that modifies the character of the speaker so as to develop that emotive internal structure necessary to empathize with the feelings of the audience. Quintilian wrote:

> The prime essential for stirring the emotions in others is, in my opinion, first to feel those emotions oneself. It is sometimes positively ridiculous to counterfeit grief, anger and indignation, if we content ourselves with accommodating our words and looks and make no attempt to adapt our own feelings to the emotions to be expressed. What other reason is there for the eloquence with which mourners express their grief, or the fluency which anger lends even to the uneducated, save the fact that their minds are stirred to power by the depth and sincerity of their feelings? Consequently, if we wish to give our words the appearance of sincerity, we must assimilate ourselves to the emotions of those who are genuinely so affected, and our eloquence must spring from the same feeling that we desire to produce in the mind of the judge...Fire alone can kindle, and moisture alone can wet, nor can one thing impart any colour to another save that which it possesses itself. Accordingly, the first essential is that those feelings should prevail with us, that we should be moved ourselves before we attempt to move others.[86]

The difficult task of *com-movere* the passions involves much more than the mastery of stylistic devices or a sort of merely technical psychological ability. It requires a deeper process of maturation through direct experience and cultivation, aimed at developing the capacity to feel those same emotions that we want to arouse in the others. But how can we learn to feel emotions and feelings, since these are not in our control? Quintilian suggested that one crucial way is using imagination to create visions in our mind that could make us experience things absent, with the same vividness and force as if they were indeed present.[87] Imagination, for him, was a capacity that depends on natural talent, but that can be also cultivated and improved: for instance, through musical education, or avoiding hampering its development in the youngsters by an exceedingly precocious consolidation of critical and analytical attitudes, or by the fear instilled by teacher, or by their dryness.[88] The capacity to adapt one's own state of mind to the situation and the audience is a quality that is very important for rhetoric: in Plato's *Phaedrus* it appeared as a psychological knowledge and in Aristotle's *Rhetoric* as a sort of psychological perspicacity. In the Roman tradition it was understood as a sort of imaginative capacity, strengthened through experience and education, to enlarge one's own sense of identity and create bridges with the others. It is this imaginative capacity of impersonation—for Quintilian, one of the most difficult tasks of the orator[89]—that Antonius evokes in a famous passage of the *De oratore*, when he explains how he prepares his cases in the courts of law: "all by myself I play with equanimity of soul three characters: my self, my adversary, and my judge."[90]

Cicero and Quintilian's continual insistence on the personal qualities of the orator, the greatness of his spirit, has been often denounced as an empty response to Plato's remark about the inconsistency of rhetoric, or even worse, as a little more than a hollow exercise of moralism.[91] However what I have tried to show in this chapter is that at the roots of such an extraordinary expansion of the limits of the *ethos* through rhetoric there is the idea that this is what is required to deal with the infinity of situations created by politics, or in Quintilian's words to "range at large over the open fields" of politics.[92] At the end of the day for both Cicero and Quintilian "no rhetoric can be better than the character of its orator."[93] Thus even more than in Aristotle, for them rhetoric became a kind of communicative *phronesis*—or an agent-based ethics (as opposed to an act-based code) as Joy Connolly has suggested—in which what counts is how an ideal vision is embodied, performed, and communicated on a public stage, among the contingencies of political life.[94] This communicative *phronesis* however attains the vast scope Cicero and Quintilian gave to it, since for them the flourishing both of society and the individual depended essentially on the capacity to communicate. This is why they arrived at reformulating the meaning of the "good life…in terms of communication."[95] In this respect we can say that the rhetorical process of formation envisioned by Cicero and Quintilian is broader than the Socratic-philosophical one: it doesn't consist only in the solitary dialectical investigation into philosophical principles, but rather involves a process of development of a enlarged communicative self, one able to move among the web of human relationships, through a continuous interplay between conflicting exigencies, contingent and ideal, individual and communal, rational and extra-rational. Forming oneself in eloquence means creating a self able to live well through this web of human relations through the medium of language.

It is a process of self-creation, then, but one that cannot be understood in solipsistic terms since within it "the self is shaped from childhood through maturity in a never-ending, circular process of self-fashioning, communal response, and self-reevaluation."[96] Indeed, if on the one hand the orator is asked to represent all the virtues of community, so as to become something like "the speaking embodiment of the *res publica*", and to propagate them through his eloquence; on the other, the possibility for him to become a symbol for the rest of the community depends on his capacity to be unique, exceptional, and thanks to this to be able to represent his community in an outstanding way.[97] It is in this second aspect that the support of philosophy, specifically in its capacity to expand a person's horizons, is crucial. And it is in this sense that philosophy (and wisdom) and rhetoric should merge, according to Cicero, bringing together an existential ideal and political one: in a sort of dialectical relationship in which the cultivation of the self and the rhetorical capacity to communicate combine and enrich one another. It is precisely this kind of dialectical relationship that we find in a passage of *De re publica*, where we read that the first duty of a statesman is to never stop examining himself so as to become an example to his fellow-citizens.[98] The passage reveals that, similarly to Plato, Cicero located the roots of justice in the psyche of the self and in a process of self-analysis in which philosophy plays a crucial role. Nevertheless, for him it is mainly through the practice of eloquence that this sort of spiritual superiority can acquire its full meaning, by manifesting and refining itself in the communal world, and thus becoming an authoritative example for other citizens.[99]

In Cicero and Quintilian's conceptions of rhetoric, as I hope to have made clear, we can find much more than theories on how to persuade. They provide a privileged perspective from which to see politics as a multidimensional activity, which interweaves a normative striving for transcendence and practical considerations to deal with contingency. Plato's critical view on rhetoric highlights the former, while Aristotle's theory of rhetoric the latter. Cicero and Quintilian's conceptions instead highlight their interconnection. In the second part of the book I will move to three influential and very different twentieth-century political theorists. My aim is to show how the question of the relation between transcendence and contingency in politics, which the ancient quarrel between philosophy and rhetoric reveals, still continues to resonate in contemporary political theory.

NOTES

1. The question of the best form of life, whether the *bios theoretikos* or *praktikos* (*vita contemplativa* or *vita activa*), is broached in clear terms in: Aristotle, *The Nicomachean Ethics*, trans. Hippocrates G. Apostle (Dordrecht and Boston: Reidel, 1980), 1097b16–20, 1098a16–20; Aristotle, *The Eudemian Ethics*, trans. Anthony Kenny (Oxford: Oxford University Press, 2011), 1215 b15–16a36. Cf. Aristotle, *Politics*, trans. C. D. C. Reeve (with introduction and notes) (Indianapolis: Hackett, 1998), 1260b28–29, 1323a–24a; Plato, *Gorgias*, trans. Donald J. Zeyl (Indianapolis: Hackett, 1987), 500c1–8.
2. Hannah Arendt, *The Human Condition* (Chicago: University of Chicago Press, 1998), 16.
3. Ibid.
4. Cicero's attempt to blend political action and intellectual reflection has generated along the centuries two opposite reactions, generally depending on whether those expressing the judgment are more inclined towards politics or philosophy. In the former case, Cicero has been celebrated as one of the very rare examples of those able to bring theory and practice together. In the latter, instead, his attempt to combine theory and practice has been criticized for producing mediocre results in both fields. John Adams is an example of the former opinion. For him "as all the ages of the world have not produced a greater statesman and philosopher united than Cicero, his authority should have great weight." John Adams, *The Political Writings of John Adams* (Washington, DC: Regnery Publishing, 2001), 121. On the other side, we can mention the famous historian Theodor Mommsen, who, under the influence of Hegel, expressed in his *Römische Geschichte* an harsh judgment on Cicero, defining him an irrelevant philosopher and a statesman without vision. Theodor Mommsen, *The History of Rome*, Vol. 4—part II (Cambridge: Cambridge University Press, 2010), 511, 609ff. On this see: Walter Nicgorski, "Cicero's Paradoxes and His Idea of Utility," *Political Theory* 12 (1984): 559; Walter Nicgorski, *Cicero's Practical Philosophy* (Notre Dame, IN: University of Notre Dame Press, 2012), 257.

5. Eugene F. Rice, *The Renaissance Idea of Wisdom* (Cambridge, MA: Harvard University Press, 1958), 39.
6. Cicero, *On the Ideal Orator (De Oratore)*, trans. James M. May and Jakob Wisse (New York: Oxford University Press, 2001), 3.55. In talking about Cicero, beyond the term rhetoric I will also use interchangeably the expressions used by him: 'oratory' and 'eloquence'. Eloquence (*eloquentia*) in particular is the expression Cicero employs more frequently in his most important work on the subject, *De oratore*, where he defends the ideal of the union between eloquence and wisdom (*eloquentia* and *sapientia*). On the different meanings of 'oratory' and 'eloquence' in Cicero and the relation with the Greek word 'rhetoric' see: James S. Baumlin and Joseph J. Hughes, "Eloquence," in *Encyclopedia of Rhetoric and Composition: Communication from Ancient Times to the Information Age*, ed. Theresa Enos (New York and London: Garland, 1996), 215.
7. William H. F. Altman, "Introduction," in *Brill Companion to the Reception of Cicero*, ed. William H. F. Altman (Leiden and Boston: Brill, 2015), 8.
8. George Kennedy, *The Art of Rhetoric in the Roman World, 300 B.C.–A.D. 300* (Princeton, NJ: Princeton University Press, 1972), 496. Cf. Jiří Kraus, *Rhetoric in European Culture and Beyond* (Prague: Karolinum Press, Charles University, 2016), 70; Renato Barilli, *Rhetoric* (Minneapolis: University of Minnesota Press, 1989), 35; Michael Mooney, *Vico in the Tradition of Rhetoric* (Princeton, NJ: Princeton University Press, 1985), 34.
9. Quintilian famously wrote that Cicero is "not his name but of eloquence itself." Quintilian, *Institutio Oratoria*, trans. Harold Edgeworth Butler (Cambridge, MA: Harvard University Press, 1963), 10.1.112. As one scholar has recently put it, we can say that Cicero "is omnipresent on Quintilian in ways large and small, the *sine quo non* of his masterwork, the standard by which he defines the arts and practitioners of oratory and eloquence." Alain M. Gowing, "Tully's Boat: Responses to Cicero in the Imperial Period," in *The Cambridge Companion to Cicero*, ed. Catherine Steel (Cambridge: Cambridge University Press, 2013), 233. On the reception of Cicero's view of oratory in the Imperial period and further on see also: M. L. Clarke, "'Non Hominis Nomen, Sed Eloquentiae'," in *Cicero*, ed. T. A. Dorey (London: Routledge & Kegan Paul, 1964); Virginia Cox and John O. Ward, eds., *The Rhetoric of Cicero in Its Medieval and Early Renaissance Commentary Tradition* (Leiden and Boston: Brill, 2006).
10. Cf. Joy Connolly, *The State of Speech: Rhetoric and Political Thought in Ancient Rome* (Princeton, NJ and Oxford: Princeton University Press, 2007), 254–9; Vincenzo Scarano Ussani, *Il retore e il potere* (Naples: M. D'Auria, 2008).

11. Friedrich W. Nietzsche, *Friedrich Nietzsche on Rhetoric and Language*, ed. Sander L. Gilman, Carole Blair, and David J. Parent (Oxford University Press, 1989), 97. Nietzsche was well acquainted with the tradition of rhetoric, on which he lectured as professor of classical philology at the University of Basle. The influence of rhetoric is visible in important strands of his thought, particularly on his view of language. Cf. Carole Blair, Sander L. Gilman, and David J. Parent, "Introduction," in *Friedrich Nietzsche on Rhetoric and Language*, ed. Carole Blair, Sander L. Gilman, and David J. Parent (New York and Oxford: Oxford University Press, 1989).

12. On the influence on the humanists of Latin rhetorical culture and in particular of Cicero's idea of eloquence see for instance: Jerrold Seigel, *Rhetoric and Philosophy in Renaissance Humanism: The Union of Eloquence and Wisdom, Petrarch to Valla* (Princeton: Princeton University Press, 1968), Ch. 1; Paul O. Kristeller, "Humanism," in *The Cambridge History of Renaissance Philosophy*, ed. Quentin Skinner, Eckhard Kessler, and Charles B. Schmitt (Cambridge: Cambridge University Press, 1988), 122–3; Marc Fumaroli, *L'âge de l'éloquence. Rhétorique et "res literaria" de la Renaissance au seuil de l'époque classique* (Paris: Albin Michel, 1994), 37–46; Quentin Skinner, *The Foundations of Modern Political Thought: Vol. I. The Renaissance* (Cambridge and New York: Cambridge University Press, 1978), 27, 35–48, 84–101; Cary J. Nederman, "The Union of Wisdom and Eloquence before the Renaissance: The Ciceronian Orator in Medieval Thought," *Journal of Medieval History* 18 (1992); Ronald G. Witt, *In the Footsteps of the Ancients: The Origins of Humanism from Lovato to Bruni* (Leiden and Boston: Brill, 2000), 201ff.

13. In general terms, we can say that Cicero follows the Isocratean ideal of a culture with a marked civic and practical character (but at the same time not too mundane or technical), centred on the use of speech and on humanistic disciplines such literature, ethics, and politics. Aristotle, instead, is a key influence for Cicero in a number of aspects: first, for the idea of the combination of philosophy and rhetoric (see: Cicero, *Tusculan Disputations*, trans. J. E. King (Cambridge, MA: Harvard University Press, 1960), 1.7; Cicero, *On the Ideal Orator*, 3.141); second, for the idea of the existence of three proofs of persuasion—*logos, ethos, pathos*—that in Cicero becomes the three tasks of the orator: *probare/docere, conciliare/delectare*, and *movere* (see Ibid., 2.115, 128, 310, 3.104; Cicero, "Brutus," in *Brutus, Orator*, trans. G. L. Hendrickson and H. M. Hubbell (Cambridge, MA: Harvard University Press, 1934), 185, 276; Cicero, "Orator," in *Brutus, Orator*, trans. G. L. Hendrickson and H. M. Hubbell (Cambridge, MA: Harvard University Press, 1934), 69); and finally, for the view of rhetoric as an unsystematizable art and an aspect of practical reason. On the influ-

ence of Isocrates and Aristotle in Cicero see: Alain Michel, *Les rapports de la rhétorique et de la philosophie dans l'oeuvre de Cicéron. Recherches sur les fondements philosophiques de l'art de persuader* (Louvain and Paris: Peeters, 2003), 101–8, 119–23; George Kennedy, *A New History of Classical Rhetoric* (Princeton, NJ: Princeton University Press, 1994), 142–3; Sarah C. Stroup, "Greek Rhetoric Meets Rome: Expansion, Resistance, and Acculturation," in *A Companion to Roman Rhetoric*, ed. William Dominik and Jon Hall (Malden: Blackwell, 2007), 23–37; William W. Fortenbaugh and David C. Mirhady, eds., *Peripatetic Rhetoric after Aristotle* (New Brunswick, NJ: Transaction Publishers, 1994), Chs. 5 and 6.

14. Connolly, *The State of Speech*, 169. The same is valid also for Quintilian, for whom a good citizen and politician cannot but be a good orator. Quintilian, *Institutio Oratoria*, 1.pr.10.

15. On the relationship between philosophy and rhetoric in Cicero, see: Michel, *Les rapports de la rhétorique et de la philosophie dans l'oeuvre de Cicéron*; Robert Gaines, "Cicero's Response to the Philosophers in De Oratore, Book 1," in *Rhetoric and Pedagogy*, ed. Winifred Bryan Horner and Michael Leff (Mahwah, NJ: Lawrence Erlbaum Associates, 1995); Emanuele Narducci, *Cicerone. La parola e la politica* (Rome: Laterza, 2009), Ch. 19; Alberto Grilli, "Cicerone tra retorica e filosofia," in *Interpretare Cicerone. Percorsi della critica contemporanea. Atti del II Symposium Ciceronianum Arpinas*, ed. Emanuele Narducci (Florence: Felice Le Monnier, 2002); Bryan Garsten, *Saving Persuasion: A Defense of Rhetoric and Judgment* (Cambridge, MA: Harvard University Press, 2006), Ch. 5; Connolly, *The State of Speech*, 121–9; Ingo Gildenhard, *Creative Eloquence: The Construction of Reality in Cicero's Speeches* (Oxford and New York: Oxford University Press, 2010); Yelena Baraz, *A Written Republic: Cicero's Philosophical Politics* (Princeton, NJ: Princeton University Press, 2012).

16. Cicero, "De Inventione," in *De Inventione, De Optimo Genere Oratorum, Topica*, trans. M. Hubbell (Cambridge, MA: Harvard University Press, 1949), 1.1.1.

17. Quentin Skinner, *Reason and Rhetoric in the Philosophy of Hobbes* (Cambridge: Cambridge University Press, 1996), 2.

18. The full passage states: "For there was a time when men wandered at large in the fields like animals and lived on wild fare…At this juncture a man—great and wise I am sure—…assembled and gathered them in accordance with a plan; he introduced them to every useful and honourable occupation, though they cried out against it at first because of its novelty, and then when through reason and eloquence they had listened with greater attention, he transformed them from wild savages into a kind and gentle folk. To me, at least, it does not seem possible that a mute and voiceless wisdom

could have turned men suddenly from their habits and introduced them to different patterns of life." Cicero, "De Inventione," 1.1.2–3.
19. Ibid., 1.5; Cicero, *De Officiis*, trans. Walter Miller (Cambridge, MA: Harvard Univesity Press, 1997), 1.11–12.
20. Cicero, *De Officiis*, 1.132.
21. According to Sean McConnell, Cicero's position on the relation between philosophy and politics (which is strictly related to that between philosophy and rhetoric) has changed along the years. If at the beginning he considered them two neatly separated subjects, he came progressively to develop the idea that philosophy could give an essential contribution to politics. In this sense, according to McConnell, the turning point could have been his exile in 58 BC. After this Cicero gradually withdrew from public life and thus could devote more and more time to philosophy and come to see under a different light its relation with politics. Sean McConnell, *Philosophical Life in Cicero's Letters* (Cambridge: Cambridge University Press, 2014), Ch. 1.
22. Cicero, *On the Ideal Orator*, 3.143.
23. Ibid., 3.60–1.
24. Ibid., 3.122. In relation to the importance of philosophy for oratory according to Cicero, in *Orator* he comes to affirm that it is Plato's Academia, rather than the workshops of the rhetoricians, who has made him an orator. Something similar is asserted in the *Tusculanae disputationes*, when he sustains that the source of his oratorical accomplishments is his study of philosophy. Cicero, "Orator," 12; Cicero, *Tusculan Disputations*, 1.6.
25. Cicero, *On the Ideal Orator*, 3.72, see also 1.16. Cf. Cicero, "Pro Archia," in *Pro Archia. Post Reditum in Senatu. Post Reditum Ad Quirites. De Domo Sua. De Haruspicum Responsis. Pro Plancio*, trans. Nevile Hunter Watts (Cambridge, MA: Harvard University Press, 1923), 12.
26. Cicero, "Brutus," 322, cf. 161. See also Cicero, *On the Ideal Orator*, 1.17–18, 20–1, 48–70, 157–8, 160–203, 2.6, 3.54, 76.
27. Cicero, *On the Ideal Orator*, 3.55. Cf. Plato, *Gorgias*, 456c–57c, 469c–69e.
28. The distinction between general and particular questions, *theses* and *hypotheses*, was a customary one in ancient rhetoric. The former were usually studied by philosophers, while the latter were studied by rhetoricians. In the *De oratore* Cicero accepts this distinction. However, in an open polemic against a technicist understanding of rhetoric, he strongly criticizes the rhetors of his time for not paying attention to the general questions and thus for reducing their discipline to a set of rules to be applied to standard cases. Cicero, *On the Ideal Orator*, 1.58–68, 2.42, 133–4, 3.04–25. However, Cicero's position on this topic has evolved along the years. In *De*

inventione he was still of the idea that "these [abstract] questions are far removed from the business of an orator." Cicero, "De Inventione," 1.6.8. Later, first in *De oratore* and then in *Orator*, he came to include in the domain of oratory these general, abstract arguments, though keeping them in a subordinate position to the specific issues at hand, since his orator is not a full-fledged philosopher but first of all a politician. This shift is consistent with the argument (see supra note 21) that Cicero came only progressively to develop the idea that philosophy can give a fundamental contribution to politics. Cicero, "Orator," 14.45–6; Gary Remer, *Humanism and the Rhetoric of Toleration* (University Park: Pennsylvania State University Press, 1996), 18.

29. Cicero, *On the Ideal Orator*, 1.56–7, 94.
30. So Cicero specifies that for those involved in practical life only need a certain familiarity with philosophical wisdom. They don't need to become experts in every domain, because their responsibility is to act and they don't have much time to study philosophy. See ibid., 1.94, 3.86–9, etc. As Nicgorski correctly points out in this respect, in *De oratore* Crassus clarifies that what interests him is not the truest philosophy, but rather that philosophy which is best suited to the orator (and therefore to his political commitment). Nicgorski, "Cicero's Paradoxes and His Idea of Utility," 558. Cicero, *On the Ideal Orator*, 3.64.
31. In the Introduction to their translation of *De oratore*, May and Wisse argue that Cicero's idea that eloquence needs to be supported by philosophy has no moral background, but is motivated only by the fact that in every particular and concrete question with which an orator has to deal, there is always implicit a more general and indefinite one. James M. May and Jakob Wisse, "Introduction," in *Cicero: On the Ideal Orator*, trans. James M. May and Jakob Wisse (New York and Oxford: Oxford University Press, 2001), 25. This may be true in the sense that for Cicero philosophy is not a discipline able to provide a knowledge about the good and the bad, which is directly and easily applicable to practice through eloquence. However, keeping in mind his general understanding of philosophy as a spiritual guide, we can say that for him philosophy has the key ethical and political function of helping to reshape and expand the moral framework of an individual and a citizen. This is what has been defended, for instance, by Bryan Garsten, Renato Grilli, or Ingo Gildenhard: Garsten, *Saving Persuasion*, 156–66; Grilli, "Cicerone tra retorica e filosofia," 60; Gildenhard, *Creative Eloquence*.
32. When centuries later Giambattista Vico defended the rhetorical humanistic model of education threatened by the diffusion of Descartes's new critical method, he felt the necessity to clarify that the ancient method is not opposed to critical thinking and moral rightness. In *De ratione* Vico writes:

"Here some learned pundit might object that, in the conduct of life, I would have our young students become courtiers, and not philosophers; pay little attention to truth and follow not reality but appearances; and cast down morality and put on a deceitful 'front' of virtue. I have no such intention. Instead, I should like to have them act as philosophers, even at court; to care for truth that both is and has the appearance of truth, and to follow that which is morally good and which everybody approves." Giambattista Vico, *On the Study Methods of Our Time*, trans. Elio Gianturco (Ithaca: Cornell University Press, 1990), 37–8.

33. See e.g., Cicero, "Paradoxa Stoicorum," in *De Oratore, Book III; De Fato; Paradoxa Stoicorum*, trans. H. Rackham (Cambridge, MA: Harvard University Press, 1968), 2–3; Cicero, "Orator," 12; Cicero, *Tusculan Disputations*, 1.1–4, 4.5–6, 5.9; Cicero, "De Legibus," in *De Republica (on the Republic) & De Legibus (on the Laws)*, trans. Clinton Walker Keyes (Cambridge, MA: Harvard University Press, 2000), 1.28, 58; Cicero, "De Natura Deorum," in *On the Nature of the Gods. Academics*, trans. H. Rackham (Cambridge, MA: Harvard University Press, 1933), 1.7–8; Cicero, "De Divinatione," in *On Old Age. On Friendship. On Divination*, trans. W. A. Falconer (Cambridge, MA: Harvard University Press, 1923), 2.1–2.

34. The idea to create a Roman tradition of philosophy was conceived by Cicero in the 40s, when the advent to power of Caesar forced him to abandon politics.

35. Cicero, *Tusculan Disputations*, 1.7. In this text, and more in general in Cicero's philosophical writings of the 40s, the hierarchy between philosophy and politics seems to change in favour of the former, so that the focus is no more on the profile of the statesman and *orator perfectus*, but rather on *perfecta philosophia*. Ingo Gildenhard, *Paideia Romana: Cicero's Tusculan Disputations* (Cambridge: Cambridge University Press, 2007), 149–56.

36. Gildenhard, *Creative Eloquence*, 2, 6.

37. Ibid., 7–10.

38. According for Cicero, this occurs in those cases when, for instance, a tyrant as he believes to be Sulla transforms a *res publica* into a *res private*, thus going against natural justice; or when a law goes against the interest of the state. Cicero, "On the Agrarian Law," in *Pro Quinctio. Pro Roscio Amerino. Pro Roscio Comoedo. On the Agrarian Law*, trans. J. H. Freese (Cambridge, MA: Harvard University Press, 1930), 3.5; Cicero, *Philippics*, trans. Walter C. A. Ker (Cambridge, MA: Harvard University Press, 1995), 5.16. Another very interesting case discussed by Gildenhard is the concept of *humanitas*, which in Cicero acquires an extremely rich semantic connotation: Gildenhard, *Creative Eloquence*, 175, 191–2, 201–16. Natural law

and justice are, of course, foundational elements in Cicero's conception of the state. See e.g., Cicero, "De Re Publica," in *De Re Publica (on the Republic) & De Legibus (on the Laws)*, trans. C. W. Keyes (Cambridge, MA: Harvard University Press, 2000), 1.21, 39, 42, 3.3; Cicero, "De Legibus," 1.17–18, 2.8; Cicero, *De Officiis*, 1.12, 157–8.

39. This kind of reading of the *Pro Murena*, which goes against the standard interpretation of this speech that takes it as an example of Cicero's manipulative use of eloquence, has been defended by Michael Leff. Michael Leff, "Cicero's Pro Murena and the Strong Case for Rhetoric," *Rhetoric and Public Affairs* 1 (1998).

40. Yelena Baraz has studied in depth the prefaces of Cicero's philosophical works of the 40s—where Cicero usually provides a justification of the choice to devote himself to philosophy—both to explore the meaning of this political-cultural project and scrutinize the rhetorical strategies he employs to justify it. Baraz, *A Written Republic*.

41. Cicero, *On the Ideal Orator*, 1.12; Cicero, "Paradoxa Stoicorum," 1. Cf. Cicero, *Tusculan Disputations*, 2.4.

42. Baraz, *A Written Republic*, 131–6.

43. Ibid., 77.

44. On the importance of the *exempla* see for instance: Cicero, "Pro Archia," 14.

45. See e.g., Cicero, "De Re Publica," 1.8, 12, 3.5–7, 6.13, 29, etc.; Cicero, *Tusculan Disputations*, 1.19, 90; Cicero, *De Officiis*, 1.22, 70–3.

46. Cicero, *On the Ideal Orator*, 1.56; Connolly, *The State of Speech*, 125.

47. Quintilian, *Institutio Oratoria*, 11.2.30, see also 1.12.16–18, 2.15.34, 2.16.16, 2.17.31, 12.1–3, 12.2.1, etc. The motto '*ut vivat, etiam quemque dicere*' Quintilian cites (and that, as he says, is a Greek aphorism) recalls Cato's famous motto of *vir bonus dicendi peritus*, or Seneca's *talis oratio, qualis vita* (*Epistolae* 114.1). See also: Cicero, *Tusculan Disputations*, 5.47. John Dugan, *Making a New Man: Ciceronian Self-Fashioning in the Rhetorical Works* (New York: Oxford University Press, 2005), 2.

48. Quintilian, *Institutio Oratoria*, 12.3.12.

49. Ibid., 1.pr.15–16.

50. Ibid., 1.pr.13–15, 12.3.12. See also: 11.1.35, 12.2.8–10.

51. See e.g., Kennedy, *A New History of Classical Rhetoric*, 9, 181–2.

52. Clarity is for Quintilian one of the main qualities of a good speech; and arrogance, a vice (very typical of the youngsters) that is pernicious in all the aspects of life and that has to be avoided at all costs. Quintilian, *Institutio Oratoria*, 1.5.1, 12.6.2. Also in Cicero we find references to arrogance as a vice quite common among philosophers. For instance: Cicero, *On the Ideal Orator*, 1.193. Cf. Cicero, *De Officiis*, 1.99.

53. For instance: Ernesto Grassi, *Vico e l'umanesimo* (Milan: Guerini, 1992); Ernesto Grassi, *Retorica come filosofia. La tradizione umanistica* (Naples: La città del sole, 1999).
54. For Quintilian "a man's character is generally revealed and the secrets of his heart are laid bare by his manner of speaking." Quintilian, *Institutio Oratoria*, 11.2.30. In humanists such as Petrarca and Valla we find the same idea. See, respectively: Eugenio Garin, *L'umanesimo italiano. Filosofia e vita civile nel Rinascimento* (Bari: Laterza, 1965), 27; Salvatore Camporeale, *Lorenzo Valla. Umanesimo e Teologia* (Florence: Istituto Palazzo Strozzi, 1972), 152. Miguel de Cervantes, another great humanist, writes in the *Don Quijote*: "Si el poeta fuere casto en sus costumbres, lo será también en sus versos; la pluma es lengua del alma: cuales fueran los conceptos que en ella se engendraren, tales serán sus escritos." [If the poet be pure in his habits, he will be pure in his verses too; the pen is the tongue of the soul, and as the thoughts engendered there, so will be his writings]. My translation. Miguel de Cervantes, *El ingenioso hidalgo Don Quijote de la Mancha*, 2 vols., vol. II (Madrid: Castalia, 1982), 157.
55. Cicero, *On the Ideal Orator*, 1.1–5; Cicero, "De Re Publica," 1.1–12. For Nicgorski, if *De re publica* is Cicero's most important political work, *De oratore* is its continuation. In the former Cicero argues that the Roman Republic is the greatest regime ever realized because of the greatness of its statesmen. And in the latter, he explains the kind of education necessary for statesmanship. Walter Nicgorski, "Cicero's Focus: From the Best Regime to the Model Statesman," *Political Theory* 19 (1991): 250. On the relation between the perfect orator and the perfect statesman in Cicero see also: Jonathan Powell, "The Rector Rei Publicae of Cicero's De Republica," *Scripta Classica Israelica* 13 (1994); Grilli, "Cicerone tra retorica e filosofia," 59; Jonathan Zarecki, *Cicero's Ideal Statesman in Theory and Practice* (London and New York: Bloomsbury, 2014), 46.
56. There are many relevant passages in Cicero's writings on the relationship between theory and practice and the necessity of their union. For instance: Cicero, "De Re Publica," 1.2, 15, 28, 3.4–6; Cicero, *De Officiis*, 1.28–9, 153–7; Cicero, "De Legibus," 1.17, 28, 58; Cicero, *Tusculan Disputations*, 1.1–3, 4.5–6, 5.9; Cicero, "De Natura Deorum," 1.7–9; Cicero, "De Divinatione," 2.1–2, etc.
57. Cicero, *On the Ideal Orator*, 1.34. Cf. Cicero, *De Officiis*, 1.156–7.
58. Cf. Nicgorski, "Cicero's Focus: From the Best Regime to the Model Statesman," 249.
59. Likewise, Joy Connolly has argued that: "Cicero's representation of the *orator perfectus* takes on significance as an intervention in ethical theory that reinvents the process of conceptualizing the good life in terms of communication." Connolly, *The State of Speech*, 139.

60. Ibid., 14. In the third book of *De oratore*, Crassus justifies his choice to talk about the *summus orator* (an orator in his highest accomplishment) by arguing that in order to understand the nature of something it is necessary to see it in its perfect form. In the first book, Crassus talks about "the Orator we are seeking", evoking the ideal city envisioned by Plato in the *Republic*. Cicero, *On the Ideal Orator*, 3.85, 1.118, see also 1.202. The connection between the figure of the perfect orator and the Platonic concept of 'ideas' is made explicit in Cicero's last work on rhetoric, *Orator*, where he writes: "Consequently in delineating the perfect orator I shall be portraying such a one as perhaps has never existed. Indeed I am not inquiring who was the perfect orator, but what is that unsurpassable ideal which seldom if ever appears…This ideal cannot be perceived by the eye or ear, nor by any senses, but we can nevertheless grasp it by the mind and imagination…these patterns of things are called ιδεαι or ideas by Plato." Cicero, "Orator," 7–11.
61. Similarly Zarecki underlines that the figure of the ideal statesman outlined by Cicero in *De re publica* (and that for Zarecki coincides in crucial aspects with that of the perfect orator) is an ideal, but with a practical meaning, since it is supposed to inspire political actions. Zarecki, *Cicero's Ideal Statesman in Theory and Practice*, 91–4.
62. There is a passage in *De oratore*, which particularly stresses the materiality of the process of self-fashioning to become an orator. It is when Antonius, in commenting on this process, says: "After doing what I set out to do, namely begetting, nourishing, and developing the strength of this orator that I am now fashioning, I shall hand him over to Crassus to be clothed and equipped." Cicero, *On the Ideal Orator*, 2.123. This process of self-fashioning is extremely difficult, according to Cicero, because of the "incredible scope and difficulty of oratory." And this explains why for him there are so few examples in history of orators who have been able to get close to the ideal of the perfect orator. Ibid., 1.16–19, cf. 1.76ff., 94–5, 118, 128, 202, 2.187, 3.84. Among the few examples of remarkable oratory and statesmanship Cicero includes Crassus and Pericles, who thanks to "his supreme learning, counsel and eloquence, was the leader of Athens for forty years." Ibid., 3.15, 3.138. Cicero's judgment on Pericles is in open contrast with Plato's negative appreciation of him as a leader who corrupted the demos. Plato, *Gorgias*, 515d–e.
63. On the topic of rhetorical self-creation an increasing number of works have been published in the last years. For example: Emanuele Narducci, *Cicerone e l'eloquenza romana* (Bari: Laterza, 1997); Martin Bloomer, "Schooling in Persona: Imagination and Subordination in Roman Education," *Classical Antiquity* 16 (1997); Erik Gunderson, *Staging Masculinity: The Rhetoric of Performance in the Roman World* (Ann Arbor: University of

Michigan Press, 2000); Dugan, *Making a New Man*; Maud W. Gleason, *Making Men: Sophists and Self-Presentation in Ancient Rome* (Princeton: Princeton University Press, 2008); Connolly, *The State of Speech*.

64. On the influence of Quintilian and Cicero on the development of the Renaissance programme of the *studia humanitatis* see for instance: Paul O. Kristeller, *Renaissance Thought and Its Sources*, ed. Michael Mooney (New York: Columbia University Press, 1979), 22ff.; Skinner, *Reason and Rhetoric in the Philosophy of Hobbes*, 21–6.

65. For Quintilian's scepticism about rules and general principles, see: Quintilian, *Institutio Oratoria*, 2.13.14, 12.5.1.

66. Ibid., 2.15.11, 2.17.25, 12.5.1, etc.

67. Confirming the importance of the *exempla*, Quintilian underlines how important is for the students to read great writers and philosophers, as well as the stories of great historical characters, who can serve as models of imitation. However, beyond the humanistic disciplines, Quintilian includes in the *curriculum* also other disciplines such as geometry, astronomy, and music. Ibid., 1.4, 1.10, 10.1.27–36.

68. As Quintilian writes "the art of speaking can only be attained by hard work and assiduity of study, by a variety of exercises and repeated trial, the highest prudence and unfailing quickness of judgment." Ibid., 2.13.15.

69. Hans-Georg Gadamer, *Dialogue and Dialectic: Eight Hermeneutical Studies on Plato* (New Haven: Yale University Press, 1980), 54.

70. Jaeger, quoted in: ibid., p. 53.

71. Eloquence requires education, natural talents, and practice, according to Quintilian. Quintilian, *Institutio Oratoria*, 2.19.

72. At the beginning of the *Institutio oratoria*, Quintilian complains that his contemporary rhetoricians neglect the early years in the development of the student, which are for him fundamental. Ibid., 1.pr.4, see also 1.1.5. An interesting parallelism could be drawn between the interest of Quintilian in the early phase of the life of a student and that of Vico (who knew Quintilian's work very well) in the origins whether of a word, a person, or a civilization.

73. Quintilian writes: "the art of oratory includes all that is essential for the training of an orator, and that it is impossible to reach the summit in any subject unless we have first passed through all the elementary stages. I shall not therefore refuse to stoop to the consideration of those minor details, neglect of which may result in there being no opportunity for more important things, and propose to mould the studies of my orator from infancy, on the assumption that his whole education has been entrusted to my charge…It has been my design to lead my reader from the very cradle of speech through all the stages of education which can be of any service to our budding orator till we have reached the very summit of the art." Ibid.,

1.pr.5–6. On the relation between natural talent and education according to Quintilian, see: Elaine Fantham, "The Concept of Nature and Human Nature in Quintilian's Psychology and Theory of Instruction," *Rhetorica* 13 (1995).
74. Javier Roiz, *La recuperación del buen juicio* (Madrid: Foro Interno, 2003), 39–40.
75. On several occasions Quintilian shows a strong optimism about the human capacity to learn. Quintilian, *Institutio Oratoria*, 1.pr.20, 1.7.2, 2.17.9, 12.11.25, etc. Cf. 2.20.1. On this point see: Fantham, "The Concept of Nature and Human Nature in Quintilian's Psychology and Theory of Instruction"; Kennedy, *The Art of Rhetoric in the Roman World*, 429.
76. For Quintilian "the material of rhetoric is composed of everything that may be placed before it as a subject." Quintilian, *Institutio Oratoria*, 2.21.1–4.
77. Ibid., 2.20.
78. See e.g., Brian Vickers, *In Defence of Rhetoric* (Oxford: Clarendon Press, 1988), 276–86; Skinner, *Reason and Rhetoric in the Philosophy of Hobbes*, 120–6; Ruth Webb, "Imagination and the Arousal of Emotions in Greco-Roman Rhetoric," in *The Passions in Roman Thought and Literature*, ed. Susanna Morton Braund and Christopher Gill (Cambridge: Cambridge University Press, 1997); Richard A. Katula, "Quintilian on the Art of Emotional Appeal," *Rhetoric Review* 22 (2003).
79. Quintilian, *Institutio Oratoria*, 6.2.1–3.
80. Ibid., 6.2.7. On the instrumental use of the emotions in Roman rhetoric cf.: Daniel M. Gross, "Introduction," in *Heidegger and Rhetoric*, ed. Daniel M. Gross and Ansgar Kemmann (Albany, NY: SUNY, 2005); Skinner, *Reason and Rhetoric in the Philosophy of Hobbes*, 124; Katula, "Quintilian on the Art of Emotional Appeal," 12–14.
81. Quintilian translates *pathos* with *adfectus* and argues that for the term *ethos* there is no adequate translation in Latin, although it is usually rendered by the term *mores*. However, he adds, this translation is inadequate because the meaning of *mores* is very general, since it refers to a state of mind in general. This is why for him it would be better to explain the meaning of *ethos* (rather than trying to translate it), in order to show its affinity with the word *pathos*. Quintilian, *Institutio Oratoria*, 6.2.8–10.
82. Ibid., 6.2.13.
83. Cicero defines style as "the fitting of the proper language to the invented matter." Cicero, "De Inventione," 1.7.9. He individuates three basic styles of oratory: the grand (or also Asiatic), the tempered, and the plain style (or also Attic). See e.g., Cicero, "Orator," 20–1, 69, 106–9. Quintilian's discussion of the style follows in many aspects that of Cicero. Quintilian, *Institutio Oratoria*, 12.10.58–72.

84. Among the various *tropoi,* Quintilian highlights in particular the importance of metaphors. Quintilian, *Institutio Oratoria,* 8.6.4–5. On *paradiastole,* see: ibid., 8.3.89. Skinner has analysed in depth the fundamental meaning of *paradiastole* and redescription in rhetoric: Skinner, *Reason and Rhetoric in the Philosophy of Hobbes,* Ch. 4.
85. Quintilian, *Institutio Oratoria,* 8.4.1. On the proximity between the orator and the musician see: Roiz, *La recuperación del buen juicio,* 33–4, 39–40, 62, 72, 112–13, 304, 331–2.
86. This principle, Quintilian says, belongs to "the secret principles of this art" and "the inmost recesses of the subject." Quintilian, *Institutio Oratoria,* 6.2.25–28, cf. 12.5.4.
87. Ibid., 6.2.29. For Quintilian eloquence "depends in the main on the state of the mind, which must be moved, conceive images and adapt itself to suit the nature of the subject which is the theme of the speech." Ibid., 1.20.30. Cf.: Katula, "Quintilian on the Art of Emotional Appeal," 7.
88. Quintilian, *Institutio Oratoria,* 2.4.7–12. Quintilian however doesn't neglect analytical and critical skills, which are relevant, for instance, to the study of geometry. Indeed, he includes this discipline in the curriculum from the very early years of study. Ibid., 1.10.34, 37. Giambattista Vico criticizes the rigid application of the Cartesian method in education, by arguing that its exclusive emphasis on the critical and analytical could inhibit the development in the youngsters of imagination, and correlated capacities as ingenuity and memory. Also Vico, however, is perfectly aware of the importance of these analytical and critical skills. See for instance: Giambattista Vico, "Il metodo degli studi del tempo nostro," in *Opere,* ed. Fausto Nicolini (Milan and Naples: Riccardo Ricciardi Editore, 1953), 177. The idea that among young people the creative faculties are stronger and that rationality matures gradually over the years is confirmed in one of the *degnità* (axioms) of the *Scienza Nuova* and represents the basis of his theory of poetic character of the first peoples: Giambattista Vico, "Prinicipi di Scienza Nuova," in *Opere,* ed. Fausto Nicolini (Milan and Naples: Riccardo Ricciardi Editore, 1953), par. 211.
89. Quintilian, *Institutio Oratoria,* 3.8.50–1.
90. Cicero, *On the Ideal Orator,* 2.102–4. Cf. Quintilian, *Institutio Oratoria,* 12.8.15.
91. Brian Vickers, for instance, has written that if you ask for (as Cicero does in *De oratore*) "the subtlety of the logician, the thoughts of a philosopher, a diction almost poetic, a lawyer's memory, a tragedian's voice, and the bearing almost of a consummate actor", enriched by an in-depth knowledge in all fields of knowledge and transformed into an eloquence so potent "that it embraces the origin and operation and developments of all things, all the virtues and duties, all the natural principles governing the

morals and minds and life of mankind, and also determines their custom and laws and rights, and controls the government of the state", than you end up giving an empty response to Plato's criticism because you pass from nothing to too much. Vickers, *In Defence of Rhetoric*, 164–5. Cf. Kennedy, *The Art of Rhetoric in the Roman World*, 227, 504. In this perspective, we could say that Cicero and Quintilian's conceptions of rhetoric represent an emblematic example of what Dilip Gaonkar has called the recurrent temptation of rhetoricians to "flee from mere rhetoric." Dilip P. Gaonkar, "Rhetoric and Its Double: Reflections of the Rhetorical Turn in the Human Sciences," in *Contemporary Rhetorical Theory: A Reader*, ed. John Louis Lucaites, Celeste Michelle Condit, and Sally Caudill (New York and London: The Guilford Press, 1999), 194.
92. Quintilian, *Institutio Oratoria*, 5.14.31.
93. The quotation continues in this way "and sometimes it [*rhetoric*] seduces him." George Kennedy, the author of this remark, alludes here to the possibility that the technical and instrumental dimension of rhetoric takes the upper hand on the ethical one. Kennedy, *The Art of Rhetoric in the Roman World*, 24.
94. Connolly, *The State of Speech*, 129.
95. Ibid., 139.
96. Ibid., 129.
97. Joy Connolly, "Virile Tongues: Rhetoric and Masculinity," in *A Companion to Roman Rhetoric*, ed. William Dominik and Jon Hall (Malden: Blackwell, 2007), 91. John Dugan has argued that in the repertoire of Roman orations we find a rich set of different and competing representations of an imagined idea of Rome as a community, in which the identity of the orator—and the *auctoritas* he claims for himself—enters as a constitutive part. So, despite the cult of the tradition, in practice the idea of Rome as a community was subject to great flexibility, which the orator could use for his own political purposes. John Dugan, "Rhetoric and the Roman Republic," in *The Cambridge Companion to Ancient Rhetoric*, ed. Erik Gunderson (Cambridge: Cambridge University Press, 2009), 180.
98. Cicero, "De Re Publica," 2.69. Quintilian similarly writes: "assuredly the man who will best inspire such feelings in others is he who has first inspired them in himself." Quintilian, *Institutio Oratoria*, 12.1.25, 29.
99. Connolly, stressing the role of eloquence in materializing wisdom, has argued that "Cicero constructs a contest over the communication of knowledge between the Roman orator and the Greek philosopher that turns on the way the orator embodies, emotionalizes, and contextualizes what he knows—making it natural by making it a product of the body, taking philosophical themes and giving them flesh and blood." Connolly, *The State of Speech*, 120.

PART II

CHAPTER 4

Politics as Transcendence: Leo Strauss

4.1 Introduction

In this chapter, with a leap of several centuries, we'll move to three influential twentieth-century political theorists: Leo Strauss, Richard Rorty, and Hannah Arendt. As explained in the Introduction, the aim of the second part of the book is to demonstrate how the themes and questions discussed in the first part—which emerge from the ancient debate between philosophy and rhetoric—strongly resonate in the thought of those modern thinkers. In effect, none of the contemporary thinkers mentioned has ever really dealt with this ancient debate in a substantive manner. In particular, none of them has engaged directly and extensively with the tradition of rhetoric, recognizing thus its values for the history of political thought. Nevertheless, as I hope to demonstrate in the following pages, the narrative that I have constructed around the relation between philosophy, politics, and rhetoric as it was discussed by Plato, Aristotle, Cicero, Quintilian, and some of the Renaissance Humanists up until Vico, can be used to illuminate the works of those modern thinkers under a different light. What we can see through this narrative is that the conceptions of politics of Strauss, Rorty, and Arendt are all characterized by a dialectical relationship between its transcendent and contingent dimensions, which are mediated through rhetoric. This dialectical relationship assumes in each of these thinkers a different form: not only in the sense of having its centre located closer to one or the other of the two poles, but also in the

© The Author(s) 2018
G. Ballacci, *Political Theory between Philosophy and Rhetoric*, Rhetoric, Politics and Society,
https://doi.org/10.1057/978-1-349-95293-9_4

sense of providing different (but not incompatible) meanings of these same two poles. As a consequence, the meaning of rhetoric also changes in each of these three thinkers.

I will start by considering the work of Leo Strauss, one of the political theorists who has done most in the twentieth century to recover the transcendent dimension of politics, understood as the never-ending search through philosophy for the first principles of common life and the question of how to live. The recovery of this transcendent dimension in politics is what attributes to Strauss's understanding of politics its foremost 'philosophical' dimension. The process put into motion by a philosophical attempt to understand politics is for him one of striving for transcendence, or eternity, since in attempting to clarify the opinions of the citizens on justice and the common good, the philosopher realizes that the principles of politics in turn depend on the wider realm in which politics is contained: the cosmos itself, or the whole. For this reason political life has always a transcending dimension and thus calls for a philosophical life, which is considered hierarchically superior to the former and thus always tempts the philosopher to abandon political life altogether. Such a risk however is avoided in the very moment the philosopher understands that her search for the first principles cannot but be perceived as a threat by the community, which sees its order continually called into question by that search and thus reacts aggressively against philosophy. This is the moment in which philosophy assumes a political dimension, by trying to understand how its activity interferes with the political context in which it takes place. It thus understands that in order to defend itself it needs to employ rhetorical stratagems: that is, make recourse to an astutely devised style that hides uncomfortable and challenging truths behind the surface of an apparent defence of edifying and socially acceptable moral principles.[1] For Strauss, Socrates epitomizes this way of understanding political philosophy; an understanding that according to him was destroyed with the consolidation of what we could broadly define as the 'modern project' and the radical process of what he calls a "lowering of sight", which brought a complete "oblivion of eternity."[2]

In this chapter I focus on these three dimensions in Strauss's thought: transcendence, as the unending search through philosophy of the first principles; contingence, the concrete and historically mutable social and political reality in which such search takes place; and rhetoric, as the form that philosophy has to assume to defend itself and justify its presence in the community through the technique of writing between the lines. The interconnection among these three dimensions shows Strauss's deep awareness of the extension of the domain in which politics unfolds: from contingency to transcendence. As I will show in the next section, in his view one of the most negative consequences of the modern revolution is precisely to have distorted the real meanings of these two dimensions: first eliminating the striving for transcendence and then, as a consequence, trivializing the meaning of contingency and dispensing with the role of rhetoric as a mediating force. However, in Strauss's view this extension does not appear, as in Cicero, as a continuum, but rather as a field characterized by a rupture. Because of that rupture Strauss understands rhetoric essentially in instrumental terms, as a more or less benevolent form of manipulation—from a sort of "pedagogical reserve"[3] to a noble lie—exercised by the philosopher to compensate for the rupture between the philosophical search of truth and the political life. On the other hand, as we have seen, in the case of Cicero (or also of Aristotle) rhetoric is seen as a power that can make the connection between these two realms more positive and less unidirectional; one in which education is carefully combined with more coercive forms of influencing and that assumes a less hierarchical form.

From the point of view of this book, the relevance of Strauss is determined not only by his compelling defence of the significance of transcendence in political life; but also by his vindication of the important, even if subordinate, role of contingency for philosophy. In line with the spirit of Socratic rationalism, Strauss conceives philosophy as a process that, starting from the point of view of lay citizens and common sense, strives to gain a critical perspective and ultimately transcend them. The domain of conventions, the 'cave', assumes a constitutive role for philosophy. It is the *conditio sine qua non* of philosophy.[4] The commonsensical evaluation of political things is the necessary starting point from which the philosopher, as a citizen herself, must start in her process of ascension. Nevertheless, the role the contingent plays according to Strauss is clearly hierarchically inferior to that of transcendence. As a consequence, differently from Cicero or Aristotle, his conception of rhetoric cannot but be an essentially instrumental one. This reductive view of rhetoric Strauss endorses corresponds to the Platonic idea of the people as ultimately irrational and incompetent, and therefore of the political order as reluctant to any sort of significant change and progress. For Strauss the only source of movement is in the hands of the few able to philosophize. The more radical choice in effect is for him not between politics and philosophy, but rather between revelation and philosophy. These are indeed the only two alternative sources of our moral and political obligations, since they are the only ones able to provide a normative account of the whole.[5] On the contrary, according to the Roman and Humanistic tradition, the function of rhetoric cannot be reduced to that of finding *a posteriori* a proper form for philosophic knowledge in the realm of politics. Rather it consists in establishing a double-way and synchronic relationship between these two realms. This position responds to the idea that politics, the practical realm, is not a passive entity that can be moulded at will by philosophical knowledge, but rather something with its own rationale that philosophy needs to understand. This important difference between Strauss and the Roman and Humanistic tradition on the relationship between theory and practice corresponds to a crucial difference on the value of politics and the role of the people in promoting change and progress.

4.2 The Modern Oblivion of Eternity

At the most general level, we can say that for Strauss the crisis of modernity is first of all a philosophical crisis. It is a crisis that has to do with the rejection by modern thinkers of the idea that society can only aspire to really improve its condition through a systematic investigation into the foundations of its principles. The moderns, Strauss argues, didn't renounce the idea of human perfectibility and progress, but came to the conclusion that these goals don't require an investigation on the foundations of the normative order, but only on 'facts'. This is why philosophy came to be replaced in its leading position by the new science emerging from the Scientific Revolution: a neutral, non-evaluative knowledge that has nothing to say about the question of how to live, since it conceives its function according to Francis Bacon's famous dictum 'knowledge is power': i.e. in merely practical terms, as an instrument to master nature.[6] The consequence of such transformation for Strauss is that the modern project remained a project without foundations; it was a project based on the idea of progress—the progressive expansion of the levels of welfare—but without an underlying reason to justify it and thus uncertain of its destiny.[7] What Strauss calls the "crisis of our time, the crisis of the West" is, in brief, a philosophical and cultural transformation that has engendered a form of hidden but very corrosive nihilism.[8]

Strauss explains the effect of replacing philosophy with the new science in terms of a radical upturn of the hierarchy of the normative order or, moreover, the annulation of that hierarchy: the great questions related to the human condition began to be assessed not in terms of what is considered hierarchically superior to human being but rather to what underlies it. Because for him human beings belong to a broader reality—the cosmos or, to use the expression preferred by Strauss, 'the whole'—whose nature is unknown, there are two ways in which the latter can be conceived in relation to the former: either as sub-human or as supra-human. The position of the human being within the whole thus must be understood according to one of these two options: "either man is an accidental product of a blind evolution or else the process leading to man, culminating in man, is directed toward man."[9] Ancient philosophy took the latter option, assuming that the cosmos has a purpose and that this purpose is normatively meaningful for the human being. Modern science instead took the other option. With the Scientific Revolution, and the resulting demise of philosophy and consolidation of the new natural sciences,[10] a new nonteleological and materialist cosmology became preponderant. This new cosmology rejected as unscientific not only the teleological view of the cosmos, but also the idea that it is composed of qualitatively different parts that can be classified according to the metaphysical categories of subhuman, human, and superhuman. The cosmos (including the human being) is made, according to this modern cosmology, of elements whose difference are quantitative rather than qualitative.

Among the most significant consequences of this revolution Strauss emphasizes the fact that the basis upon which the ancient conception of natural right came to be completely undermined and with it the same possibility of developing a philosophical discussion about the proper ends of human beings. A normative analysis was, in effect, progressively replaced by a descriptive one: no more a discussion about how the human beings should act, but rather of how they actually act.[11] This is evident in the case of modern political science, particularly that of Hobbes. Being founded on such a cosmology, the new political science epitomized by Hobbes accepted the idea that to understand something means to understand its causes and thus "to understand the higher in terms of the lower: the human in terms of the subhuman, the rational in terms of the subrational, the political in terms of the subpolitical." Additionally Hobbes's new political science denied that "the common good is something that is."[12]

At the core of what Strauss calls the 'modern project' there is therefore an attempt to "to prove the necessary coincidence of the rational and the real, or to get rid of that which essentially transcends every possible human reality."[13] It is here that we find the source of modern nihilism, according to Strauss's analysis, and here is the basis for his idea of a return to the spirit of classical thought. But the possibility of such a return, as Strauss knew, must face a very strong objection: the fact that it presupposes also the return to an antiquated cosmology that modern science puts in question.[14] Strauss's response to this objection is clear: the difference between the modern and the ancient understanding of the human being in relation to the whole is to be found in the fact that the latter, even if within a teleological framework, leaves the question open; it is a matter of ongoing enquiry. As he writes:

> Whatever the significance of modern natural science may be, it cannot affect our understanding of what is human in man. To understand man in the light of the whole means for modern natural science to understand man in the light of the sub-human. But in that light man as man is wholly unintelligible. Classical political philosophy viewed man in a different light. It was originated by Socrates. And Socrates was so far from being committed to a specific cosmology that his knowledge was knowledge of ignorance. Knowledge of ignorance is not ignorance. It is knowledge of the elusive character of the truth, of the whole. Socrates, then, viewed man in the light of the mysterious character of the whole ... to articulate the situation of man means to articulate man's openness to the whole.[15]

For Strauss what differentiates the ancients from the moderns is that the former understood the problem of the human in the perspective of a whole, which is considered ultimately mysterious. On the other hand, the moderns replaced this perspective of openness in the understanding of the human with a closed one; a perspective that assumes, to use the words of a like-minded theorist, Eric Voegelin, "the structure of the external world as it is constituted in the system of mathematized physics is the ontologically real structure of the world."[16] It is this premise that for Strauss (and for Voegelin) makes normative inquiry into the human ends impossible.

Strauss diagnosed such a change of perspective—what he would later come to describe as a radical 'lowering of horizons'—in his first writings on Jewish thinkers and early modern philosophy in the 1920s, where he focuses on the modern critique of revealed religion.[17] In his first published book, a work on Spinoza published in the 1930, he interpreted the *Theological-Political Treatise* as an outright attack on religion's authority: the reclamation of the "freedom to live apart from one's own theologico-political community" made on behalf of philosophy; that is, the reclamation of the "freedom of the philosopher."[18] Strauss saw Spinoza's philosophy as the paradigmatic form of the attack that the Enlightenment brought to revealed religion: an attack that aimed to undermine its authority not through reasoned argument, but by mockery. It is an attitude that Strauss compared to a "Napoleonic strategy", which consists in leaving "the seemingly impregnable fortress of orthodoxy in the rear, telling itself that the enemy would not and could not venture any sally" and hoping that the new world it began to construct in replacement of orthodoxy could be proclaimed victorious simply by history.[19] The problem with such a solution however is that it doesn't represent a real victory over religion: revelation was not refuted, but only made object of ridicule and consigned to a primitive past by an act of the will.[20] Refutation would have required for Strauss something much more ambitious: to provide the "proof that the world and human life are perfectly intelligible without the assumption of a mysterious God" and thus that the human being is "himself theoretically and practically a master of his life."[21]

The momentous implication of that failure for Strauss is that the crucial problem of the foundations of communal life and the question of how to live were not really debated by post-Enlightenment thinkers. Even if the focus of his book on Spinoza is on epistemological questions, he soon came to understand that the question of the relation between reason and revelation is, first of all, a political question. Through the study of Jewish and Islamic medieval philosophy, Strauss recovers an understanding of revealed religion not much as a form of belief and knowledge, but rather as a form of authority: the ultimate source of the law.[22] In this perspective the question raised by the modern critique of religion appears under a different light: as a political problem concerning the relation between law and knowledge, rather than an epistemological one.[23] What is the foundation of the law: revelation or reason? This is for Strauss the "fundamental question" and the substance of what he calls the 'theological-political problem': whether we should live a life "of obedient love" toward God and its principles, or a life of "free insight."[24] It is question then that has an essentially political dimension as it concerns the foundation of the just order for the individual and the community and the scope of our moral obligation.

We can see then that Strauss's analysis of the decline of ancient tradition of natural right in *Natural Right and History* dovetails with his earlier analysis of the modern neglect of the theologico-political problem. In both cases, the modern epoch is characterized as an epoch established on the refusal to treat the question of the foundations of the moral and political order as open, and as a question accessible to rational inquiry.[25] The understanding and elucidation of such a question was rendered impossible in turn by the refusal of modern thinkers to take into serious consideration the possibility that philosophy could give an alternative foundation—equal in scope and completeness—than that provided by religion. This refusal was motivated by three main kinds of reasons, which for Strauss characterizes what he calls the three 'waves' of modernity.

Machiavelli and Hobbes are the two most relevant representatives of the 'first wave' of modernity. They are for Strauss responsible of the epochal turn taken by political philosophy, replacing the reflection on what Machiavelli would famously define the "imagined republics and principalities that have never been seen nor known to exist in reality", with that on those that actually exist.[26] The passage from an 'idealist' to a 'realist' conception of human being entails for Strauss replacing, as a point of reference for the reflection on politics, what is superior and transcends human being with what is lower to the human being: the instinct of survival and the self-interested desire of power and glory. Machiavelli is considered by Strauss to be the "founder of modern political philosophy": the first thinker really able to break away from the grip of tradition. As a second Columbus, Machiavelli discovered a completely unknown moral continent.[27] By consciously forsaking the Socratic search for the essence of justice, he founded a new practical philosophy, committed to understanding politics not according to supra-human standards, but rather from the perspective of the 'low, real' reality of the conflict and the intrinsic contingent dimension of political life: *Fortuna*.[28] From here, Machiavelli developed also a new, restricted version of virtue: a merely practical and instrumental kind of virtue, exclusively concerned with the attainment of mundane goals such as the foundation and preservation of the state, prosperity and glory.[29] But what appeared to Machiavelli and his followers as the discovery of a new continent for Strauss represents a radical contraction of horizons.[30]

Hobbes is the other great exponent of the first wave of modernity identified by Strauss. He is the thinker who attempted to construct a theory of the state on the new ground prepared by Machiavelli and refound political philosophy in a realistic and scientific fashion.[31] Strauss emphasizes Hobbes's absolute belief in the impossibility for humans to know the principles of the cosmos.[32] Every kind of teleological view of the cosmos was for him absurd, since human beings can only know what they themselves produce. Morality thus assumed with Hobbes a completely different meaning from that of the past, to the extent that the self-evident human passions and needs, the *primum naturae*, came to substitute the fundamental human ends as its base. Accordingly, the notion of natural law changed into a subjective notion of right, based on the right of self-preservation.[33] This transformation, according to Strauss, is the key to understand Hobbes's political philosophy and the developments of the discipline after him. Strauss sees in Hobbes one of the founding fathers of liberalism and of a new conception of politics based on a conflictive idea of the human being, which denies its political nature and that happiness depends on the pursuit of virtue, and instead proclaims that what is just coincides with what is legally permissible. The individual, isolated and fearful of her peers, becomes with Hobbes the measure of all things, taking the place of what was the prerogative of nature.[34]

In Strauss's interpretation then, Machiavelli and Hobbes have in common two crucial and interrelated aspects, both emblematic of the new modern spirit: first of all, the denial that political science should be concerned with the search of the common good as a transcendent ideal; second, the aspiration to recast political science as an exclusively practical science, concerned with the management of political reality and its contingencies. Nevertheless, both of them were thinkers in-between two epochs; thinkers still identifiable with a tradition of political theory, understood as a tradition that doesn't completely avoid reflection on the great normative questions of politics and ethics.[35] The problem for Strauss is rather that the response they gave are the wrong ones, since in trying to give a more practical content to political science they completely disregard its other crucial dimension: the striving for transcendence.

Much more drastic is the situation with the 'third wave' of modernity identified by Strauss and represented by two figures: Nietzsche and Heidegger, the greatest exponents of what Strauss calls 'radical historicism'. Together with positivism, historicism is for Strauss the main obstacle to the restoration of a proper understanding of politics. Despite the influence both thinkers had on him, Strauss believes that their philosophies represent at the same time the highest manifestation and one of the main causes of the contemporary state of crisis.[36] If historicism is the product of the "discovery", or "experience of history", in its mature form it came to imply the idea that:

all human thought is dependent on unique historical contexts that are prepared by more or less different contexts and that emerge out of their antecedents in a fundamentally unpredictable way: the foundations of human thought are laid by unpredictable experiences or decisions.[37]

Strauss recognizes that only in its radical form is historicism coherent with its philosophical premises. Radical historicism applies the basic insight of historicism all the way down: denying the same distinction between facts and values, it assumes that also the former (like the latter) cannot be studied objectively by science. It thus comes to deny the same possibility of scientific progress and the alleged universality of science as a method of knowing. From here it draws the only possible conclusion: that the possibility of human emancipation is ultimately meaningless, since human thinking is inevitably limited by time. As Strauss writes, for a radical historicist the most fundamental existential condition is "the experience, not of bliss, but of suffering, of emptiness, of an abyss."[38] This extreme form of nihilism and relativism is certainly more consistent than the less radical one we find in moderate historicism (as for instance in the historicism of positivist science). But clearly this conclusion cannot be accepted by Strauss. To assert that history is ultimately meaningless indeed is tantamount with denying the same possibility of a meaningful thinking: a thinking that can provide direction by enquiring into the ultimate questions. In this sense, the exaltation of contingency made by the radical historicist perfectly dovetails with the positivist denial of the possibility of investigating ultimate transcendent ends. They bring us to the same conclusion: a form of nihilism and relativism caused by the incapacity to find absolute truths about questions of value.[39]

Also, more moderate forms of historicism, like that exemplified by Max Weber, cannot escape this conclusion. Weber believed in the emancipatory power of science. But at the same time, he was convinced that science cannot provide any support to decide among conflicting values. For Weber, Strauss explains, "there is a variety of unchangeable principles of right or goodness which conflict with one another, and none of which can be proved to be superior to the others."[40] This sort of position is for Strauss the emblematic manifestation of the consequences of the epochal transformation in the conception of knowledge brought about by modernity: the passage from the idea of science as an evaluative contemplation of nature to that as a neutral instrument to control nature. The modern attempt to conquer contingency through science has thus brought to the conclusion that all is contingent and thus that we don't have any basis upon which to found our judgments of value. Modern philosophy, in Strauss's analysis, began "with the elevation of all knowledge to science, or theory" and ended "with the devaluation of all knowledge to history, or practice."[41] But this whole transformation entails for him a fatal obscuring of the difference between theory and practice and thus a misunderstanding of both concepts: first there was "a reduction of praxis to theory (this is the meaning of so-called [modern] rationalism)" and then "the rejection of theory in the name of praxis that is no longer intelligible as praxis."[42] In particular it entails the abandonment of the ultimate aim of theory—to inquiry into the mysterious whole and to understand the human condition in this transcending perspective—and with it the "estrangement from man's deepest desire and therewith from the primary issues."[43]

4.3 The Recovery of Classical Philosophy: From Contingency to Transcendence

It should be clear by now why Strauss believes that the most distinctive feature of the modern revolution is what he calls a radical "lowering of sight"; a closure of horizon that forecloses the possibility of understanding the human condition in the perspective of a future emancipation by way of a striving toward a transcending standard.[44] It is on this analysis that Strauss came to invoke a return to the spirit of classical political philosophy. For him it was essential to re-activate the reflections about the foundations of collective life. This, in turn, required recovering the possibility of developing a philosophy not based on the modern dogma that knowledge about the whole is impossible and thus that searching for it is useless. It is this premise that brought modern thinkers into a condition Strauss calls a "cave below the Platonic cave", or a "second cave." Differently from the Platonic cave, this second cave is for Strauss "unnatural,"[45] because to the 'natural' difficulties of philosophizing of the former it adds also an historical and cultural obstacle: the prejudice (since not substantiated by any conclusive argument, according to Strauss) of the moderns about the impossibility to ever reach the truth about the whole.[46] Strauss then considers necessary to escape this second prejudice the moderns created in combating what they believed to be the prejudice of the tradition. Only this could make possible a return to the 'first', Platonic cave, and thus to reactivate philosophy in its original, Socratic sense as a process of inquiry that moves from the premise our own ignorance. This, in turn, means for Strauss nothing more nor less than to re-propose the most basic question—how should we live?—and hence to remake the problem of the foundation of the law the main object of investigation.[47]

In promoting a return to the origins of western civilization Strauss is clearly in debt to the teachings of his former professor, Heidegger. But the return avowed by Strauss is of a different kind: not to the pre-philosophical origins of this tradition but rather to the politically philosophical and philosophically political ones. It is a return to Socrates rather than to the pre-Socratics.[48] Indeed for Strauss the problem is not so much the consolidation of a metaphysics of presence that alienated Being from the world, but rather the consolidation of a set of prejudices that made impossible the access to basic questions about justice and the common good, both philosophically and, as Strauss says, 'naturally'.[49] That is, for Strauss the alienation of modernity is an alienation from the 'natural' political dimension of human life, which consists for him in the normal disposition every individual has to question oneself and one's fellows about the justice and goodness of their actions.[50] Such a disposition, which is at first a practical disposition motivated by the necessity to orient our actions, can develop into a theoretical investigation by giving birth to philosophy in its primary political meaning. It is the realization that the political order is limited and conventional and that there is a discrepancy between how it is and how it should be, which is at the basis of political philosophy as it put in motion the search for the natural order.

Now, according to Strauss, with the progressive consolidation of historicism and positivism not only philosophy as a quest for knowledge of the whole (and its alternative, religion) was put in question, but also the political awareness human beings normally, or naturally, have. Because historicism and positivism belittle political opinion as a pre-scientific and thus an insignificant kind of knowledge, for Strauss they put at risk also "those simple experiences of right and wrong which are at the bottom of the philosophical contention that there is natural right."[51] In his view indeed there is a fundamental connection between the understanding at the level of common sense over basic questions about right and wrong and philosophical reflection on them.[52] Philosophy assumes in Strauss's view the form of an ascent: the Socratic "ascent from what is first for us to what is first by nature."[53] But because modern thinkers believe that all knowledge should assume the form of scientific knowledge, the basis from which such an ascent should start—the opinions of the lay citizens—was turned by them into an impossible starting point: something to be avoided rather than the point of departure for the inquiry. This has been particularly deleterious in the domain of politics and ethics; a domain on which Strauss believes humans are naturally inclined to develop opinions. It is because of this that, for him, modern political science has become increasingly estranged from the concrete phenomena it studies.

Beyond the influence of positivism, the weight of the tradition has contributed to this result, according to Strauss. Classical political philosophy, he says, can claim a sort of original character, to the extent that it could approach such phenomena 'naturally', without the screen of tradition.[54] Modern political science, on the contrary, is the result of a long tradition of systematic reflection, which inevitably created a screen to the things it studies. But the Scientific Revolution gave a great contribution to make this screen particularly thick, as a consequence of the gradual implementation of its conception of science into the domain of moral and social sciences. The result of this process was that the whole *modus operandi* of political science was modified in the direction of an increasing abstraction, which can be seen: first, in the creation of a gulf—both in terms of the content and the language—between science and opinions; and, second, in a new method that doesn't attempt anymore to generalize from particular experiences but rather to apply abstract theories directly to particular cases.[55]

To the abstraction of modern political science Strauss opposes the concreteness of ancient political philosophy. Beyond the lack of a consolidated tradition what grants to the latter a more direct access to political affairs is the fact that it studies them from within: from the point of view of the lay citizens and politicians. It speaks the same kind of language spoken in the public square and its point of departure is common sense: the "articulation of reality that precedes all scientific articulation… that wealth of meaning, which we have in mind, when speaking of the world of common experience or of the natural understanding of the world."[56] Modern political science, on the contrary, denies any scientific value to this pre-scientific domain and in particular to its normative judgments. It reduces lay opinions to a sort of neutral and uniform material through a process of abstraction that filters its political, normative, values, and inevitably detaches reflection and theorization from its originating experiences.[57] Clearly, Strauss clarifies, classical political philosophy aimed at challenging and transcending common opinions by way of a rational analysis aimed at detecting their contradictions. But this doesn't entail depriving those opinions of all meaning.[58] The goal was rather to improve them, making them more coherent, not dispense with them altogether, because the presupposition was that there was an element of truthfulness in them.[59] Modern political science, concludes Strauss, finds itself in a paradoxical situation: on the one hand, it deprives commonly accepted opinions of any substantive meaning but, on the other, to the extent that it cannot develop alone the criteria of relevance to choose its object of research, finds itself always dependent on those same opinions to know in which direction to proceed.[60]

Strauss underlines also another reason why classical political philosophers could study political things from within. Because his function, he explains, was similar to that of a judge: impartial, but not neutral or indifferent, to the questions on which he decides. That is, the exercise of his function doesn't imply the suspension of his role as citizen.[61] A political science, detached, neutral, and therefore unable to establish the criteria of relevance, was inconceivable because the basic political fact—that there is a natural order that determines what is just and good for the community—was for the ancient mind a self-evident fact. And also the language used by the classical political philosopher confirms his proximity to the political phenomena he studies. Certainly not without technicalities, his language was much closer to the language spoken in the public square. It was a language whose features and, in particular, whose vagueness and concreteness reflected the vagueness and concreteness of its subject—political and ethical affairs—in a way that the 'objective' language of modern political science cannot do.[62]

What Strauss tried to recover from classical (political) philosophy then is not only its striving towards transcendence but also its necessary embeddedness in the contingent dimension of political life. Indeed, as the case of Socrates testifies, both dimensions are for him necessary to recover the original political character of philosophy and the primacy of the problem of the foundation of the law. But Socrates is also the emblematic manifestation for Strauss of the tension between philosophy and politics. He is the one who, according to Cicero, brought philosophy down to earth.[63] And he is the one who first showed that the investigation that starts from opinions cannot but transcend them as soon as the philosopher discovers that such opinions are inconsistent and contradictory. In this moment he starts looking for the truth in nature itself, thus transcending the limits of the city and its conventions.[64] It is at this point that the tension between his role as philosopher and as citizen arises. Because in this moment he understands that to fulfil its duty as philosopher—"never condescending to what lies near at hand"[65]—the participation in the life of the city could become an impediment, since such endeavour requires a total dedication.[66] Inquiring into the principles of the city requires inquiry into the principles of the whole and because such whole is infinite and ultimately ungraspable this inquiry can never reach a conclusion.[67] In this sense philosophy acquires the meaning of an existential and political choice: it becomes a way of life and the ultimate authority.

On the other hand, the tension arises also from the perspective of the city. The philosopher's inquiry puts the laws (*nomoi*) of the city in contrast with nature (*physis*) and thus inevitably arrives at questioning the legitimacy of the former and its divine origins.[68] In this sense, the philosopher inevitably represents a destabilizing presence for the community: something like a stranger living in a city and posing a threat to its order and stability; a threat that is continuous, since by its own nature philosophic inquiry cannot produce any definitive, stable solutions.[69] In this sense, for Strauss, classical philosophy is primarily *political*: not only because it deals with political things but also because it realizes that it cannot but generate a reaction from the city and thus that from the very beginning it needs to reflect about its role in the city. Such reflection, Strauss underlines, was central in ancient political philosophy. As he says: "in its original form political philosophy broadly understood is the core of philosophy or rather 'the first philosophy'."[70] Even if as a transcending endeavour, classical political philosophy realized that it should always maintain a connection with the common sense of the city. In this sense, it was the "branch of philosophy which is closest to political life, to non-philosophical life, to human life."[71]

Strauss sees philosophy, in its original, Socratic version, as an endeavour that divides itself in two directions: a more theoretical investigation of the principles of the political realm, which in turn requires the investigation of the transcending whole, and a more practical reflection about how such activity interferes with the contingent life of the city. For Strauss classical political philosophy is the enquiry into the human condition in light of something that transcends it: "the mysterious character of the whole."[72] It is this transcending dimension that puts philosophy in tension with politics; but at the same time it is also because of this striving towards knowledge that philosophy should lead politics.[73] On the other hand, the tension between philosophy and politics obliges philosophy to become aware of the political dimension of its activity, of its contingent situation, so to speak. To develop this form of awareness means to develop a practical rationality, which constitutes an essential part of philosophy, but which cannot be completely dissociated from the other side: philosophy as an investigation on the transcending whole.[74] These are the original meanings of theory and practice that modern political science (and modern philosophy in general) according to Strauss came to lose. Because of this double dimension—theoretical and practical—classical political philosophy could reach a comprehensiveness that today is lost:

> It is both political theory and political skill; it is as open minded to the legal and institutional aspects of political life as it is to that which transcends the legal and institutional; it is equally free from the narrowness of the lawyer, the brutality of the technician, the vagaries of the visionary, and the baseness of the opportunist. It reproduces, and raises to its perfection, the magnanimous flexibility of the true statesman.[75]

The problem with the new political science, Strauss detects, is not only that it renounced the open investigation of ultimate principles but also that it lost its connection with the domain of opinion, that is, with all its partisan disputes, but also with the moderating effect that derives from constant contact with the problems and exigencies that emerge in such a domain. Because of this double connection to transcendence and contingency, Strauss sees (classical) political philosophy as a sort of prudent idealism.[76] An 'idealism' since it is open to the search for the ultimate truths about justice and the good; but a 'prudent' idealism since it is aware of the limitations that not only political actions, but also philosophy should respect to the extent that it realizes its position in the city and thus its political dimension. A crucial element of such prudence is represented according to him by rhetoric, which plays a key role in connecting the two dimensions. It is to this crucial aspect of his theory that I want move in the last part of this chapter.

4.4 Strauss's Philosophical Rhetoric: Or on the Art of Writing Between the Lines

Strauss's famous 'rediscovery' of the ancient and forgotten 'art of writing' and of the distinction between the exoteric and esoteric is certainly one of the most controversial aspects of his thought. But at the same time it is also one of the most intriguing. As is testified by the controversy that the thesis has generated, the meaning and implications of this rediscovery are not to be confined to questions of methodology for the history of ideas but concern central aspects of Strauss's philosophical and political ideas. The rediscovery occurred firstly through his engagement with two central medieval philosophers: the Jewish Maimonides and his Islamic teacher Alfarabi.[77] It is through the study of these two non Christian thinkers that Strauss made his breakthrough to the idea of recovering the spirit of classical philosophy, which means the primacy of political philosophy and thus of a particular 'art of writing'.[78]

In Strauss's reading Maimonides and Alfarabi developed a different approach to the question of revelation and, in particular, of its relation to philosophy than that characteristic of the Christian philosophers of the Middle Ages. As indicated before, for Strauss the relation between revelation and philosophy was understood by the two philosophers, first of all, as a question related to the political and legal order of the community rather than a matter of belief and dogma.[79] It was a question of the ground of the fundamental law that governs the city: whether it should be based on blind obedience to the divine command or on an unbound search for truth through reason. Emphasizing the significance of the theologico-political problem, Strauss could develop an original interpretation of Maimonides and Alfarabi not as Aristotelian thinkers, who believed in the possibility of conciliating reason and revelation, but rather as Platonists who believed in the impossibility of reconciling them. What Strauss came to understand by engaging with Maimonides and Alfarabi is that, because they lived in deeply religious societies, they understood that they could defend the philosophic way of living as an alternative foundation for the law of the city only through an art of writing that disguised their true beliefs. This art would create an exoteric surface to make the lay reader (the many) believe that they are defending the divine commands and the opinions of the city; and, at the same time, make an esoteric core in which they present their true beliefs as understandable only to the most careful and intelligent readers (the few).[80] But Strauss came also to realize is that this particular art of writing was a technique commonly employed by philosophers from the age of Plato, until the modern neglect of the theologico-political problem and the tension between philosophy and the city made it obsolete.

Beyond the fear of prosecution, Strauss identifies two other reasons that justify the use of this rhetorical art of concealing. But each of them derive from the basic tension between philosophy and the city and from the theologico-political problem: that is, from the problem of the ultimate source of our normative commitments.[81] The second reason has to do not with the philosopher's fear but with his sense of responsibility: the responsibility that emerges from recognizing that revealing to the general public certain philosophical truths, or revealing all the truths, that go against conventional wisdom and laws can put the order of the community at risk. It is this sense of responsibility, a form of political prudence and "pedagogical reserve", that is the motive most frequently discussed by Strauss in his writings on this topic.[82] He explains it in this way:

> Philosophy or science, the highest activity of man, it the attempt to replace opinion about 'all things' by knowledge of 'all things'; but opinion is the element of society; philosophy or science is therefore the attempt to dissolve the element in which society breathes, and thus it endangers society. Hence philosophy or science must remain the preserve of a small minority, and philosophers or scientists must respect the opinions on which society rests. To respect opinions is something entirely different from accepting them as true. Philosophers or scientists who hold this view about the relation of philosophy or science and society are driven to employ a peculiar manner of writing which would enable them to reveal what they regard as the truth to the few, without endangering the unqualified commitment of the many to the opinions on which society rests.[83]

There is, finally, a third motive that justifies the employment of such a technique and that we could define also as 'pedagogical', but in a different manner. Philosophy is a hard and challenging endeavour. A technique of writing that, hiding its "treasures" to the majority, lets them be glimpsed by the few and thus encourages them to undertake the "very long, never easy, but always pleasant work" of philosophy by exciting their curiosity.[84] In the same way, this technique can serve also a method to select the few able to philosophize.[85]

Each of these three motivations depend, to different degrees, on the premise that between philosophy and politics, or between the philosopher and society, there is an intrinsic tension. In the first case (prosecution), the tension between politics and philosophy is not insurmountable in principle. If society can be enlightened and persuaded to accept philosophy, as the Moderns think, then it will be no more necessary for the philosopher to use that art of writing. In the second case, instead, the tension is stronger since it is based on an understanding that truth is always dangerous for society at large. In this case thus the need of this art of writing is stronger.[86]

Finally, in the last case, this tension is expressed in the form of an elitist view that divides society in two groups—the many and the few—and which considers necessary a form of benevolent manipulation to initiate the latter to philosophical life and isolate them from the seductions of mundane life. This in turn implies that, in the first case, the tension cannot be expected to disappear altogether because society can never fully understand philosophy; it can never completely abandon conventionalism. Instead of a straightforward "prosecution" then we will have the more typical form of "ostracism" against those who continuously put in question the conventional truths, the truths of the majority.[87]

We are allowed therefore to consider this rhetorical technique as one, even if it is one that assumes different forms and degrees. Its general objective is to make philosophy and politics as much as possible compatible and to conciliate the erotic, divinely maniac, and thus imprudent, search for truth by the philosopher, with the prudent behaviour society requires. It is clearly the same kind of rhetoric that we saw in Plato and that Strauss labels as "Socratic rhetoric" (even if Socrates is represented by Xenophon rather than Plato):

> Socratic rhetoric is meant to be an indispensable instrument of philosophy. Its purpose is to lead potential philosophers to philosophy both by training them and by liberating them of the charms which obstruct the philosophic effort, as well as to prevent the access to philosophy of those who are not fit for it. Socratic rhetoric is emphatically just. It is animated by the spirit of social responsibility. It is based on the premise that there is a disproportion between the intransigent quest for truth and the requirements of society, or that not all truths are always harmless. Society will always try to tyrannize thought.[88]

According to Strauss this sort of political and rhetorical sensibility to communicate with non philosophers is a fundamental skill that the philosopher has to develop. But what kind of rhetoric is that? And how does this rhetoric impinge on his way of philosophising? Strauss calls it the "highest kind of rhetoric."[89] But the boundaries of this rhetoric seem quite limited, to the extent that its main function (apart from its pedagogical role in relation to potential philosophers) consists essentially in giving a public mask to disguise the real essence of philosophy in order to make its presence in society possible. It is a rhetoric that doesn't teach much more than "revealing by not revealing and not revealing by revealing."[90] Compared with

Cicero, Quintilian, or Aristotle's conceptions of rhetoric then its scope appears much narrower. As we know, the art of discourse associated with Socrates is dialectic, not rhetoric.

The narrowness of this form of rhetoric has to do above all with the fact that—differently from the conceptions of Cicero, Quintilian, and Aristotle—it operates mostly according to an instrumental logic: rhetoric is an instrument that philosophy needs to employ in its relations with the city to protect both itself and the city.[91] In this sense, as we have seen before, it can be described as a form of moderation. It is the moderation that derives, first of all, from the insight into the primary political dimension of philosophy and its intrinsic tension with the city and, second, from the awareness the philosopher has of his own ignorance, as long as human wisdom cannot but be knowledge of ignorance.[92] Once the philosopher has realized these aspects of philosophy, he comes to the conclusion that he has to speak rhetorically, with "a new awakeness, caution, and emphasis" and explain his ascension from law to nature with a "a lucid, comprehensive, and sound argument which starts from the 'common sense' embodied in the accepted opinions and transcends them."[93] The part of his discourse that aims to transcend the accepted opinions however is exclusively directed to the few that can philosophize, not to the general public. It is true that the exoteric, or public, part of this discourse is not only moved by a "pedagogical reserve" that aims to avoid harming society but also has an "edifying character" in the sense of transmitting morally appropriate values.[94] But it is difficult to see how, according to this conception, edification can be something more than a corroboration of common sense. The difference with Cicero's conception of rhetoric in this respect is significant. As we have seen, eloquence for the Ciceronian orator/statesman was also and crucially a way to spread through the people his philosophical knowledge and made thus materialize it in the realm of practice.

Seen from this perspective, Straussian Socratic rhetoric seems to be one that promotes a monological discourse going from the philosopher to the city, rather than a two-way communication between them. In other words, this rhetoric seems an art concerned with how to speak to the city, but much less with how to listen to what the city has to say. Because of its essentially instrumental character, it is a form of communication much more interested in obtaining a certain effect rather than the quality of process of communication itself. Certainly we can say that this form of rhetoric promotes in the philosopher a certain receptiveness towards the inputs coming from the city. The Socratic philosopher knows that he cannot disregard the opinions of the city, not only for his own safety but also because he is aware that disregarding the opinions of the city "would amount to abandoning the most important access to reality which we have."[95] As we have seen before, indeed, one of great merits of classical political philosophy according to Strauss is precisely that it "did not separate wisdom from moderation."[96] But apart from that starting moment, it seems that in Strauss's conception of philosophy that kind of receptiveness towards the public square does not play any real role in influencing the way philosophy proceeds once it has started to transcend that realm.[97] Moderation is for Strauss not a theoretical virtue, since "thought" he argues "must be not moderate, but fearless, not to say shameless."[98] It is a practical matter that doesn't seem to have any significant bearing on the way the philosopher theorizes. The Socratic philosopher, as Strauss underlines, "remains" in his inquiry "chiefly, if not exclusively, concerned with the human things."[99] But his method of inquiry remains thoroughly philosophical and dialectical. Rhetoric is an instrument and does influence the one who employs it.

In comparison with Ciceronian, or Aristotelian, rhetoric Strauss's is much less involved with political affairs, to the extent that it is essentially an instrument developed and used by a philosopher. In turn its relationship with philosophy is a relationship much less dialogical and much more hierarchical. Certainly the Ciceronian philosopher-statesman is divided between his activity as philosopher and politician. His relation with the popular audience is clearly not symmetrical. He teaches and engages in deliberation, but also leads and manipulates. But as we have seen, his rhetoric operates much more as a mediating force between these two realms. And something similar happens also in Aristotle, since for him one of the main functions of rhetoric as a civic art of deliberation is finding a proper compromise between the common good and particular interests, or on a different level between the rational and the extra-rational. On the other hand, the absolute preponderance Strauss concedes to philosophy makes the former much more independent and impermeable to the inputs coming from the public sphere and from its practical engagement. It is a political philosophy, but more philosophical and less political than the Ciceronian one.

Clearly, as Thomas Pangle has written, in Strauss the necessity of rhetoric arises also for political and moral reasons. The philosopher needs to justify the rule of reason to people—common people, non-philosophers—

who don't necessarily accept the premise that reason should be the supreme standard. Thus, in order to do that, he needs to start without assuming such premises and keep in mind that what is asked for is a moral and political justification, rather than a theoretical one.[100] This implies that somehow the philosopher has to abandon his activity and start reflecting politically, as we have said. But the point is that, differently from the Ciceronian philosopher-statesman, the Straussian philosopher doesn't seem to share the same idea that philosophy can benefit from its involvement with politics. As Strauss writes "it is ultimately because he means to justify philosophy before the tribunal of the political community, and hence on the level of political discussion, that the philosopher has to understand the political things exactly as they are understood in political life."[101] That is, the development of this political and rhetorical sensibility is essentially motivated (to repeat the argument) by the instrumental motive of wanting to defend its presence within society. It is a question of necessity, rather than of mutual respect.

Strauss's rhetorical sensibility cannot be questioned. The relation between form and content and thus of rhetoric is for him a crucial one. The importance that he attributes to the formal aspects of Plato's works for their interpretation—their dialogical form, the relations of one part of the dialogue with the whole, and of one dialogue with the other dialogues, the dramatic aspects that characterize the dialogues, the things said as well the things unsaid—testifies such sensibility.[102] More generally, despite all his anti-historicism, Strauss's hermeneutic implies necessarily keeping in consideration the rhetorical aspects of a work: the intention of its author, the audience to which it is addressed, and its form.[103] Moreover, it is clear that Strauss was aware of the great importance of rhetoric in ancient thought, particularly in relation to political philosophy, even though he didn't write anything specifically on this topic.[104] Nevertheless the fact is that he always starts from the premise of an absolute priority of philosophy over politics; the premise that "philosophy—not as a teaching or body of knowledge, but as a way of life—offers, as it were, the solution to the problem that keeps political life in motion."[105] Starting from such a Platonic premise, the mechanism of mediation between these two poles cannot but assume a minor and preponderantly instrumental role. But this can be problematic from a democratic point of view. As argued also by Benedetto Fontana, Strauss's conception of rhetoric is based on the Platonic dichotomies—between philosopher and intellectual, philosophy and ideology, truth and opinion, private-esoteric discourse and public-exoteric one, few and many—which are in turn the result of that prioritization of philosophy over politics, and whose ultimate result is the anti-democratic and elitist negation of a substantive political role by the 'people.'[106] Despite his elitist and anti-democratic presuppositions, his own differentiation between philosophy and politics/rhetoric (*contentio* and *sermo*, *ratio* and *oratio*), Cicero tried to build a bridge between them through the figure of the orator-statesman and a form of rhetoric that presupposes and promotes a much more politically active idea of citizenry. The absence of any reference to such figure in Strauss's works is telling in this respect.[107]

Affirming that in Strauss rhetoric has mainly an instrumental role doesn't mean however to deny that for him it cannot contribute in any positive way to the philosophic endeavour. Necessity and constriction can certainly have a positive value for him, as it is satisfied by the fact that he chose to use as epigraph to his *Persecution and the Art of Writing* the following quotation by W.E.H. Lecky: "[t]hat vice has often proved an emancipator of the mind, is one of the most humiliating, but, at the same time, one of the most unquestionable, facts in history."[108] An important example of this is represented by Jewish philosophy in the Middle Age. In comparison to Christian philosophy, Strauss notes, religious authorities exerted a much stronger censure on Jewish philosophers. But this he adds, was ultimately beneficial since it obliged them to retire to the private sphere and by consequence permitted them to escape the supervision of the ecclesiasts and develop a far greater inner freedom.[109] Nevertheless we shouldn't forget in this regard that one of the fundamental reasons Strauss suggests, in agreement with the bulk of the tradition of philosophy, the superiority of philosophy over politics is precisely its great self-sufficiency in comparison to the conditioning necessities that characterize the latter (starting with those that derive from the belonging from a specific political community).[110]

Notes

1. This is, clearly, a quite generic account of the meaning of political philosophy according to Strauss. Catherine and Michael Zuckert individuate at least four different, even if interconnected, meanings political philosophy in Strauss: Catherine H. Zuckert and Michael Zuckert, *Leo Strauss and the Problem of Political Philosophy* (Chicago: University of Chicago Press, 2014), 8–12. On this see also: Steven B. Smith, "Philosophy as a Way of Life: The Case of Leo Strauss," *The Review of Politics* 71 (2009).

2. Leo Strauss, "What Is Political Philosophy?", in *What Is Political Philosophy? And Other Studies* (Chicago: University of Chicago Press, 1988), 55; Leo Strauss, "The Three Waves of Modernity," in *An Introduction to Political Philosophy: Ten Essays*, ed. Hilail Gildin (Detroit: Wayne State University Press, 1989).
3. Catherine Zuckert and Michael Zuckert, *The Truth About Leo Strauss* (Chicago and London: University of Chicago Press, 2006), 136.
4. Pawel Armada, "Leo Strauss as Erzieher: The Defense of the Philosophical Life or the Defense of Life against Philosophy," in *Modernity and What Has Been Lost: Considerations on the Legacy of Leo Strauss*, ed. Pawel Armada and Arkadiusz Górnisiewicz (Indiana and Cracow: Jagiellonian University Press and St. Augustine's Press, 2011).
5. The choice between revelation and reason has inevitably a political dimension, as it concerns the question of how to live and our ultimate allegiance and thus the question of authority. This is why Strauss refers to it as the theologico-*political* problem. Politics however doesn't stand on the same level of neither revelation, nor philosophy, because it cannot elevate itself from the level of opinions. As Strauss writes: "One cannot seriously question the claim of philosophy in the name, e.g., of politics or poetry. To say nothing of other considerations, man's ultimate aim is what is really good and not what merely seems to be good, and only through *knowledge* of the good is he enabled to find the good." Strauss cited in: Heinrich Meier, *Leo Strauss and the Theologico-Political Problem* (Cambridge: Cambridge University Press, 2006), 6.
6. From the contemplative science of the ancients in search of the eternal truths and the foundations of the political and moral order, to the practical science of the moderns whose aim was to "relief man's estate", this was the great transformation brought about by modernity according to Strauss. E.g., Leo Strauss, "La Crise De Notre Temps," in *Nihilisme Et Politique* (Paris: Payot & Rivages, 2001), 80, 84–5.
7. Leo Strauss, *The City and Man* (Chicago: Rand McNally & Company, 1964), 3–5; Strauss, "La Crise De Notre Temps," 80, 84.
8. Strauss, *The City and Man*, 1.
9. Leo Strauss, "Social Social Science and Humanism," in *The Rebirth of Classical Political Rationalism: An Introduction to the Thought of Leo Strauss*, ed. Thomas L. Pangle (Chicago: University of Chicago Press, 1989), 7.
10. E.g., Leo Strauss, "Progress or Return?," in *The Rebirth of Classical Political Rationalism: An Introduction to the Thought of Leo Strauss*, ed. Thomas L. Pangle (Chicago: University of Chicago Press, 1989), 240.
11. Leo Strauss, *Natural Right and History* (Chicago: University of Chicago Press, 1953), Chs. 5 and 6.

12. Leo Strauss, "An Epilogue," in *Liberalism, Ancient and Modern* (Ithaca: Cornell University Press, 1989), 207.
13. Strauss, "What Is Political Philosophy?," 51; Strauss, "The Three Waves of Modernity," 91.
14. Strauss, *Natural Right and History*, 7–8. Cf. Smith, "Philosophy as a Way of Life: The Case of Leo Strauss," 41.
15. Strauss, "What Is Political Philosophy?," 38–9.
16. Eric Voegelin, *History of Political Ideas, Vol. 6: Revolution and the New Science*, ed. Barry Cooper (Columbia: University of Missouri Press, 1998), 164.
17. Strauss, "The Three Waves of Modernity," 96.
18. Steven B. Smith, "Leo Strauss's Discovery of the Theologico-Political Problem," *European Journal of Political Theory* 12 (2013): 400.
19. Leo Strauss, *Philosophy and Law: Contributions to the Understanding of Maimonides and His Predecessors* (Albany: State University of New York, 1995), 32. On Strauss's account of the Napoleonic strategy of the Enlightenment and its mockery of orthodoxy see: David Janssens, *Between Athens and Jerusalem: Philosophy, Prophecy, and Politics in Leo Strauss's Early Thought* (Albany: State University of New York Press, 2008), 92ff.
20. Strauss, *Philosophy and Law*, 29–30.
21. This is what for Strauss Spinoza's *Treatise* was unable to offer and thus the reason why this philosopher didn't succeed in his attempt to refute Judaic orthodoxy through reason Leo Strauss, *Spinoza's Critique of Religion* (New York: Schocken Books, 1982), 28–9.
22. See for instance: Hillel Fradkin, "Philosophy and Law: Leo Strauss as a Student of Medieval Jewish Thought," *The Review of Politics* 53 (1991).
23. Leora Batnitzky, "Leo Strauss and the 'Theological-Political Predicament'," in *The Cambridge Companion to Leo Strauss*, ed. Steven B. Smith (New York: Cambridge University Press, 2009), 49–51. On how Strauss came to develop his understanding of the political dimension in the relation between philosophy and religion, see: Martin D. Yaffe and Richard S. Ruderman, eds., *Reorientation: Leo Strauss in the 1930s* (New York: Palgrave Macmillan, 2014).
24. Strauss, *Natural Right and History*, 74. In the last years, the theologico-political problem has been recognized more and more as a central theme in Strauss. See for instance: Meier, *Leo Strauss and the Theologico-Political Problem*; Batnitzky, "Leo Strauss and the 'Theological-Political Predicament'."
25. The refusal to take the normative distinction between the noble and the base, the just and the unjust, as an open question susceptible of rational analysis, however, doesn't mean for Strauss that modern thinkers felt into

a complete nihilism. He argues that modern thinkers maintain Biblical morality, but divested it of its theological apparatus and foundation in faith, which they considered rationally unjustifiable. This operation however couldn't but leave morality without any form of foundation, as the rejection of faith and theology was not replaced by a philosophical justification. Strauss, "Progress or Return?," 239–40.
26. Niccolò Machiavelli, *The Prince*, trans. Peter E. Bondanella (Oxford and New York: Oxford University Press, 2005), 53.
27. Strauss, "The Three Waves of Modernity," 91.
28. The substitution of the 'high' for the 'low' as the standard for human actions is evident, according to Strauss, in Machiavelli's advice to the Prince to imitate the beast. The beast replaces God as the standard. That is, the human being is invited to transcend her limits toward the subhuman, not the superhuman. Leo Strauss, *Thoughts on Machiavelli* (Chicago: University of Chicago Press, 1978), 78.
29. Strauss, "What Is Political Philosophy?," 42; Strauss, *Natural Right and History*, 178–9.
30. "Machiavelli does not bring to light a single political phenomenon of any fundamental importance which was not fully known to the classics. His seeming discovery is only the reverse side of the oblivion of the most important elements of political philosophy: all things necessarily appear in a new light if they are seen for the first time in a specifically dimmed light. A stupendous contraction of the horizon appears to Machiavelli and his modern liberal successors as a wondrous enlargement of the horizon." Strauss, *Thoughts on Machiavelli*, 295.
31. Strauss however believes that Hobbes's political philosophy has to be understood independently from his natural science. Leo Strauss, "On the Basis of Hobbes's Political Philosophy," in *What Is Political Philosophy? And Other Studies* (Chicago: University of Chicago Press, 1988), 177.
32. Strauss, *Natural Right and History*, 173–7, 180–2.
33. Ibid., 180.
34. Ibid., 180–2.
35. This, according to Strauss's reading, is particularly true for Machiavelli. For Strauss, indeed, the real scope of Machiavelli's revolution can be grasped only from the perspective of the classical tradition of political thought. Strauss, *Thoughts on Machiavelli*, 12.
36. The "second wave" of Modernity is represented according to Strauss's tripartite schema by Rousseau and Kant. Strauss, "The Three Waves of Modernity," 94–8.
37. Strauss, *Natural Right and History*, 22.
38. Strauss, "What Is Political Philosophy?," 54. According to the radical version of historicism also the same discovery of the 'truth' of historicism—

the historical and limited character of all forms of thought—is not the result of theoretical or philosophical progress, but rather an 'event': something that happened by chance in a determinate moment of history and that produced belief rather than knowledge. Strauss, *Natural Right and History*, 29. On radical historicism for Strauss see also: Strauss, "What Is Political Philosophy?," 26–7; Strauss, "Progress or Return?," 241; Leo Strauss, "The Origins of Political Science and the Problem of Socrates," *Interpretation: A Journal of Political Philosophy* 23 (1996): 136.

39. Strauss, *Natural Right and History*, 25–6; Strauss, "What Is Political Philosophy?," 54.
40. Strauss, *Natural Right and History*, 74. See also: Strauss, "The Origins of Political Science and the Problem of Socrates," 133; Strauss, "What Is Political Philosophy?," 23–4. The position of Strauss on Weber, to whom he devotes many pages in *Natural Right and History*, is once again similar to that expressed by Eric Voegelin (who has also dedicated many pages in his *The New Science of Politics*). Both thinkers consider Weber the thinker in which positivism has reached its highest philosophical expression thus providing the clearest manifestation of its deep contradictions. Eric Voegelin, "The New Science of Politics (1952)," in *Modernity without Restraint: The Political Religions, the New Science of Politics, and Science, Politics, and Gnosticism*, ed. Manfred Henningsen (Columbia and London: University of Missouri Press, 2000), 98–105.
41. Batnitzky, "Leo Strauss and the 'Theological-Political Predicament'," 46. Cf. Meier, *Leo Strauss and the Theologico-Political Problem*, 58.
42. Strauss cited in Batnitzky, "Leo Strauss and the 'Theological-Political Predicament'," 46.
43. Strauss, "What Is Political Philosophy?," 55.
44. "It is safer to understand the low in the light of the high, then the high in the light of the low. In doing the latter one necessarily distorts the high, whereas in doing the former one does not deprive the low of the freedom to reveal itself fully as what it is." Strauss, *Spinoza's Critique of Religion*, 2.
45. Strauss, *Philosophy and Law*, 136.
46. On the idea of the 'second cave' see: Janssens, *Between Athens and Jerusalem*, 102–8; Meier, *Leo Strauss and the Theologico-Political Problem*, 57–60.
47. Janssens, *Between Athens and Jerusalem*, 99.
48. Robert Pippin has expressed some serious doubts about the possibility to return to the supposedly natural access to political questions of the ancients, as defended by Strauss, arguing that this request cannot escape (despite Strauss's intention) its historicist premises. Robert Pippin, "The Unavailability of the Ordinary: Strauss on the Philosophical Fate of Modernity," *Political Theory* 31 (2003).

49. On the influence of Heidegger on Strauss about the idea of a return to the origin and on their differences, see: Steven B. Smith, *Reading Leo Strauss: Politics, Philosophy, Judaism* (Chicago: University of Chicago Press, 2006), 115–20; Daniel Tanguay, *Leo Strauss: An Intellectual Biography* (New Haven: Yale University Press, 2007), 123ff.; Richard Velkley, "On the Roots of Rationalism: Strauss' Natural Right and History as Response to Heidegger," *Review of Politics* 70 (2008).
50. The political and moral predisposition that for Strauss human beings naturally develop can be seen, for instance, in that sort of religious apprehension engendered by the intuition that our freedom must have limits and in the sense of dignity that originates from the conscience of the hiatus between the 'as it is' and 'as it should be'. Strauss, *Natural Right and History*, passim.
51. Ibid., 32.
52. Such fundamental connection is explained by Strauss very clearly: "All political action aims at either preservation or change. When desiring to preserve, we wish to prevent a change to the worse; when designing to change, we wish to bring about something better. All political action is then guided by some thought of better and worse. But thought of better and worse implies thought of the good. The awareness of the good which guides all our actions has the character of opinion: it is no longer questioned but, on reflection, it proves to be questionable. The very fact that we can question it directs us towards such a thought of the good as is no longer questionable—towards a thought which is no longer opinion but knowledge. All political action has then in itself a directedness towards knowledge of the good ... If this directedness becomes explicit, if men make it their explicit goal to acquire knowledge of the good life and of the good society, political philosophy emerges." Strauss, "What Is Political Philosophy?," 10.
53. Strauss, *The City and Man*, 240.
54. Strauss, "What Is Political Philosophy?," 27.
55. Ibid., 27–8; Strauss, "An Epilogue," 210–15.
56. Strauss, *Natural Right and History*, 77. For Strauss's characterization of classical political philosophy, see especially: Leo Strauss, "On Classical Political Philosophy," in *What Is Political Philosophy? And Other Studies* (Chicago: University of Chicago Press, 1988).
57. Strauss, "An Epilogue," 212–13.
58. As Behnegar notes "the only way to overcome an opinion is to become aware of its inherent contradictions, which is not likely to happen if one does not take seriously that opinion's claim of truth." Nasser Behnegar, "The Intellectual Legacy of Leo Strauss (1899–1973)," *Annual Review of Political Science* 2 (1999): 107.

59. This account of the attitude towards the opinions is clearly more in accordance with Aristotle than with Plato. Here we have to take for granted Strauss's Socratic reading of Plato. On Aristotle's method of "saving the appearances" see: Martha Nussbaum, *The Fragility of Goodness: Luck and Ethics in Greek Tragedy and Philosophy* (Cambridge: Cambridge University Press, 2001), 274ff.
60. Strauss, "An Epilogue," 213–14.
61. It is precisely this double role of citizen and philosopher that creates the tension which transformed philosophy into political philosophy.
62. Strauss, "An Epilogue," 217; Strauss, "What Is Political Philosophy?," 29.
63. Cicero, *Tusculan Disputations*, trans. J. E. King (Cambridge, MA: Harvard University Press, 1960), 5.10.
64. Strauss, "On Classical Political Philosophy," 90; Strauss, *The City and Man*, 20.
65. Plato, *The Theaetetus of Plato*, trans. Jane Levett (Indianapolis: Hackett, 1990), 174a.
66. From this perspective, therefore, we can say that the philosopher's involvement with politics began reluctantly, "like the performance of a duty in an alien place." Stuart Umphrey, "Why Politiké Philosophia?," *Man and World* 17 (1984): 444.
67. "Because of the elusiveness of the whole, the beginning or the questions retain a greater evidence than the end or the answers; return to the beginning remains a constant necessity" Strauss, "What Is Political Philosophy?," 21.
68. Strauss, *The City and Man*, 20.
69. Aristotle, *Politics*, trans. C. D. C. Reeve (with introduction and notes) (Indianapolis: Hackett, 1998), 1324a16.
70. Strauss, *The City and Man*, 20.
71. Strauss, "What Is Political Philosophy?," 10.
72. Ibid., 39.
73. "There is a necessary conflict between philosophy and politics" writes Strauss "if the element of society necessarily is opinion", because philosophy attempts to replace opinion by knowledge. Leo Strauss, "On a Forgotten Kind of Writing," in *What Is Political Philosophy? And Other Studies* (Chicago: University of Chicago Press, 1988), 229.
74. "... the meaning of the common good is essentially controversial, due to its comprehensive character. Thus the temptation arises to deny, or to evade, the comprehensive character of politics and to treat politics as one compartment among many." Strauss, "What Is Political Philosophy?," 16–17.
75. Ibid., 28.

76. In a similar way Benedetto Fontana has characterized Strauss's view as the result of "a synthesis of a deeply realistic analysis of the flux of reality and a critical reconstruction or reconstitution of that reality." Benedetto Fontana, "Reason and Politics: Philosophy Confronts the People," *Boundary 2* 33 (2006): 12. On this combination of 'prudence' and 'idealism' in Strauss, see also: Smith, *Reading Leo Strauss*, 121.
77. Leo Strauss, *Persecution and the Art of Writing* (Chicago: University of Chicago Press, 1988), 8.
78. Thomas L. Pangle, *Leo Strauss: An Introduction to His Thought and Intellectual Legacy* (Baltimore: Johns Hopkins University Press, 2006), 58–9. For a detailed account of this fundamental turn in Strauss's line of research during the '30s see: Heinrich Meier, "How Strauss Became Strauss," in *Reorientation: Leo Strauss in the 1930s*, ed. Martin D. Yaffe and Richard S. Ruderman (New York: Palgrave Macmillan, 2014).
79. Leo Strauss, "Introduction," in *Persecution and the Art of Writing* (Chicago: University of Chicago Press, 1988), 9–10.
80. Zuckert and Zuckert, *Leo Strauss and the Problem of Political Philosophy*, 54–5.
81. Leo Strauss, "Persecution and the Art of Writing," in *Persecution and the Art of Writing* (Chicago: University of Chicago Press, 1988), 22–5.
82. Michael L. Frazer, "Esotericism Ancient and Modern," *Political Theory* 34 (2006): 36, 40. On the idea of "pedagogical reserve" see: Zuckert and Zuckert, *The Truth About Leo Strauss*, Ch. 4.
83. Strauss, "On a Forgotten Kind of Writing," 221–2. Cf., Strauss, "Persecution and the Art of Writing," 32–6; Leo Strauss, "The Law of Reason in the Kuzari," in *Persecution and the Art of Writing* (Chicago: University of Chicago Press, 1988) 110; Leo Strauss, "How to Study Spinoza's Theologico-Political Treatise," in *Persecution and the Art of Writing* (Chicago: University of Chicago Press, 1988), 183; Leo Strauss, "Liberal Education and Responsibility," in *Liberalism, Ancient and Modern* (Ithaca: Cornell University Press, 1989), 14.
84. Strauss, *Persecution and the Art of Writing*, 36.
85. On the importance of the pedagogical motive for esotericism, see: Arthur Melzer, "On the Pedagogical Motive for Esoteric Writing," *Journal of Politics* 69 (2007); Frazer, "Esotericism Ancient and Modern."
86. See: Frazer, "Esotericism Ancient and Modern."
87. Strauss, "Persecution and the Art of Writing," 32–3. As Frazer notes, Strauss offers only these two examples of extremely liberal societies in which such form of social coercion was almost inexistent: the third Republic in France and post-Bismarckian Wilhelmian Germany. Such scarcity of examples however also suggests that a weaker form of prosecution, or social ostracism, is not only a 'contingent' fact, but rather a regu-

lar feature of politics, and thus that the weaker version of esotericism is always a necessity. Frazer, "Esotericism Ancient and Modern," 40.
88. Leo Strauss, *On Tyranny (Revised and Enlarged)* (Ithaca, NY: Cornell University Press, 1975), 27.
89. Ibidem.
90. Leo Strauss, "The Literary Character of The Guide for the Perplexed," in *Persecution and the Art of Writing* (Chicago: University of Chicago Press, 1988), 52.
91. Similarly Moshe Halbertal has called Strauss's understanding of esotericism "instrumental", since it is devised mostly as a technique to minimize the risks to disseminate knowledge to society. Moshe Halbertal, *Concealment and Revelation: Esotericism in Jewish Thought and Its Philosophical Implications* (Princeton, NJ: Princeton University Press, 2007), 149.
92. "There is no knowledge of the whole but only knowledge of the parts, hence no partial knowledge of parts, hence no unqualified transcending, even by the wisest man as such, of the sphere of opinion" Strauss, *The City and Man*, 20.
93. Ibidem. The consistent denial of the common good is for Strauss impossible "as every other consistent manifestation of the break with common sense." Strauss, "An Epilogue," 219.
94. Strauss, "Persecution and the Art of Writing," 36.
95. Strauss, *Natural Right and History*, 123–24. Cf. Batnitzky, "Leo Strauss and the "Theological-Political Predicament"," 52.
96. Strauss, *Natural Right and History*, 123.
97. Cf., Batnitzky, "Leo Strauss and the "Theological-Political Predicament"," 52.
98. Strauss, "What Is Political Philosphy?," 32.
99. Strauss, *The City and Man*, 20.
100. Thomas Pangle, "Introduction," in *The Rebirth of Classical Political Rationalism: An Introduction to the Thought of Leo Strauss*, ed. Thomas Pangle (Chicago: University of Chicago Press, 1989), xviii.
101. Strauss, "On Classical Political Philosophy," 94.
102. For instance Strauss, *The City and Man*, 52–61.
103. Pangle, "Introduction," xviii–xix.
104. About Strauss's awareness of the relevance of rhetoric in ancient culture, I can quote this passage: "… This expression is clearly metaphoric. Any attempt to express its meaning in unmetaphoric language would lead to the discovery of a terra incognita, a field whose very dimensions are as yet unexplored and which offers ample scope for highly intriguing and even important investigations. One may say without fear of being presently convicted of great exaggeration that almost the only preparatory work to

guide the explorer in this field is buried in the writings of the rhetoricians of antiquity." Strauss, "Persecution and the Art of Writing," 24. See also his reflections on ancient rhetoric in: Strauss, "On Classical Political Philosophy," 82–3.

105. Ibid., 91; Strauss, "Persecution and the Art of Writing," 37. Cf. Pangle, "Introduction," xvi.

106. Fontana, "Reason and Politics: Philosophy Confronts the People." See e.g., Strauss, "Persecution and the Art of Writing," 33; Strauss, "The Literary Character of The Guide for the Perplexed," 59; Strauss, *The City and Man*, 39–40.

107. Even if Fontana defends an idea of rhetoric as a potential catalyst of democratic processes, similar to that I defend in this book, he is less inclined to enlist Cicero among those who contribute to such an idea of rhetoric. Fontana, "Reason and Politics: Philosophy Confronts the People," 30–4. See also: Benedetto Fontana, "The Democratic Philosopher: Rhetoric as Hegemony in Gramsci," *Italian Culture* 23 (2005); Benedetto Fontana, Cary J. Nederman, and Gary Remer, "Introduction: Deliberative Democracy and the Rhetorical Turn," in *Talking Democracy: Historical Perspectives on Rhetoric and Democracy*, ed. Benedetto Fontana, Cary J. Nederman and Gary Remer (University Park: Pennsylvania State University Press, 2004).

108. Strauss, "Persecution and the Art of Writing," 22.

109. Ibidem.

110. Strauss, *On Tyranny*, 79–91, cf. 179.

CHAPTER 5

Politics as Contingency: Richard Rorty

5.1 Introduction

In this chapter I move to a philosopher whose background, ideas, and style are quite distant from Strauss, but who also provides a very interesting point of comparison with the tradition of ancient rhetoric: Richard Rorty. Exploring the philosophy of Rorty through the lens of that tradition allows us to see from a different perspective the meaning of transcendence and contingency in politics, and how rhetoric mediates between them. More specifically, what I propose in what follows is a parallel reading of Rorty and the rhetorical-humanistic tradition of Cicero, Quintilian, and Vico, on a theme on which they have at the same time a strong affinity and strong divergence: the relation between self-cultivation and political commitment. What these thinkers share with Rorty is an idea of the human world as a largely linguistic artefact and hence that individual and collective progress depends principally on linguistic skills—eloquence, or, in Rortyan terminology, the art of redescription—and the hermeneutic capacity to navigate through this linguistic medium. What differentiates them instead is that, according to Cicero, Quintilian, or Vico, self-creation and political commitment are two interdependent and complementary tasks, while for Rorty they are two endeavours that have to be kept separate. Also in the case of Rorty, as in that of Strauss, the relation between transcendence and contingency plays a key role in his conception of politics. And once again, also for him rhetoric is key in mediating between

© The Author(s) 2018
G. Ballacci, *Political Theory between Philosophy and Rhetoric*, Rhetoric, Politics and Society,
https://doi.org/10.1057/978-1-349-95293-9_5

these two dimensions. In his philosophy, transcendence assumes a different aspect: that of a continuous endeavour to change and enlarge one's own identity (personal or collective) through the art of redescription (that is, through rhetoric). The recognition of contingency as the basic condition of human life, on the other hand, is for Rorty the result of embracing a fully antifoundationalist and historicist view. However, as I will argue, it is mainly because of a too radical notion of contingency that Rorty is unable to find a better compromise between self-cultivation and political commitment and, as a consequence, to formulate a vision of politics more substantively progressive.

If Rorty has been labelled "arguably the most controversial" among American philosophers, certainly the separation he postulates between the private and the public realms is one of his most controversial ideas.[1] This separation is the result of a reflection started at the very beginning of his career and which continued for the rest of his life. As Rorty explains in the autobiographical "Trotsky and the Wild Orchids," he started studying philosophy with the hope of finding "some intellectual or aesthetic framework" to (using an expression he took from Yeats) "hold reality and justice in a single vision," where by "reality" we are to understand the "private, weird, snobbish, incommunicable interests" that give one's own self-image a sense of uniqueness and autonomy and by "justice" the sense of responsibility to fight for a better world. In the same essay he also explains that it is in *Contingency, Irony, and Solidarity*—the book in which this question took central stage—that he came to the conclusion that "there is no need to weave one's personal equivalent of Trotsky and one's personal equivalent of my wild orchids together."[2] How relevant this split is for Rorty's thought can be immediately grasped by reflecting on the fact that it concerns the two main motives animating it: the defence of a poeticized, ironic culture of individual self-creativity, on the one hand, and of a liberal and progressive democratic society, on the other. But the conclusion he reached—that these two commitments should be kept separate—is quite puzzling. As Richard Bernstein has written, it is often difficult to avoid thinking that, despite all his professed progressivism, ultimately Rorty's political theory does not seem to offer much more than an "apologia for the status quo."[3] This sort of disappointment is not uncommon among Rorty's readers, and it is a disappointment many of them associate with the split between the private and the public realms. Actually, over the years, Rorty came to regret the rigidity with which he drew this split in *Contingency, Irony, and Solidarity* and to recognize that the relation between these two realms is more complex.[4] Indeed, as we will see, this rigidity contradicts important aspects of his own general vision. Nevertheless it is quite telling that, despite later qualifications and partial concessions, Rorty has never provided an alternative view on this topic as fully elaborated as the one we find in that book.

Thus the position Rorty takes there has become, since the book's publication, one of the main targets of his critics. In reducing the idea of philosophy to a literary genre and thus relegating it to the private realm, Rorty has been accused of promoting a "de-theorization of politics" and "de-politicization of philosophy."[5] The problem, according to this criticism, is that if together with philosophy's pretension to truth we also dispense with the idealizing moment implicit in this claim we run the risk of losing any foothold from which we can question the accepted beliefs and practices of a society.[6] In a similar vein, Rorty's split between private and public realms has been attacked for revealing an incapacity to find a productive compromise between the Romantic impulse to self-creation and the pragmatic defence of solidarity, and thus to clarify how radical redescriptions can be politically relevant. According to Nancy Fraser, who advanced this criticism, such an incapacity can be seen in the fact that Rorty often seems to reduce all "abnormal" discourses to an overly "aestheticized, narcissized, and bourgeoisified" kind of discourse with no political utility and to depict the public space as an "overly communitarian and solidary" one where no radical change is possible. The case of feminism for her is a clear example of why the private is political and why radical, creative redescriptions are crucial for transforming not only one's own life but also that of the community.[7] The critical point then has to do with the fact that Rorty's division between the private and the public ends up relegating all the disrupting and creative power of contestation—in particular, the capacity of irony to uncover the arbitrariness of state power—to the private realm, with the consequence that in his account it is difficult to find the resources for promoting political change.[8] Moreover, in making self-creation essentially a private matter, Rorty has been accused also of betraying one of the most important legacies of pragmatism: the idea that democracy cannot live on abstract principles alone, but should be embodied in a concrete form of life, an *ethos*, and that the vitality of democracy depends on the capacity of its citizens to reform themselves.[9]

As suggested above, in Rorty the relationship between the "existential" and the "political" is crucial: "self-creation and human solidarity" are his two main commitments—as he says, both "equally valid" and "yet forever incommensurable."[10] The highest aspiration of associated life should consist for him precisely in "optimizing the balance between leaving people's private lives alone" so that they can maximize their possibility of self-creation, and "preventing suffering" by way of enlarging solidarity. Indeed, Rorty thinks that this is the core of political liberalism and the reason for its superiority as a political system.[11] For him the separation between the goals of self-creation and of fostering human solidarity, the existential and the political, is justified by the fact that between them not only are there no systematic synergies, but there can even be dangerous interferences. Similarly to Nietzsche, Heidegger, and Foucault, Rorty believes that common sense and social conformity always exercise a negative pressure against individual projects of self-creation. But against these thinkers he also argues that the purpose of transforming these projects into political ones is intrinsically authoritarian, because it threatens pluralism. This does not mean, however, that Rorty does not recognize that some kind of positive transaction between the private and the public is not only possible, but also necessary. Political progress, on his account, cannot happen without imaginative individuals who create new and more attractive vocabularies. But he believes that this transaction, and therefore the same progress, ultimately depend on nothing more than "the accidental coincidence of a private obsession with a public need."[12] This is the great paradox of his political theory, which has been denounced over and over again by Rorty's critics: he identifies in individual creativity a crucial factor for promoting progress, yet he is at the same time unable to offer a more positive account of how to reconcile such creative power with the necessities of society. It is because of this deficiency that, at the end of the day, Rorty's "liberal hope" appears somehow hollow, nothing more than a mere hope.

Rorty's critics are right to argue that the difference between his irreverent and radical critique of philosophy and his somehow uninspiring and conformist political theory depends to an important extent on his incapacity to find a better compromise between the public and the private. At the same time we have to acknowledge that Rorty's position on this question is more complex and that it is possible to find in his writings resources to draw a less dichotomous and more positive view of the relation between these two realms. For instance, in the important essay "Feminism and Pragmatism," in which Rorty explains the propagation of feminist discourses to the rest of society, we have the impression that, as Nancy Fraser puts it, "the oppositions between the public and the private, the community and the individual, the political and the aesthetic are exploded."[13]

Some recent interpretations of Rorty have confirmed this more benevolent kind of reading. William Curtis for instance has tried to recompose Rorty's dichotomy between the private and the public, differentiating his concept of irony into two versions: one, understood as an openness to question one's own values, which should be embraced by all citizens, and a second and more radical version, which is the prerogative of the "strong poets," whose relevance is mainly private. The political version of irony constitutes for Curtis one of the founding virtues of liberalism, which he defines, with the support of Rorty, as an ethically thick ideology, a form of life that combines the existential and the political.[14]

Like Curtis, many of Rorty's interpreters have focused on his idea of irony. The political relevance of irony dwells essentially in its capacity to question the certainty of our own self-image and thus to foster an "ethos of 'presumptive generosity'" and openness towards the other.[15] Irony, however, functions mainly in a negative manner: through a rhetoric of contestation that critically remarks upon the contingent and arbitrary character of hegemonic identities. But in Rorty's philosophy we find not only an apology for irony in line with his post-modern and romantic inclination, but also a defence of a politics of consensus more in line with his liberalism and pragmatism. It is a politics made possible by relational faculties such as imagination, empathy, rhetorical and hermeneutic skills, which allow for the interconnecting of different vocabularies and discourses. This relational dimension is central to Rorty's understanding of rationality, normativity, society, and self-creation, as much as his idea of irony.[16] If the latter serves to question our self-image and start the process of enlargement of one's own identity, it is only through the former that this enlargement can occur through the creation of links between different vocabularies. And it is in Rorty's account of this relational dimension that we can detect an unexpected but very significant proximity with the rhetorical-humanistic tradition, and in particular with that of Cicero, Quintilian, and Vico. It is a proximity that has to do with the idea of self-creation, understood as a process of self-enlargement. It is a process described by Rorty as a continuous effort to transcend the frontiers of one's own identity by connecting more and more vocabularies; and by the rhetorical-humanistic tradition as an ongoing harmonious development of all the human potentialities through the cultivation of eloquence. For both Rorty, and that tradition then, the capacity to master language creatively is key for self-creation. On what they disagree however is on the possibility to make this process at the same time valuable for the individual and the community. If Rorty's strong humanism has not passed unnoticed, it has never been the subject of a deep analysis.[17] So, what I hope to show in this chapter is that examining Rorty's humanism through the lens of key humanist thinkers such as Cicero, Quintilian, and Vico, on the central theme of self-creation, is a productive exercise that permits important insights on Rorty and on humanism itself. This analysis allows us not only to bring new light on an important conundrum in Rorty's thought, but also to consider the prospects of humanism in our times. And finally, this analysis also allows us to see a different manifestation of why transcendence, contingency, and rhetoric are important in politics.

5.2 Rorty's Humanism: The Priority of Language and Politics over Truth and Philosophy

In the preface to the volume in the Library of Living Philosophers series dedicated to Rorty, Randy Auxier writes: "Rorty is a humanist in the sense that one might apply the term to Cicero, Seneca, and Epictetus, the *eloquent* humanist; or to Pico della Mirandola and Montaigne, the *wise* humanist; or to Emerson and Dewey, the *prudent* humanist."[18] Eloquence, wisdom, and prudence, Auxier reminds us, are the cardinal virtues of rhetoric. According to him, in Rorty we find all of these virtues, but it is prudence in which he excelled. In what follows we will explore Rorty's humanism, taking into consideration all the dimensions mentioned by Auxier. One of the conclusions we will reach, however, is that it is precisely the virtue of prudence that Rorty's humanism fails fully to endorse.

Probably the most general sense in which Rorty can be considered a humanist has been highlighted by Richard Bernstein. In summing up Rorty's legacy, Bernstein has referred to a "deep and persistent humanism…characteristic of his life and thinking," clarifying that he considers Rorty a humanist because he "challenged any and all attempts to argue that there are any constraints upon us—except those that come from our fellow human beings."[19] The plea to shift the focus from the search for truth to the enhancement of solidarity, indeed, certainly represents Rorty's main theme and the basic reason for the unreserved identification he came to develop with the tradition of pragmatism. As he puts it: "in the end, the pragmatists tell us, what matters is our loyalty to other human beings clinging together against the dark, not our hope of getting things right."[20]

Such prioritization of the sphere of human affairs is unquestionably also one of the defining features of humanism. It is the meaning that, for instance, Hannah Arendt attributed to Cicero when she defined him a "true humanist" since he believed that "neither the verities of the scientist nor the truth of the philosopher nor the beauty of the artist can be absolutes" and therefore that ultimately "the question of freedom...[is] the decisive one."[21] Actually Arendt may be exaggerating a little, because Cicero's stoicism made him believe in the existence of a natural law conceived by divine reason, which should serve as a model for human institutions and morals. In this sense, Rorty could be more properly approximated to the antifoundationalism *ante litteram* of Protagoras, according to whom human beings are the measure of all things. But the crucial fact here is that as we have seen for also for Cicero, there was a shift of perspective towards the realm of human affairs and specifically of politics, where freedom rather than truth is what really matters. And precisely as happened for the sophists, for Cicero too rhetoric came to take central stage because in this sphere things occur mainly through language.

In Rorty we find a similar connection between antifoundationalism, attention toward the power of language, and the shift from philosophy to politics. First came antifoundationalism and the idea of the power of redescription. In "Trotsky and the Wild Orchids" he recounts how, as a young philosopher, he reached a point when the more philosophy he read, the clearer it became in his mind that finding absolute standpoints—the "fabled place 'beyond hypotheses,'" which can assure that a justification of a philosophic position is, ultimately, noncircular—was impossible.[22] The next step consisted in debunking the idea of philosophy as a founding discipline and redescribing it as one of the activities we have to defend our positions, not because it is closer to truth, but rather because their new vocabularies offer better ways to look at things. The category of truth then came to lose all its aura, being downgraded to a simple "compliment we pay to entities or beliefs that have won their spurs, paid their way, proved themselves useful, and therefore been incorporated into accepted social practices."[23]

In *Philosophy and the Mirror of Nature*, Rorty's humanism took the form of this attack on the primacy of epistemology, on which philosophy has traditionally based its claim of authority over the rest of culture. Philosophy as epistemology, he proposed, should be substituted by an alternative way of philosophizing he described as "therapeutic" and "edifying" and whose main purpose would be the substitution of outworn vocabularies with new ones and the creation of connections among different vocabularies.[24] Philosophy should become something like a "conversational" art that helps to "keep the conversation going."[25] And if philosophy were to evolve into a conversational art, then it is clear that it should develop hermeneutical skills. Indeed in this book Rorty found in Gadamer an important ally. "Hermeneutics," Rorty wrote, "is the name philosophy should take…once we decide to focus more on how things are said rather than on the possession of truths"; and *Bildung*, that is, self-transformation through education in order to find "a new and more interested way of expressing ourselves, and thus of coping with the world," the goal of thinking.[26] If "edifying" and "therapeutic" philosophies have the task of challenging, through a continuous engagement with "abnormal discourses," the closure and hypostatization of "normal" ones (those a particular community in a specific moment considers the standards of rational argumentation),[27] hermeneutics for Gadamer is the art that, starting from the assumption about the universality of the experience of misunderstanding, strives to find a "fusion of horizons."[28] They move from similar premises and promote similar political goals.

In his subsequent works Rorty would abandon the strictly metaphilosophical focus of *Philosophy and the Mirror of Nature* and start to spell out the political implications of his positions.[29] *Contingency, Irony, and Solidarity* in particular is a key text in this regard. It is in this work that he offers the most comprehensive profile of his "liberal utopia": a society whose democratic-liberal institutions and values are understood as the outcome of historical contingencies and defended not by appealing to ultimate philosophical justifications, but rather pragmatically for their capacity to promote solidarity and protect its members from suffering. Such a society would be a progressive one; however, it would be one where change is not considered a matter of truth—a category that became almost completely useless—but rather of new vocabularies able to expand solidarity and freedom.[30] Politics as described in *Contingency, Irony, and Solidarity* becomes something that depends entirely on the capacity to create and persuade; where persuasion is obtained through aesthetically and practically attractive new discourses, more than through philosophical argumentation. Creating new stories, capable of stimulating our imagination to strengthen solidarity, inspiring our hope for the future and showing new solutions to old problems—this is how Rorty thinks we can promote political change. Politics, in brief, becomes rhetoric, or as he says, literature[31]; and the capacity to redescribe, the main vehicle of progress.

As we have seen, ancient rhetoric also considered the technique of redescription (or *paradiastole*) a central aspect of its art, since through it the orator could present reality in different ways, according to whatever circumstances require, highlighting one moral aspect rather than another, emphasizing one emotion rather than another.[32] For such an activity, both the tradition of rhetoric and Rorty identify in tropes, and above all in metaphors, a particularly important instrument. Quintilian, for one, refers to metaphor (*translatio*) as "the most beautiful of the tropes"; tropes that are particularly useful for redescription since they permit translating the meaning of a term from its original context to a new one and thus to accomplish "the supremely difficult task of providing a name for everything."[33] For Rorty, metaphors are "growing-points of language": voices from outside the logical space of a particular vocabulary, which enlarge the realm of its possibilities and reweave its beliefs.[34] They are for him such a primary tool for change that he comes to define "intellectual and moral progress" as "a history of increasingly useful metaphors."[35] Recalling the legacy of Romanticism, according to which "anything could be made to look good or bad by being redescribed," Rorty concludes that "a talent for speaking differently, rather than for arguing well...is the chief instrument of cultural change."[36]

But in Rorty's works we do not find any real engagement with the tradition of rhetoric. When he talks about what for him is a key advancement in Western culture—"the idea that truth was made rather than found"[37]—it is to the Romantic tradition, the French Revolution and German Idealism, that he makes reference; not to the tradition of rhetoric or, for instance, to Vico's motto *verum et factum convertuntur*, which proclaims the convertibility between the true and the created, and his thesis about the poetic origin of civilization. In this respect, it is noteworthy that, after the publication of *Philosophy and the Mirror of Nature*, Rorty's interest in Gadamer's hermeneutic vanished altogether. As Gadamer came more and more to understand, rhetoric and hermeneutics are complementary arts, one focused on communication and the other on comprehension; and both have an essentially social dimension.[38] Their neglect, as Danish and Wain suggest, seems to indicate that Rorty came to understand the potential of redescription more in line with the existentialist Romantic-Nietzschean tradition, as a way of making difference and uniqueness proliferate, than in the rhetorical-humanistic sense of using it to create social and political cohesion.[39]

Nevertheless, the assonances between Rorty's vision of a postphilosophical, literary culture and that of the rhetorical-humanistic tradition are strong, being rooted in a common rejection of truth as the category most important for human affairs and the consideration of the human world as a linguistic artefact. It is because of this shift from truth to language that, as we have seen, rhetoric assumes in humanism a central place, as the binding force that keeps all the areas of knowledge together.[40] Something similar occurs in Rorty, in his endorsement of what he describes as an epochal transformation, from the Enlightenment to Romanticism: the "transition from a philosophical to a literary culture."[41] It is the passage from a philosophical-scientific idea of knowledge, as a realm divided into specialized fields, all them regulated by philosophy, to a more fluid conception, where philosophy loses its leading position and literature comes to assume the same key function of rhetoric in humanism, as disciplinary frontiers become porous and everything is treated as "text" and considered as "permanent possibilit[y]...for redescription, reinterpretation, manipulation."[42] The main character of such a culture, accordingly, is no longer the philosopher, but rather the novelist, the poet, the journalist, the filmmaker, or more generally the literary critic.[43] All these figures can be included in the portrait of what Rorty calls the "humanistic intellectual."[44] The "humanistic intellectuals" are people who "read a lot more books in the hope of becoming a different sort of person" and "in order to enlarge their sense of what is possible and important—either for themselves as individuals or for their society."[45] They have a political and moral ascendancy, not thanks to a "special access to moral truth," but rather because they have "exceptionally large range of acquaintance," they "have been around" and "have read more books" and thus are "in a better position not to get trapped in a [single] vocabulary" and to understand the needs of those who use different vocabularies from their own.[46] Their specialty consists in finding analogies between different vocabularies, in "placing books in the context of other books, figures in the context of other figures," and putting them in dialogue. This is how they make their contribution to society, helping in the task of "reweaving its fabric of beliefs."[47]

As in traditional philosophy, then, so too in Rorty wisdom plays an essential political and moral role. But his idea of wisdom, or more generally of culture, is of a different sort: one that cannot be understood according to the traditional philosophical metaphor of "depth"—a reason that penetrates beyond the realm of appearance towards real essences—but rather according to the much more humanistic and rhetorical metaphor of "width" or "enlargement."[48] There is also in Rorty a clear sense of transcendence, of going beyond what is given. But such transcending occurs in a different direction: horizontally rather than vertically. It is this metaphor of "width", or "enlargement", that best reveals the humanistic-rhetorical sensibility of Rorty's thought. Expanding the frontiers of our culture, and therefore our political and moral horizons, becomes for him a matter of creating connections between different discourses: something like "sewing together a very large, elaborate, polychrome quilt."[49] This is why in his view reason is displaced by imagination as "the cutting edge of cultural evolution."[50] It is through imagination indeed that "our minds gradually [grow] larger and stronger and more interesting by the addition of new options—new candidates for belief and desire."[51]

The metaphor of "width" used by Rorty for describing his idea of culture echoes in effect the encyclopedic ideal of Cicero, Quintilian, the Humanists, and Vico. Vico, in particular, is emblematic in this respect. He describes his *New Science* as a work that embraces "all the wisdom, human and divine."[52] It is a work that, as he says in the second edition of 1730, has to be read with an "associative mind," because in such a mind "there is no thing that cannot be associated with innumerable others of other sorts."[53] Differently from Diderot and d'Alembert's *Encyclopédie,* composed with a dissociative and analytic logic, the *New Science* embodies a more associative and inclusive encyclopedic ideal.[54] It is a work that collects an enormous number of facts, subjects, and ideas, whose common nature is discovered through ingenuity and fantasy[55] and which are made to cohere into a unique story through the art of narration. In extolling such an imaginative work, Vico was of course following the teachings of the rhetorical-humanistic tradition, which considered imagination a central faculty for *inventio* (one of the five basic canons of rhetoric) and its associated *ars topica*: the creative art of finding the 'places', or arguments, from which to start a discourse.[56] But as I have argued in Chap. 3, imagination is also important for rhetoric in a much more immediate political sense, since it is through an imaginative thinking and feeling from the other's point of view that the orator can empathize with the audience and improve her chances of persuading it.[57] In similar terms, for Rorty imagination is crucial in the process of persuasion, through which we can extend the reach of solidarity. Indeed the possibility of extending our solidarity depends for him not so much on convincing people of the rationality of some moral truths, but rather on a "sentimental education": a process guided by the capacity of the imagination to establish connections, through which we come to "see strange people as fellow sufferers."[58] It is also in this more direct political sense that for Rorty imagination is the key political faculty: in that it educates our feelings, putting us in the place of others through a work of redescription, and hence expanding "the reference of the terms 'our kind of people' and 'people like us.'"[59]

We can see then why the Rortyan "humanistic intellectual" is so much in harmony with the humanistic ideal of the Renaissance man of learning and action and its predecessor, the Ciceronian perfect orator. These ideals promote a "wide" rather than a specialist education as a key factor not only for personal improvement but also for engaging with one's own fellow citizens, since it contributes to the development of a capacity to create connections among persons, disciplines, and discourses, and thus to enhance the kind of judgment necessary to deal with the variety of situations that human interaction creates.[60] A cultivated person, according to this humanistic perspective, is someone who, as Arendt puts it, "knows how to choose his company among men, among things, among thoughts, in the present as well as in the past."[61]

5.3 Rorty's Antihumanism and the Unpersuasiveness of the Public/Private Division

Having unravelled the sense of Rorty's affinity with the rhetorical-humanistic tradition, I can now move on to their main point of difference. The premise from which we should move to deal with this topic is the fact that according to both, becoming proficient in the sort of literary wisdom and the art of redescription we have just explored also means undergoing a fundamental change in one's own self-understanding. One of the implications is that we cannot deal with Rorty's idea of redescription, considering linguistic mastery as a mere instrument through which one can change things by way of redescribing it. Rorty does have a pragmatic understanding of language, according to which what counts is the result, but for him how we understand ourselves depends to a larger extent on how we describe ourselves.[62] This is why it is more meaningful to compare Rorty with the substantive conception of rhetoric of Cicero, Quintilian, and their followers—according to whom eloquence produces not only an external change but also a modification of the ethos of the speaker—rather than with the merely instrumental one of the sophists.[63]

As I have argued, the central feature of the rhetorical-humanistic tradition is the idea that personal cultivation and involvement in political life are interdependent endeavours, which find their combination in eloquence. In contrast to the Platonic perspective, this tradition defends the necessity of combining the *vita contemplativa* with the *vita activa*, arguing that the latter without the former would be a mere struggle for power and the former without the latter a hollow and sterile endeavour. What for this tradition can guarantee the union between these private and public endeavours is precisely the art of rhetoric—on the one hand, because eloquence is the medium through which theoretical wisdom can be transmitted to the people and transformed into political action, and on the other, because practicing eloquence means practicing politics and therefore the guarantee of a continuous connection with the concrete problems of the community. The best illustration of such a combination is given in Cicero's and Quintilian's figure of the *perfectus orator*, which represents an ideal both for the individual and the citizen; an ideal in which outstanding political and ethical virtues are combined with vast knowledge and find their concrete manifestation in eloquence. Eloquence becomes here the highest manifestation of a practical reason, which can be reached only through a transformation of one's own ethos; so that, as Quintilian says, greatness of the spirit is indeed the most important attribute of an orator.

Despite his humanistic sensibility, however, Rorty sees the relationship between self-creation and public commitment in different terms. His most important work, *Contingency, Irony, and Solidarity*, "tries to show how things look if we drop the demand for a theory which unifies the public and private, and are content to treat the demands of self-creation and of human solidarity as equally valid, yet forever incommensurable."[64] It is in this book that he defends in the most elaborate way the idea of the split between them. And, even if over the years Rorty gradually came to soften this position, it is undeniable that the belief about the necessity to create some kind of separation is, as Keith Topper has suggested, a central element of his postmetaphysical liberalism: it is the "way out" he offers from "what he sees as a prototypical case of deadlock in contemporary social and political theory, namely the stalemate regarding the relation between the private and the public."[65] The question of how to maintain a proper separation between these two domains is a central question for liberalism. And the separation proposed by Rorty is his solution to respect at the same time his liberal credo of avoiding cruelty and his Romantic-Nietzschean penchant for self-creation.[66]

Rorty introduces the split between the private and the public in *Contingency, Irony, and Solidarity* by establishing a division between two types of intellectuals: on one hand, ironist, aestheticist, and irrationalist figures such as Nietzsche, Heidegger, Foucault, and Proust; on the other, liberals and public intellectuals such as Mill, Dewey, Habermas, and Orwell. In the first group "the desire for self-creation, for private autonomy dominates," and with it a strong scepticism for socialization, which they consider intrinsically "antithetical to something deep within" them. They are archetypes of "what private perfection…can be like," because they are masters in creating new vocabularies to redescribe themselves. In the second group what stands out is the "desire for a more just and free human community" and the capacity to produce vocabularies of justice and solidarity.[67] Because of this, the latter group severely reproaches the pursuit of private perfection by the ironists because, mocking universality and consent, they cannot reconcile it with the pursuit of justice. These two different existential orientations are for Rorty not merely different, but incommensurable. Both can be described as linguistic undertakings, but they diverge insofar as they engender different vocabularies: "the vocabulary of self-creation is necessarily private, unshared, unsuited to argument. The vocabulary of justice is necessarily public and shared, a medium for argumentative exchange."[68] The liberal intellectual strives to create discourses that strengthen the beliefs that keep together a community, while the master ironist strives to "create the taste by which he will be judged."[69]

What is important to underline is that the separation between these two spheres of action is for Rorty a practical solution and, as he says, a negative point.[70] It is the consequence of recognizing a philosophical impossibility, once we accept antifoundationalism and historicism. It is here that the question of contingency enters in the scene. Indeed, if the vocabularies we speak are, as Rorty believes, the products of historic contingencies and if we human beings are only contingent "centerless webs of beliefs and desires,"[71] then reconciling self-creation and public commitment under a single general account is impossible, since it would require a metaphysical idea of human nature and an ahistorical vocabulary that are not available.[72] Politically, keeping these endeavours separate is the only possible solution for Rorty that allows one to pursue both, even if separately. On the other hand, the purpose of unifying them cannot but lead to antidemocratic solutions, as was the case for Hitler's and Mao's totalitarian fantasies about the creation of the new man.[73]

The great inconvenience with such a solution, however, is that it does not provide any conceivable ways, beyond mere chance, in which to employ the creative resources of self-creation for political ends. As we have seen, even if for Rorty the contribution of great individualities is crucial to change society for the better,[74] the possibility that this could happen is a question of mere chance, or as he says, something that cannot be anticipated since it lies "somewhere down the line."[75] This sort of fatalism contrasts starkly with the picture we get from the rhetorical-humanistic tradition, which finds in the figure of the orator and his art the main agent for political change—that which is able to give birth to and maintain a community—being a substantial part of such a power the product of the process of self-cultivation. In the Rortyan narrative, instead, creativity is associated almost exclusively with private self-creation, so that it becomes difficult to understand on which resources we can count to promote what he calls an "Emersonian self-creation on a communal scale."[76] This difficulty in Rorty's theory can be traced back to the rather elitist and fractured picture of society he sometimes seems to endorse. In *Contingency, Irony, and Solidarity*, for instance, Rorty reifies society into a stark dichotomy between an elite of brilliant ironists devoted to the creative, but exclusively private, project of self-cultivation and a mass of "commonsensical" citizens, from whom no real political change can be expected.[77] Even if Rorty describes the separation between the private and the public as a critical response to what he defines as the "Platonic attempt" to unify them, such a division closely echoes that established by Plato between the few and the many.[78] In the citizens who populate Rorty's liberal society we find no trace of political grandeur. They are, in his words, "bland, calculating, petty, and unheroic" individuals whose daily and too mundane private affairs drain all their energies. "The prevalence of such people," he recognizes, "may be a reasonable price to pay for political freedom."[79] The only figures sketched with heroic traits are those (radical) ironists—intellectuals, artists, and the like—who have the courage and creativity to continuously reinvent themselves.[80]

If we accept Curtis's distinction between a radical and a more moderate sense of irony, we see that only the former possess the creative energies necessary to promote change. Indeed if the more moderate version of irony generates an attitude of open-mindness, it is only the more extreme one that impels one to produce new vocabularies, installing radical and continuous doubts about one's own "final vocabulary" and thus the desire to seek autonomy.[81] But this more radical version of irony, similarly to

Plato's philosophy, has for Rorty a very problematic relation to politics: it stands in perfect opposition to common sense, which he calls "the watchword of those who unselfconsciously describe everything important in terms of the final vocabulary" and who "tak[e] for granted that statements formulated in that final vocabulary suffice to describe and judge the beliefs, actions, and lives of those who employ alternative final vocabularies."[82] The radical ironists can challenge the self-image of society, but they cannot provide the rhetoric of hope and empowerment that is necessary to foster solidarity. Indeed, in contrast to the metaphysicians who promise to emancipate their subjects by providing them discourses that uncover and set free their real nature, the ironists cannot make such promises simply because they do not believe that such a nature exists.[83] Above all, the incapacity of the radical ironists "to take themselves seriously because always aware...of the contingency and fragility of their final vocabularies, and thus of their selves" is difficult to combine with the need of stability and order a community necessarily has.[84] For Rorty, radical irony engenders a discourse of disruption that posits a permanent risk to the necessary cohesion of society; a discourse, on the other hand, whose positive political contribution is often hampered by a too complex and sophisticated style. Political language for him can only be commonsensical, simpleminded, since its aim is to strengthen the common "truths" and sense of solidarity that keep together the community, not emphasizing individual idiosyncrasies, as the ironic language does. It has to be much more like Orwell's *1984* or *Animal Farm*, than like Proust's *À la recherche*.

However, as we know, for Rorty, without the acumen of radically ironic redescriptions society cannot gain a critical distance from its own self-image and accept the substitution of its old, solidified vocabularies. What is interesting here is that, confirming once again an unexpected proximity to Plato, for Rorty this crucial public role can be exercised only in disguise, by covering these redescriptions under the mask of a commonsensical and responsible rhetoric to avoid giving the impression of putting the stability and order of society too much at risk.[85] Rorty invites radical ironists to recognize that their redescriptions could cause harm, since "threatening one's final vocabulary, and thus one's ability to make sense of oneself in one's own terms...suggests that oneself and one's world are futile, obsolete, powerless."[86] That is why, more than "commonsensical" citizens, this ironist needs "as much imaginative acquaintance with alternative final vocabularies as possible, not just for her own edification, but in order to understand the actual and possible humiliation of the people who use these alternative final vocabularies."[87] That is, radical irony can perform its political function only with the help of imagination, which allows us to see "the similarities between ourselves and people very unlike us"[88] and therefore to be more empathetic toward people who do not share the same ironic attitude. As we have seen before, indeed, it is precisely because of their exceptionally broad range of acquaintance and familiarity with different vocabularies that the literary critics are taken as moral advisers.[89] In brief, then, for Rorty irony can play a political role only if used with tact, and accompanied by that imaginative empathy and hermeneutic ability typical of the humanistic intellectual. Its rhetoric of disruption needs to be complemented and tamed by a rhetoric of consensus, necessary to persuade the members of one's own community about the advantages of changing their self-image and, at the same time, the potential of new members to join the practices and values of that community.[90]

Now, putting together all these virtues—irony, imagination, the capacity to redescribe, a hermeneutic sensibility—we obtain the outline of what *phronesis* would be like according to Rorty. Indeed this is how he described his view of philosophy in *Philosophy and the Mirror of Nature*: as the form of practical reason necessary for having a conversation, which results from a process of "edification" made up of acculturation and practice.[91] It is thanks to this process of edification through the encounter with a great variety of vocabularies that the "literary critics" and "humanistic intellectuals" can develop the communicative and relational capacities necessary to act politically. This form of *phronesis* is crucial because it helps us to be ironic, even radically ironic, in public without causing arbitrary harm: it develops what Rorty characterizes as the "taste" necessary to mediate between abnormal and normal discourses, as it allows us to see "normal discourse in terms of its own motives" rather than "only from within our own abnormal discourse" and to make us understand when "someone's refusal to adopt our norms...is morally outrageous and when it is something which we must...respect."[92]

The kind of "taste" Rorty talks about can be associated with one of the most important principles in rhetoric: *decorum*, a principle that combines ethical and aesthetic considerations to determine the more appropriate discourse according to the circumstances.[93] The relevance of *decorum* is particularly evident in Cicero's conception, where it assumes an important role in instructing the orator about how to find the proper combination of more principled considerations about justice, on the one hand, and practical ones related to the specific context on the other.[94] Translated into

Rorty's jargon, this is the principle that instructs us how to employ irony, and particularly its more radical version, for public purposes. The Ciceronian orator, with his combination of self-cultivation and political commitment, is a character particularly skilled in such mediation. In Chap. 3, I have explained the way in which Cicero portrays him as someone at the same time able to communicate with the people, through common-sensical vocabularies, and to look beyond common opinion through philosophical insight.[95] For this reason the orator always remains in an ambiguous position: at centre of the public stage, but always with an eye to what is beyond. He is aware that self-cultivation and politics have different and often conflicting exigencies.[96] So when he speaks in public, he is always careful to avoid his more unconventional views patently hurting with commonly held opinions, precisely as both Rorty and Strauss (in different ways) prescribe.

In Cicero's *De oratore*, those who lack eloquence and *decorum* are called "tactless" (*ineptus*); an attribute which is said to be particularly common among the cultivated Greek people.[97] The same kind of tactlessness seems to abound also in Rorty's radical ironists, who do not know how to adapt their disruptive discourses of self-creation to the exigencies of political life. Since their specialty consists in creating "the taste by which [they] will be judged," they have problems in accommodating their discourse to communal norms, as *decorum* prescribes.[98] They are exceptionally eloquent in redescribing themselves, but normally quite ineloquent (or *inepti*) when it comes to politics. They are Romantic geniuses, not Ciceronian orators. Even if they are formed by the culture to which they belong—since their redescriptions cannot but start from the textual resources provided by such culture[99]—they are somehow strangers in their own community. They understand themselves through abnormal discourses and do not usually have the capacity to bring their descriptions into dialogue with the normal discourses of society. The possibility that such a fluency could develop at the same time as a kind of practical reason is indeed reduced by Rorty to a question of mere chance, about which there is not much to be said.

This sort of fatalism about the relation between society and some of its most inventive minds not only contrasts with Rorty's progressive view (because moral and political progress for him cannot happen without the creativity of those minds), but also with the fact that he has always admonished those who, in devoting themselves too eagerly to the creative project of self-creation, run the risk of falling away from the rest of society.[100] At the same time this fatalism seems to disregard the fact that, enlarging one's own sense of identity through a continuous engagement with different vocabularies and imaginative literature is crucial not only for the political goal of expanding solidarity but also for the existential one of self-creation. Both the creation of bridges between different groups and the search of one's own personal autonomy indeed require one to combat what Rorty calls "egotism": an excessive self-satisfaction and self-confidence that render us incapable of changing and taking other points of view into consideration.[101]

5.4 AT THE BOTTOM OF RORTY'S PUBLIC/PRIVATE DIVISION

I want to conclude this chapter by suggesting a possible explanation of why Rorty ended up in such a cul-de-sac and thus also a way to overcome it. As we have seen, Rorty refuses to combine the private and the public in a general account, for instance in a conception of *phronesis*, because this would inevitably imply defending one particular Truth about human nature. Such a defence is for him not only theoretically impossible, once we adopt an antifoundationalist vocabulary, but also politically problematic, since our institutions have the obligation to guarantee pluralism. But is Rorty's conclusion the only one possible? Well, only if we think that the only possible way to combine the public and the private is to provide a comprehensive theory that solves the problem once and for all, rather than through thoroughly contingent, practically oriented, and fuzzy solutions, which can be applied and tested and then continuously reinvented. Cicero's famous theoretical eclecticism, which many have interpreted as a proof of an incapacity to produce a really original and deep philosophy, can be seen under this perspective also as spurring from an awareness about the necessity to always adapt theory to practice. On the contrary, despite all his effort to demystify philosophy, it seems that at the end of the day Rorty has remained trapped in a too philosophical anti-philosophical posture, which prevented him from developing a more constructive political theory. Indeed people such as Alessandro Ferrara, Jean Elshtain, Jürgen Habermas, Richard Bernstein, and Ernesto Laclau have all in some way suggested that Rorty's thinking is constructed on a series of exclusive dichotomies, in which the position he takes results from a dialectical negation of the opposite view that precludes developing the argument in new directions.[102] It is because of this, I think, that he has not been able to truly move from the task of deconstructing the primacy of philosophy over politics to that of drawing the consequences of such ideas.

But if the main goal of Rorty's project consists in replacing dialectical argumentation with poetical redescription, then there is nothing to prevent him from creating an account, certainly provisional, multifaceted, or even vague, of how to attempt to establish positive interactions between private self-creation and public commitment without falling into metaphysical presuppositions. Rorty is certainly right in underlining that these two endeavours (similarly to philosophy and politics) are animated by different impulses, call for different attitudes, and express themselves in different vocabularies, and in warning that the attempt to combine them could be a threat to pluralism. But at the same time, his account reveals why it is politically and morally very problematic to keep them separate. On the one hand, the radical irony that abounds in the champions of self-creation is an indispensable political tool for questioning hegemonic vocabularies. On the other, this irony can be employed in the public sphere without causing unnecessary harm only with the help of political and relational skills, such as an imaginative capacity to create connections and an ability to persuade. Society needs the radical ironist; and the radical ironist needs political reason in order to be a good citizen.

Keith Topper has underlined that the separation between the private and the public is for Rorty more of a "practical compromise" than a theoretical solution to the problem that could emerge from an attempt to keep them together. By insisting on the impossibility of creating a theoretical framework to combine these two endeavours, he says, Rorty hoped to persuade us to focus on finding practical solutions to accommodate them.[103] Nevertheless, I think the inflexibility with which Rorty has often defended such idea and his incapacity to explore other alternatives can be explained also by the fact that his reflection on this topic has developed mainly at a theoretical level, through a dialectical inversion of a position he wanted to confute (namely, that self-creation and political commitment are commensurable and can be combined within a general account). It is because of this that Rorty has developed a notion of contingency so radical and absolute, as to prevent him to explore possible (and contingent) solutions to overcome the split between the private and the public. In this respect, as Wolin suggests, the idea of the incommensurability between self-creation and political commitment became part of Rorty's "ultimate vocabulary."[104] But according to his ironist credo, Rorty should have attempted to overcome this ultimate vocabulary. Indeed, the existence of a tension between these two goals is not something like an ultimate truth, but rather a contingent and concrete fact—certainly, one particularly significant in our modern individualist societies—with political consequences. Rorty himself gave different formulations of their relationship, revealing not only their tension, but also, as we have seen, their interconnection and mutual dependency. Nevertheless, in his work the vocabulary of tension gradually became too literalized, preventing him from developing a new one. This would perhaps have allowed him to formulate a less conformist and uninspiring political theory.

In this chapter I have not provided any substantive proposal about how to develop such positive interaction between self-creation and public commitment, beyond reminding us of the way in which the rhetorical-humanistic tradition did so and noting how Rorty came close to this idea but eventually took a different position. Here the point could be made that to revitalize a notion of *phronesis* in our epoch is an anachronism. In particular, the notion of *phronesis*—understood as the capacity to link the particular with the universal and specifically with the ultimate aim of living well—seems unfit for Rorty's vocabulary. He regarded the distinction between moral deliberation and prudential calculation as obsolete, because for him Freud's critique of the unified subject has revealed our moral development to be "far more finely textured, far more custom-tailored to our individual case, than the moral vocabulary which the philosophical tradition offered us."[105] Nevertheless, as I have emphasized in Chap. 3, we have to recall that the idea of *phronesis* in the rhetorical-humanistic tradition is one that pivots around relational, rather more substantive, qualities. It is an idea of *phronesis* that can be put in dialogue with post-modern theories of subjectivity, which stress its intersubjective and contingent dimension. As we have seen, Rorty endorses a similar kind of communicative *phronesis* as an essential instrument both for moral and political progress; a *phronesis* behind which we find a conception of the self "as relational 'through and through.'"[106] It is a wider and more imaginative description of this relational self and its interactions with society—one that reveals the positive interactions between self-creation and political commitment—that we would have expected from Rorty.

NOTES

1. Charles B. Guignon and David R. Hiley, "Introduction: Richard Rorty and Contemporary Philosophy," in *Contemporary Philosophy in Focus*, ed. Charles B. Guignon and David R. Hiley (Cambridge and New York: Cambridge University Press, 2003), 1.
2. Richard Rorty, "Trotsky and the Wild Orchids," in *Philosophy and Social Hope* (London: Penguin Books, 1999), 7–8, 13.
3. Richard J. Bernstein, *The New Constellation: The Ethical-Political Horizons of Modernity/Postmodernity* (Cambridge, MA: MIT Press, 1992), 233.
4. See e.g., Richard Rorty, "Response to Daniel Conway," in *Richard Rorty: Critical Dialogues*, ed. Matthew Festenstein and Simon Thompson (Cambridge, UK and Malden, MA: Polity Press, 2001), 91; Richard Rorty and Eduardo Mendieta, *Take Care of Freedom and Truth Will Take Care of Itself: Interviews with Richard Rorty* (Stanford, CA: Stanford University Press, 2006), 50; Richard Rorty, Derek Nystrom, and Kent Puckett, *Against Bosses, Against Oligarchies: A Conversation with Richard Rorty* (Chicago: Prickly Paradigm, 2002), 61–4; Richard Rorty, "Reply to J. B. Schneewind," in *The Philosophy of Richard Rorty*, ed. Randall E. Auxier and Lewis E. Hahn (Chicago: Open Court, 2010), 506; Richard Rorty, "Reply to Raymond D. Boisvert," in *The Philosophy of Richard Rorty*, ed. Randall E. Auxier and Lewis E. Hahn (Chicago: Open Court, 2010).
5. Thomas McCarthy, "Private Irony and Public Decency: Richard Rorty's New Pragmatism," *Critical Inquiry* 16 (1990): 366–7.
6. Ibid., 370. A similar argument can be found in: Alessandro Ferrara, "The Unbearable Seriousness of Irony," *Philosophy and Social Criticism* 16 (1990).
7. Nancy Fraser, "Solidarity or Singularity? Richard Rorty between Romanticism and Technocracy," *Praxis International* 8 (1988): 266. For Rorty's response to Fraser, see: Richard Rorty, "Intellectual Autobiography," in *The Philosophy of Richard Rorty*, ed. Randall E. Auxier and Lewis Edwin Hahn (Chicago: Open Court, 2010), 20; Rorty, Nystrom, and Puckett, *Against Bosses, against Oligarchies*, 61–2.
8. See: Terence Ball et al., "Review Symposium on Richard Rorty," *History of the Human Sciences* 3 (1990); Chantal Mouffe, "Deconstruction, Pragmatism and the Politics of Democracy," in *Deconstruction and Pragmatism*, ed. Chantal Mouffe (London: Routledge, 1996); Christopher Voparil, *Richard Rorty: Politics and Vsision* (Lanham, MD: Rowman & Littlefield Publishers, 2006), 134.
9. Voparil, *Richard Rorty*, 135–43.

10. Richard Rorty, *Contingency, Irony, and Solidarity* (Cambridge and New York: Cambridge University Press, 1995), xv.
11. Ibid., 63.
12. Ibid., 37, cf. 17.
13. Nancy Fraser, "From Irony to Prophecy to Politics: A Response to Richard Rorty," *Michigan Quarterly Review* 30 (1991): 262; Richard Rorty, "Feminism and Pragmatism," in *Truth and Progress: Philosophical Papers, Volume 3* (Cambridge: Cambridge University Press, 1998). Fraser, however, believes that the positive step Rorty takes in this essay to reconcile his public/private split is insufficient, since for her his account of the subversive practices of feminist groups is still tainted by a too poeticized, apolitical, and elitist conception of "abnormal discourses."
14. William M. Curtis, *Defending Rorty: Pragmatism and Liberal Virtue* (Cambridge: Cambridge University Press, 2015), 96–8. Similarly to Curtis, Tracy Llanera has shown how in Rorty's later writings self-creation and solidarity can be seen as complementary, even if distinct, dimensions of a single endeavour to create a larger self. Tracy Llanera, "Rethinking Nihilism: Rorty Vs. Taylor, Dreyfus and Kelly," *Philosophy and Social Criticism* 42 (2016).
15. Stephen K. White, *The Ethos of a Late-Modern Citizen* (Cambridge, MA: Harvard University Press, 2009), 128–31.
16. Christopher Voparil, "Taking Other Human Beings Seriously: Rorty's Ethics of Choice and Responsibility," *Contemporary Pragmatism* 11 (2014).
17. Richard J. Bernstein, "Richard Rorty's Deep Humanism," *New Literary History* 39 (2008); Randall Auxier, "Preface," in *In the Philosophy of Richard Rorty*, ed. Randall E. Auxier and Lewis Edwin Hahn (Chicago: Open Court, 2010); Krzysztof P. Skowronski, *Values, Valuations, and Axiological Norms in Richard Rorty's Neopragmatism* (Lanham, MD: Lexington Books, 2015), Ch. 3.
18. Auxier, "Preface," xix.
19. Bernstein, "Richard Rorty's Deep Humanism," 13, 19.
20. Richard Rorty, "Pragmatism, Relativism, and Irrationalism," in *Consequences of Pragmatism: Essays, 1972–1980* (Minneapolis: University of Minnesota Press, 1982), 166.
21. Hannah Arendt, "The Crisis in Culture," in *Between Past and Future* (New York: The Viking Press, 1968), 224–5.
22. Rorty, "Trotsky and the Wild Orchids," 10.
23. Richard Rorty, "Cultural Politics and the Question of the Existence of God," in *Philosophy as Cultural Politics: Philosophical Papers, Volume 4*. (Cambridge, UK and New York: Cambridge University Press, 2007), 6–7.

24. Richard Rorty, *Philosophy and the Mirror of Nature* (Princeton: Princeton University Press, 1979), 12, 360.
25. Ibid., 372, 78.
26. Ibid., 359. The penultimate chapter of *Philosophy and the Mirror of Nature* is entitled "From Epistemology to Hermeneutics," where the expression 'hermeneutics' is taken from Gadamer.
27. Ibid., 320–1, 60, 77.
28. Hans-Georg Gadamer, *Truth and Method (Second, Revised Edition)* (London and New York: Continuum, 1993), 179.
29. Cf. Rorty, *Philosophy and the Mirror of Nature*, 7. Rorty, *Contingency, Irony, and Solidarity*, xvi.
30. E.g., Richard Rorty, "Universality and Truth," in *Rorty and His Critics*, ed. Robert Brandom (Cambridge: Blackwell, 2000), 7.
31. Rorty, *Contingency, Irony, and Solidarity*, 94.
32. On *paradiastole* see supra note 84 in Chap. 3.
33. Quintilian, *Institutio Oratoria*, trans. Harold Edgeworth Butler (Cambridge, MA: Harvard Univsity Press, 1963), 8.6.4–5. Cf. Cicero, "Orator," in *Brutus, Orator*, trans. G. L. Hendrickson and H. M. Hubbell (Cambridge, MA: Harvard University Press, 1934), 134. Cicero, however, specifies that the success of a metaphor depends on giving the impression of not invading an alien place, but occupying one to which it belongs. Cicero, "Brutus," in *Brutus, Orator*, trans. G. L. Hendrickson and H. M. Hubbell (Cambridge, MA: Harvard University Press, 1934), 274.
34. Richard Rorty, "Philosophy as Science, as Metaphor, and as Politics," in *Objectivity, Relativism, and Truth: Philosophical Papers, Volume 1* (Cambridge and New York: Cambridge University Press, 1991), 12–13. Cf. Rorty, *Contingency, Irony, and Solidarity*, 44.
35. Rorty, *Contingency, Irony, and Solidarity*, 9.
36. Ibid., 7, 73.
37. Ibid., 3.
38. Gadamer has defined hermeneutics as the "inversion" of rhetoric. Gadamer, *Truth and Method (Second, Revised Edition)*, 188. On Gadamer's views on rhetoric and the humanistic tradition see also: ibid., 17ff.; Hans-Georg Gadamer and Riccardo Dottori, *A Century of Philosophy* (New York: Continuum, 2004), 50–65.
39. Robert Danisch, "The Absence of Rhetorical Theory in Richard Rorty's Linguistic Pragmatism," *Philosophy and Rhetoric* 46 (2013); Kenneth Wain, "Strong Poets and Utopia: Rorty's Liberalism, Dewey and Democracy," *Political Studies* 41 (1993).
40. As we have seen in Chap. 3, it is precisely in these terms that Ernesto Grassi has explained the general sense of the rhetorical humanistic tradi-

tion: Ernesto Grassi, *La filosofia dell'umanesimo. Un problema epocale* (Naples: Tempi Moderni, 1988); Ernesto Grassi, *Vico e l'umanesimo* (Milan: Guerini, 1992). A similar characterization of this movement can be found also in other distinguished scholars such as Eugenio Garin or Marc Fumaroli: Eugenio Garin, *L'umanesimo italiano. Filosofia e vita civile nel Rinascimento* (Bari: Laterza, 1965); Marc Fumaroli, *L'âge de l'éloquence. Rhétorique et "res literaria" de la Renaissance au seuil de l'époque classique* (Paris: Albin Michel, 1994).

41. Richard Rorty, "Philosophy as a Transitional Genre," in *The Rorty Reader*, ed. Christopher J. Voparil and Richard J. Bernstein (Malden, MA: Wiley-Blackwell, 2010), 477.
42. Richard Rorty, "Nineteenth-Century Idealism and Twentieth-Century Textualism," in *The Rorty Reader*, ed. Christopher J. Voparil and Richard J. Bernstein (Malden, MA: Wiley-Blackwell, 2010), 132.
43. E.g., Rorty, *Contingency, Irony, and Solidarity*, 81; Rorty, "Nineteenth-Century Idealism and Twentieth-Century Textualism," 139–41, 49.
44. Richard Rorty, "The Humanistic Intellectual: Eleven Theses," in *Philosophy and Social Hope* (London: Penguin Books, 1999), 127–30.
45. Ibid., 127.
46. Rorty, *Contingency, Irony, and Solidarity*, 80; Richard Rorty, "Redemption from Egotism: James and Proust as Spiritual Exercises," in *The Rorty Reader*, ed. Christopher J. Voparil and Richard J. Bernstein (Malden, MA: Wiley-Blackwell, 2010), 392–3.
47. Rorty, "Philosophy as Science, as Metaphor, and as Politics," 18.
48. Rorty, "Ethics without Principles," 82; Rorty, "Redemption from Egotism: James and Proust as Spiritual Exercises," 247.
49. Rorty, *Contingency, Irony, and Solidarity*, 80–1. Cf. Richard Rorty, "Philosophy as a Kind of Writing," in *Consequences of Pragmatism: Essays, 1972–1980* (Minneapolis: University of Minnesota Press, 1982), 92.
50. Rorty, *Contingency, Irony, and Solidarity*, 87.
51. Rorty, "Introduction," in *Objectivity, Relativism, and Truth: Philosophical Papers, Volume 1* (Cambridge and New York: Cambridge University Press, 1991), 14.
52. Giambattista Vico, "Autobiografia," in *Opere*, ed. Fausto Nicolini (Milan and Naples: Riccardo Ricciardi Editore, 1953), 39.
53. Vico cited in: Andrea Battistini, "On the Encyclopedic Structure of the New Science," *New Vico Studies* 12 (1994): 28.
54. Ibid., 39.
55. E.g., Giambattista Vico, "Dell'antichissima sapienza italica," in *Opere*, ed. Fausto Nicolini (Milan and Naples: Riccardo Ricciardi, 1953), 292, 303.

56. Giambattista Vico, "Prinicipi di Scienza Nuova," in *Opere*, ed. Fausto Nicolini (Milan and Naples: Riccardo Ricciardi Editore), par. 497–8; Vico, "Autobiografia," 17–18.
57. E.g. Cicero, *On the Ideal Orator (De Oratore)*, trans. James M. May and Jakob Wisse (New York: Oxford University Press, 2001), 2.102; Quintilian, *Institutio Oratoria*, 1.2.30, 6.2.29–31.
58. Rorty, *Contingency, Irony, and Solidarity*, xvi, cf. 93.
59. Richard Rorty, "Human Rights, Rationality, and Sentimentality," in *Truth and Progress: Philosophical Papers, Volume 3* (Cambridge: Cambridge University Press, 1998), 176.
60. Those who aspire to become good orators and politicians should be "reading and listening to everything, and busying themselves with every fitting pursuit and with general culture." Cicero, *On the Ideal Orator*, 1.256, see also 1.18, 3.72. Cf. Rorty, *Philosophy and the Mirror of Nature*, 360.
61. Arendt, "The Crisis in Culture," 226.
62. E.g. Rorty, "Feminism and Pragmatism," 220; Richard Rorty, "Professionalized Philosophy and Transcendentalist Culture," in *Consequences of Pragmatism: Essays, 1972–1980* (Minneapolis: University of Minnesota Press, 1982), 66.
63. Danisch, "The Absence of Rhetorical Theory in Richard Rorty's Linguistic Pragmatism," 162.
64. Rorty, *Contingency, Irony, and Solidarity*, xv. Cf. Rorty, "Trotsky and the Wild Orchids," 6–8, 13.
65. Keith Topper, "Richard Rorty, Liberalism and the Politics of Redescription," *The American Political Science Review* 89 (1995): 955.
66. Cf. Curtis, *Defending Rorty*, 101.
67. Rorty, *Contingency, Irony, and Solidarity*, xiii–xiv.
68. Ibid., xv. Cf. Rorty, "The Humanistic Intellectual: Eleven Theses," 127–8.
69. Rorty, *Contingency, Irony, and Solidarity*, 97.
70. Rorty, Nystrom, and Puckett, *Against Bosses, Against Oligarchies*, 62–3.
71. Rorty, *Contingency, Irony, and Solidarity*, 88.
72. E.g., Rorty, "Introduction," 13; Richard Rorty, "Priority of Democracy to Philosophy," in *Objectivity, Relativism, and Truth: Philosophical Papers, Volume 1* (Cambridge and New York: Cambridge University Press, 1991), 182.
73. Rorty, *Contingency, Irony, and Solidarity*, xii, 84ff., 142, 198; Richard Rorty, "Pragmatism as Romantic Polytheism," in *Philosophy as Cultural Politics: Philosophical Papers, Volume 4* (Cambridge and New York: Cambridge University Press, 2007), 29, 40; Richard Rorty, "Moral Identity and Private Autonomy: The Case of Foucault," in *Essays on*

Heidegger and Others: Philosophical Papers, Volume 2 (Cambridge and New York: Cambridge University Press, 1991), 196–7.
74. As Rorty says on one occasion, "we need a constant supply of wild-eyed visionaries to keep coming up with fresh descriptions" since "practice changes only because there are uncommon men and women who suggest how things might be done differently." Rorty, "Reply to Raymond D. Boisvert," 572.
75. Rorty and Mendieta, *Take Care of Freedom and Truth Will Take Care of Itself*, 50.
76. Richard Rorty, "Truth without Correspondence to Reality," in *Philosophy and Social Hope* (London: Penguin Books, 1999), 34.
77. Rorty, *Contingency, Irony, and Solidarity*, 87.
78. Ibid., xiii–xv; Rorty, "Trotsky and the Wild Orchids," 12–13.
79. Rorty, "Priority of Democracy to Philosophy," 190.
80. Cf. White, *The Ethos of a Late-Modern Citizen*, 107. On Rorty's elitism see: Sheldon S. Wolin, "Democracy in the Discourse of Postmodernism," *Social Research* 57 (1990); Fraser, "Solidarity or Singularity? Richard Rorty between Romanticism and Technocracy."
81. Cf. Curtis, *Defending Rorty*, 96–9.
82. Rorty, *Contingency, Irony, and Solidarity*, 73–4.
83. Ibid., 90
84. Ibid., 73–4.
85. Rorty, "The Humanistic Intellectual: Eleven Theses," 127–8. On Rorty's esotericism see: Melvin Rogers, "Rorty's Straussianism; or, Irony against Democracy," *Contemporary Pragmatism* 1 (2004). Despite his concerns about the harm irony could cause to society and its orders, however, Rorty also recommends that "the crust of conventions...should be as superficial as possible" and that "the glue which holds society together... as flexible as possible." Rorty, "Philosophy as Science, as Metaphor, and as Politics," 18. This ambivalence testifies to the conundrum in Rorty's thought on the relationship between change and order, consensus and critique.
86. Rorty, *Contingency, Irony, and Solidarity*, 90.
87. Ibid., 93.
88. Rorty, "Human Rights, Rationality, and Sentimentality," 181.
89. E.g. Richard Rorty, "Postmodernist Bourgeois Liberalism," in *Objectivity, Relativism, and Truth: Philosophical Papers, Volume 1* (Cambridge and New York: Cambridge University Press, 1991), 201; Richard Rorty, "Justice as a Larger Loyalty," in *Philosophy as Cultural Politics: Philosophical Papers, Volume 4* (Cambridge and New York: Cambridge University Press, 2007).

90. Rorty, *Contingency, Irony, and Solidarity*, 48, 60, 84. Rorty's essay "Feminism and Pragmatism" provides one of the most well-elaborated accounts of how, for him, the process through which a society changes its self-image by introducing new vocabularies that come from marginalized groups occurs. Here we can see how Rorty describes the mutual interplay between a rhetoric of difference, necessary for questioning the normal vocabulary of society, and one of consensus, through which the new, extended vocabulary is progressively accepted and normalized. Cf. supra note 13.

91. Rorty, *Philosophy and the Mirror of Nature*, 360. Cf. Voparil, "Taking Other Human Beings Seriously: Rorty's Ethics of Choice and Responsibility," 91.

92. Rorty, *Philosophy and the Mirror of Nature*, 360, 366, 372. This form of practical reason is what, for instance, makes us realize that the expression "corresponds to how things are" is "an automatic compliment paid to successful normal discourse" that cannot be extended to abnormal discourse. The attempt "to extend this compliment to feats of abnormal discourse" therefore is "a lack of tact." Ibid., 372.

93. E.g., Cicero, "Orator," 70 and also 102–6, 108–11, 129–33; Cicero, *On the Ideal Orator*, 3.208ff.; Quintilian, *Institutio Oratoria*, 6.6.11; Isocrate, "Panathenaicus," in *Isocrates, Vol. 2.*, trans. George Norlin (Cambridge, MA: Harvard University Press, 1929), 30.

94. On the importance of *decorum* in Cicero see, for instance: Daniel Kapust, "Cicero on Decorum and the Morality of Rhetoric," *European Journal of Political Theory* 10 (2011); Michael Leff, "Cicero's Pro Murena and the Strong Case for Rhetoric," *Rhetoric & Public Affairs* 1 (1998); Alain Michel, *Les rapports de la rhétorique et de la philosophie dans l'oeuvre de Cicéron. Recherches sur les fondements philosophiques de l'art de persuader* (Louvain and Paris: Peeters, 2003), 130–3, 310–18.

95. E.g., Cicero, *On the Ideal Orator*, 1.12, 16–18, 20–1, 48–70, 160–203, 2.6, 3.54, 72.

96. Cicero also distinguishes between two kinds of discourses: one more adapted for philosophical conversation among friends, which commands a more rational and impassioned style (*sermo*), and another public, aimed at action, interested in concrete questions, emotively charged and with a not-too-complex style (*contentio*). His ideal orator has to be proficient in both. See: Cicero, *De Officiis*, trans. Walter Miller (Cambridge, MA: Harvard University Press, 1997), 1.132.

97. Cicero, *On the Ideal Orator*, 2.18–20.

98. Rorty, *Contingency, Irony, and Solidarity*, 97.

99. Rorty, *Philosophy and the Mirror of Nature*, 366.

100. Rorty's criticism of what he calls the "Foucauldian Left" can be read precisely in this sense: as a reminder to those who think that giving an essential contribution to society occurs by creating more and more sophisticated theories, that in truth they are devoting more to themselves than to society. See e.g., Rorty, "Nineteenth-Century Idealism and Twentieth-Century Textualism," 158. Rorty, "A Spectre Is Haunting the Intellectuals: Derrida on Marx," 220.
101. Cf. Llanera, "Rethinking Nihilism: Rorty Vs. Taylor, Dreyfus and Kelly."
102. Ferrara, "The Unbearable Seriousness of Irony," 83, 99–100; Ernesto Laclau, "Deconstruction, Pragmatism, Hegemony," in *Deconstruction and Pragmatism*, ed. Chantal Mouffe (London and New York: Routledge, 1996), 65; Jean B. Elshtain, *Real Politics: At the Center of Everyday Life* (Baltimore, MD: Johns Hopkins University Press, 1997), 322; Jürgen Habermas, "Richard Rorty's Pragmatic Turn," in *Rorty and His Critics*, ed. Richard Rorty and Robert Brandom (Malden, MA: Blackwell Publishers, 2000), 32–3; Bernstein, "Richard Rorty's Deep Humanism," 25.
103. Topper, "Richard Rorty, Liberalism and the Politics of Redescription," 956, 962. Cf. Rorty, *Contingency, Irony, and Solidarity*, xv, 68.
104. Wolin, "Democracy in the Discourse of Postmodernism," 14.
105. Rorty, *Contingency, Irony, and Solidarity*, 33.
106. Áine Mahon, *The Ironist and the Romantic: Reading Richard Rorty and Stanley Cavell* (London: Bloomsbury, 2014), 133.

CHAPTER 6

Politics as Transcendence and Contingency: Hannah Arendt

6.1 Introduction

After analysing the works of two theorists from opposite poles of the continuum between transcendence and contingency, in this final chapter I move to Hannah Arendt, who steers a middle course between them. Her vision of politics is one that is able to give expression to both dimensions—transcendence and contingency—but in a more balanced way than those of Strauss and Rorty. It is an equilibrium that, in a sense, recalls that of Cicero. Seen from the perspective of the relation between philosophy and politics, however, the position of Arendt is ambiguous. Trained as a philosopher, she came to develop a pointedly critical stance towards the bulk of western philosophy, which she accused of a deep and generalized lack of sensibility towards politics, an entrenched inability to understand it in its proper terms. But at the same time, her reflections on politics are clearly shaped by a constant engagement with major figures in philosophy (for instance, Socrates, Plato, Aristotle, Kant, Nietzsche, Marx, or Heidegger). Nevertheless, such engagement has been for the most part essentially critical. When it comes to politics, among the major figures of the tradition of philosophy Arendt sets aside but two: Socrates and Kant (even if a quite peculiar Kant). Her inspiration to think about politics came more from actual political experiences—the Greek *polis*, the Roman republic, or the American Revolution—or from thinkers who better fit the

© The Author(s) 2018
G. Ballacci, *Political Theory between Philosophy and Rhetoric*, Rhetoric, Politics and Society,
https://doi.org/10.1057/978-1-349-95293-9_6

category of political theorists, rather than philosophers, such as Machiavelli or Montesquieu.

In this sense, then, we may say that Arendt's refusal to be included among the ranks of the 'philosophers', or the 'professional thinkers', is not an exaggeration, or a provocative pose. It is something deeper, as it concerns her identity, her answer to what she considered the very important question: *who are you?*[1] For someone like her, who devoted a whole life to the study of what she considered probably the most ennobling among human activities, politics, it should not have been a secondary question to be seen as a political theorist, rather than a member of a philosophic tradition she considered burdened by a long history of incomprehension towards this activity. One would have a hard time finding in the history of philosophy a pronouncement on the value of politics as passionate as the one she makes in the last pages of her book *On Revolution*. There, she recalls those "famous and frightening lines" that the chorus utters in Sophocles' tragedy, *Oedipus at Colonus*, and then the answer of the legendary founder and spokesman of Athens: Theseus. For him only "the *polis*, the space of men's free deeds and living words, which could endow life with splendour" enables ordinary men to bear life's burden.[2] Declarations of the same tenor, of course, can be found coming from politicians, as in the notorious speech Pericles gave to his fellow-citizens, or in some excerpts of Thomas Jefferson or of other founding fathers. But if we want to find such exaltations of the *vita activa* in intellectuals, if not philosophers strictly speaking, a good place to look is the rhetorical humanistic tradition we have explored in this book: to Roman thinkers such as Cicero, or Quintilian, for instance; or to humanists such as Brunetto Latini, Coluccio Salutati, or Leonardo Bruni, who centuries later would praise the *vita activa* on similar terms. Indeed it is not by chance that that when in one occasion Arendt tried to epitomize the existential value of politics, she referred precisely to the fundamental Roman concept of *humanitas*, which for her expresses "the very height of humanness" that can be only reached throwing oneself into the "venture into the public realm."[3]

As we know, these Roman and humanistic authors have rarely been included among the lists of the serious, systematic, 'authentic' philosophers. And it seems that this view was to some extent shared by Arendt herself, who on one occasion came to speak of a "strange lack of philosophic talent" characterizing Roman culture, or in another of Augustine as the only real philosopher it was able to produce.[4] In this aspect Arendt is pretty much in line with the tradition of philosophy in which she was educated, and specifically with the German tradition of Hegel or Heidegger, who see in Roman philosophy a mere reproduction, hollow, and even unfaithful, of Greek thought (a kind of judgment that Heidegger extended to the humanists).[5] By contrast, in terms of political capacity, her admiration for the Romans was great. For Arendt they are "perhaps the most political people we have known", and to them she attributed a "political genius."[6] In this sense, we can say that the Roman political experience is undoubtedly an important source of inspiration, even though maybe not as crucial as the Greek *polis*, in her attempt to recover a more authentic meaning of politics. Even more so, if we consider the obvious relationships between Rome and two political thinkers Arendt admired greatly: Machiavelli and Montesquieu.

Despite the evidence of this influence, however, the relation between Arendt and Roman culture and politics has been quite neglected by scholars working on her. There are of course numerous republican readings of her work. But these works tend to underline and analyse Arendt's republican traits, remaining inside the limits of her thought. They don't usually expand the analysis to engage directly with the similarities (and differences) between Arendt and Roman thinkers, such as Cicero or Quintilian, and in particular they don't touch on one central element of their political conception: rhetoric.[7]

But rhetoric is important not only for Roman political thought and Roman political practice. It was central also for Greek political thought and its practice. In particular it was a central component of the *polis*; an historical example that, as is well known, is for Arendt of very great importance. Both the Greek *polis* and the Roman *res publica* represent two key sources of inspiration for Arendt in her lifelong attempt to recover a more authentic meaning to politics.[8] Similarly to Strauss, this meaning is for her concealed under a whole conceptual framework built by the tradition of philosophy through the centuries. This is why she believes that to reconstruct such meaning requires an enormous work of 'deconstruction'[9] of that tradition and an original reflection on those rare historic experiences, in which the 'miracle of politics' has occurred. Now, because rhetoric is a central element in both the Greek *polis* and the Roman *res publica* it is not surprising that in her writings we find many elements that testify to a clear rhetorical sensibility. Indeed, we can definitely agree with David Marshall who has written that Arendt's general "conception of politics—a conception that turned not on power, traditionally conceived, but on debate—

was essentially rhetorical."[10] A proximity between Arendt and ancient rhetoric in effect has been detected by more than one of her scholars, despite the fact that we cannot find many references in her works to that tradition. As these scholars have argued, this proximity has to do first of all with the scope of judgment and persuasion in a context such as the political domain, which is characterized by a plurality of partially incompatible points of view.[11] For instance, Marshall has convincingly argued that Aristotle's *Rhetoric* has been an important source for Arendt to develop her account of judgment.[12] And judgment, as we know is a topic that has come to play a very important role in her understanding of politics. In this respect it is noteworthy that for Arendt Aristotle's *Rhetoric* is a text that "belongs to his political writings no less than his Ethics."[13]

Now, if rhetoric can be considered the 'other' side of philosophy—the reclamation of practice over theory—then it is not surprising that Arendt's theory of politics could have many points of intersection with it. As I hope to demonstrate in this chapter, these points bring to the fore a very significant proximity to the conception of politics, which is understood in both cases as an activity characterized by contingency and an irreducible pluralism and thus inevitably resting on judgment and persuasion. But if we expand our comparison to include Cicero then we can see that the affinity between Arendt and a certain tradition of rhetoric go beyond the recognition of the importance of contingency and plurality in politics. It involves also the recognition of its transcendent dimension. Arendt's conception of politics is, in effect, characterized by a humanism that is strongly evocative of Cicero. For her, politics is the most ennobling activity, since it permits the transcendence of human finitude by leaving a legacy that can aspire to an immortal status. In this sense, then, what is remarkable is that her analysis highlights not only the necessity of judgment and persuasion, but also that of distinction and excellence. The similarity with Cicero (and above all, the Cicero that emerges from his rhetorical writings) has to do essentially with the attempt to combine this agonistic and existential dimension of politics with the deliberative and discursive one: or more specifically, with the idea that the greatness of politics consists in letting the former be expressed through the latter. My aim in this chapter then is to unfold the rhetorical character of Arendt's political theory: first, by overviewing her political critique against philosophy; second, by analysing how her view of politics underscores the interconnection between the contingent and the transcendent; and finally by exposing the central role in that idea of judgment and persuasion.

6.2 Arendt's Political Critique of Philosophy

Without running the risk of oversimplification, we may say that Arendt's polemical attitude towards philosophy consists essentially in a critique of its incapacity to conjugate thinking and acting, or philosophy and politics, theory and practice. She is perfectly aware of the intrinsic tension between these two poles; to the point that we may even consider the attempt to make sense of it the key motive of her whole intellectual life.[14] Reflecting on thinking, Arendt has realized how that activity—the silent dialogue within the self—requires solitude, an estrangement from our involvement in the common world perceived by senses. But on the other hand, she has also realized that thinking, even if it deals only with general and abstract ideas, can only emerge from the particular, concrete experiences we have in the common world. Thus in order not to get lost in empty abstractions, the thinker needs always to come back to what she calls the "redeeming grace of companionship" of others.[15] The great critique she makes of the bulk of western philosophy therefore is not that that tradition has always diagnosed and emphasized the tension between thought and practice. Rather, the problem for her is that philosophy has transformed that tension into an almost irreconcilable opposition, making it impossible to establish a more constructive relation between thinking and acting:

> Our tradition of political thought began when Plato discovered that it is somehow inherent in the philosophical experience to turn away from the common world of human affairs; it ended when nothing was left of this experience but the opposition of thinking and acting, which, depriving thought of reality and action of sense, makes both meaningless.[16]

A judgment like this can appear peremptory, to say the least. But it definitely expresses a belief deeply rooted in Arendt.[17] In *On Revolution*, to mention another example, she refers to the opportunity to reconcile the age-old rift between thinking and acting—which originated in the aftermath of the Periclean Age, when "the men of action and the men of thought parted company and thinking began to emancipate itself altogether from reality"—as the "great hope of the modern age." It is a hope however, that according to her remained completely unfulfilled, precisely because of "the enormous strength and resiliency of our tradition of thought."[18] In Arendt's account, at the origins of this deep chasm between philosophy and politics is the wrong answer Plato gave to a concrete and deeply shocking circumstance: the execution of Socrates at the hands of a society in the process of political breakdown.[19] It is in this context, indeed, that according to her Plato came to develop a definitive distrust towards the chaotic and always changing political realm and, in particular, towards persuasion—the typical way of conducting political affairs in the *polis*—as a reliable method to implement reason there.[20] It is from an urgency to protect the life of the philosopher in the *polis* that, for Arendt, Plato arrived at suggesting what she calls a "tyranny of reason"[21]: a theory of politics obtained by transforming the purely philosophic experience of the contemplation of the ideas—a solitary, silent, and perfectly motionless act—into an instrument of command in the political realm, where normally things are conducted through dialogue among a plurality and in a constant flux of contingencies. In order to undertake this operation, Arendt argues, Plato resorted to an analogy: ideas were transformed from objects of contemplation into standards for practice, in the same way the craftsman uses an ideal model to produce his objects. The force of coercion in this ideal model lies precisely in its transcendent and absolute status: the philosopher-king, as the craftsman, applies ideas as unquestionable standards for action, because they are transcendent, untouched by the mutability of practice and outside the bounds of reasonable discussion. But this Platonic solution is for Arendt not only intrinsically authoritarian and antipolitical, but also one that reifies the dichotomy between knowing and acting. First of all, such a solution is based an undemocratic division between an intellectual elite, which knows and thus can decide alone, and an unwise and dull multitude that merely executes commands. Second, it brings in the free realm of politics the inevitable dose of violence, which is intrinsic to production (*poiesis*), supplanting dialogue and persuasion with a means–ends logic.[22] What for her is the political faculty par excellence, judgment—a faculty which is quintessentially political since it requires a dialogue among different points of view[23]—is reduced to a mechanical subsuming of the particular case into general laws generated in the abstract.

Arendt's critique of Platonic political philosophy, trenchant as it may be, is emblematic of her position towards the bulk of western philosophy. According to her, following the example of Plato, philosophy has always shown a diffuse reluctance to deal with politics on its own terms. As she writes:

> Escape from the frailty of human affairs into the solidity of quiet and order has in fact so much to recommend it that the greater part of political

philosophy since Plato could easily be interpreted as various attempts to find theoretical foundations and practical ways for an escape from politics altogether. The hallmark of all such escapes is the concept of rule, that is, the notion that men can lawfully and politically live together only when some are entitled to command and the others forced to obey.[24]

For Arendt, dealing with politics in its own terms means, in the first place, taking it as a *praxis* whose value lies within itself, rather than as an instrument to reach some higher goals. Hence for her trying to eliminate some of its essential, even if sometimes uneasy, features, is tantamount to denying its very essence. In her approach to politics Arendt has always strived to come to terms with what she considers its basic conditions, *in primis* plurality and natality. If politics is understood as the free interaction among a plurality of individuals with different perspectives on the world and each of whom is endowed with the capacity to start a new course of action, then contingency and difference end up inevitably being two of its basic features. From here, she concludes that dialogue and persuasion—as a way to deal with this difference of opinions—and judgment—as a capacity to deal with contingency—are two pillars on which politics should rest.[25] It is precisely this non-instrumental idea of politics that identifies in judgment and persuasion the only possible ways to practice it without destroying its essential contingent and pluralist dimension, a fundamental point Arendt shares with the political-rhetorical conceptions of Aristotle, Cicero, Quintilian, and the humanists.

6.3 Politics Between Contingency and Transcendence

Starting from the most general aspect—what we can call the ontological and epistemological levels—the proximity between this tradition of rhetoric and Arendt is revealed by the fact that, against philosophy, in both cases the privileged link between appearance and politics (and of rhetoric itself) is not asserted as a deficiency to be overcome, but as an inescapable matter of fact. Arendt recognizes explicitly appearance as the proper dimension of politics in various occasions, and with a quite clear polemical intention against philosophy's usual condemnation of appearance as that which conceals the real essence of things.[26] For her "in politics, more than anywhere else, we have no possibility of distinguishing between being and appearance. In the realm of human affairs, being and appearance are indeed one and the same."[27] This reversal is a direct consequence of the fundamental condition of plurality reigning in the public realm, which in her view implies a sort of dismantling of the univocality of the essence of things constituting reality. Differently from the other manifestations of human action, the reality of politics can only emerge amidst plurality, as it is inevitably (and paradoxically) dependent on the public space it engenders. Indeed if the activity of labour, which makes possible the reproduction of the vital cycle, is anonymous, and that of work always subordinated to the final product which outlasts it, political activity depends inevitably on a public space where "everything that appears...can be seen and heard by everybody and has the widest possible publicity."[28] Because the speeches and deeds of which politics is made leave behind nothing tangible and durable, they can only become 'meaningful', and in this particular sense 'real', when perceived by a plurality in a public space. Political reality, therefore, is a reality that exists only *inter homines esse*, only at the level of appearance.[29]

As we have seen, in the tradition of rhetoric of Isocrates, Aristotle, Cicero, or Quintilian, the level of appearance is claimed without complexes as the proper level of politics. On the opposite side, Plato's original attack on rhetoric, on behalf of philosophy, is motivated precisely by the argument that, according to him, the former can act only superficially, working with what seems but is not, rather than with what really is. This is why in the *Gorgias* he compares rhetoric with cosmetics and sustains the view that it can be no more than a simulacrum of justice and an appearance of the real science of politics. Faced with this charge, the strategies of Isocrates, Aristotle, Cicero, and Quintilian consist not in denying the privileged dwelling of rhetoric in the realm of appearance, but rather in recomposing the Platonic separation between appearance and essence and denying the equivalence between the dyad surface/essence and that of falsity/truth. We saw how Aristotle claims, as the proper dimension of rhetoric and politics, the probable (or the verisimilar, *eikos*) rather than the truthful; but he underlines at the same time that these two conditions share the same nature and are graspable by the same faculty. The same kind of argument can be found also in Quintilian, who argues that what is to be expected from an orator is to expose a plausible argument, rather than the truth, because in the realm of human affairs "there are many true things that are not very credible, and false things are frequently plausible."[30] And the same view could be found again at the very end of this tradition: in Giambattista Vico's criticism against Cartesianism. For Vico indeed, Descartes's *mathesis universalis*, with its exclusive emphasis on truth, is unfit for the sphere of human affairs—marked by contingency and freedom—and risks undermining the capacity to grasp the verisimilar and to understand the intricacies of the human mind.[31]

Now, to identify the domain of political action with the level of appearance entails of course recognizing as well that contingency is its normal state of affairs. In the case of Arendt, indeed, it is absolutely clear how in all her descriptions of human action she always strives to emphasize this feature: the uniqueness and novelty that every action bears. As a result of the basic condition of 'natality'—the fact that every human being is endowed with a capacity to start a completely new course of actions, to perpetually escape "even the most reified order of presence"[32]—to Arendt human action appears as a sort of "miracle...the infinite improbability which occurs regularly."[33] If we add to the condition of natality that of plurality, then, we can see why according to her, human interaction is inevitably unlimited in its developments and unpredictable, and thus always characterized by a deeply contingent dimension.[34] But political action means for Arendt, as it is in the tradition of rhetoric, above all speech.[35] The consequence is that, in both cases, emphasizing the contingent nature of action is the effect of a recognition of the political realm as a space inevitably populated by an irreducible plurality of opinions. Such a plurality of points of view is of course the very assumption upon which the practice of rhetoric is based: the idea that in political matters it is always possible for every argument to argue *in utramque partem* (which means that disagreement is the very premise on which rhetoric is based). Arendt, on the other hand, not only fully accepts such an assumption but reclaims the plurality of opinions as a vital feature of political life rather than a flawed condition. Thus for her every attempt to supersede once and for all this plurality of opinions by the implementation of scientific truth, as a certain philosophical idea of politics aspires to do, is tantamount to destroying the very essence of politics.

In her deconstructive reading of the tradition of philosophy, Arendt traces the dichotomy between truth and opinion back to Plato's deep scepticism about the world of the *polis*. In her essay "Philosophy and Politics", she explains that the notion of *doxa*, commonly translated as opinion, originally meant for Socrates and his fellow citizens the articulation through discourse of the world as it appears to each of us, from his or her own particular perspective (*doxai* derives from *to dokei moi*, appears to me). Everyone who enters into the public realm has inevitably a particular stance on it, a particular opinion on the events that appear in there.[36] In opposing opinions to truth, she argues, Plato drew the most anti-Socratic conclusion he could have drawn: because what Socrates wanted was not to definitely transcend opinions and install a dictatorship of truth, but rather to help his fellow citizens to find the truth present in their opinions in order to make the city more truthful. For Socrates a plurality of opinions was something normal: it is this plurality of *logoi* that constitutes the human world, insofar as humans live together as a speaking community.[37]

In agreement with Socrates, for Arendt opinions are an essential element in a public sphere marked by the condition of plurality. It is in the very nature of public affairs not to have the same evidence as rational truths, because they concern a common world—the *inter-est*, what is in-between human beings, at the same time unifying and connecting them—that is in a constant flux of transformation (because of the condition of natality) and that is perceived and judged from a plurality of points of view. It is for this reason that political affairs always call for a debate between different opinions; because differently from 'rational truths' that can be reached by the individual alone through logical thinking, 'political truths' are disputable and therefore invite thinking to exit the self and confront with others. This plurality of points of view has for Arendt a sort of ontological role for the political phenomena, since "only where things can be seen by many and in a variety of aspects without changing their identity... can worldly reality truly and reliably appear."[38] But this plurality has to be recomposed through of dialogue and persuasion, in order to move from strictly personal opinions to shared, and however always relative, 'truths'. As she writes:

> No opinion is self-evident. In matters of opinion, but not in matters of truth, our thinking is truly discursive, running, as it were, from place to place, from one part of the world to another, through all kinds of conflicting views, until it finally ascends from these particularities to some impartial generality.[39]

The validity of opinions "depends on free agreement and consent; they are arrived at by discursive, representative thinking; and they are communicated by means of persuasion and dissuasion."[40] But for Arendt this "unending discourse among men" (as the other great figure together with Socrates and Kant that inspired her in this respect, G. E. Lessing, called it) is not only intrinsic to the nature of politics, but also very positive because strictly related to freedom.[41] Because "opinions", as she explains, "will rise wherever men communicate freely with one another and have the right to make their views public."[42] Here, the connection with ancient rhetoric is made explicit. Arendt recalls how for the Greeks the creation of the *polis* as a space where violence was banned in favour of dialogue was something to be immensely proud of; it was the institution marking the difference between them and the barbarians. This is why they considered persuasion the "specifically political form of speech" and rhetoric "the truly political art."[43]

If for Arendt opinions have a strong connection to freedom through the practice of dialogue, truth is for her something potentially rather despotic. Persuasion, she notes, is not only different from physical coercion, but, as the Greek philosophers knew well, also from another and subtler but no less compelling form of coercion: that exerted by truth.[44] Philosophic truth, at least according to Plato or Aristotle, is something beyond speech and demonstration; a self-evident object of contemplation, whose cogency compels rather than convinces (at least for those able to see it). It is the speechless result with which philosophical argumentation carried out through dialectic culminates. In this respect, in "Philosophy and Politics" Arendt underlines the rigid dichotomy that Plato established between dialectic, the philosophic way of arguing between the few, based on rationality and whose ultimate aim is truth, and rhetoric, the political way of speaking with the multitude, based on opinions and aiming at persuasion. It is a division, that according to her Aristotle considered a matter of course,[45] and that after them has generally been accepted by the philosophic tradition at large, which as we have seen generally opposes the dialectical-philosophical discourse to the rhetorical-political one, associating the latter with manipulation and lack of critical insight.

In Arendt's reading, this polarity originates in the fact that for Plato the multitude is irremediably incapable of proceeding along the rational path of dialectical argumentation and thus is always doomed to endure dogmatic beliefs about issues that, for a philosopher, can only be the object of an ongoing process of questioning. It is for this reason, she concludes, that Plato came to think that the only way to address the multitude is through rhetoric: because rhetoric, differently from dialectic, does not convince through the compelling evidence of rationality but rather resorts to extra-rational ways of persuasion.[46] However, for Arendt the Platonic opposition between rhetoric and opinions, on the one hand, and dialectic and truth, on the other, has a very different meaning if seen from a political perspective. Because, politically speaking, truth introduces into the public sphere an element of coercion that goes against that openness to a free interchange of ideas, which is its necessary condition, and even more, the *raison d'être* of politics. It is for this reason that she came to affirm that "it may be in the nature of the political realm to be at war with truth in all its forms," because[47]:

> the modes of thought and communication that deal with truth, if seen from a political perspective, are necessarily domineering; they don't take into account other people's opinions, and taking these into account is the hallmark of all strictly political thinking.[48]

When someone affirms a truth, she doesn't want to start a dialogue, but to conclude it. The validity reclaimed by truth is indeed indisputable. It doesn't admit replies. On the contrary, for Arendt it belongs to the very essence of the different 'truths' affirmed in the public sphere to be relative, dependent on one's own position in the world, on one's own relationship with the other members who populate the public sphere. The urge to substitute truth for opinion, then, for Arendt risks blocking precisely the process that leads to the formation of the only 'truth' admissible in the realm of human affairs—relative and temporary 'truths'—leaving therefore the individual devoid of any kind of beliefs. This is why she accused Plato of having distorted the great lesson Socrates left us: that the task of the philosopher is to make opinions more truthful, not to eliminate them once and for all.

> Only through knowing what appears to me—only to me, and therefore remaining forever related to my own existence—can I ever understand truth. Absolute truth, which would be the same for all men and therefore unrelated, independent of each man's existence, cannot exist for mortals. For mortals the important thing is to make doxa truthful, to see in every doxa truth and to speak in such a way that the truth of one's own opinion reveals itself to oneself and to others.[49]

It is evident then that Arendt and the rhetorical humanistic tradition share a very important point about the fundamental question of the political value of truth. This, indeed, didn't escape Arendt. In "Crisis in Culture", crucially one of her writings where she deals explicitly with the question of judgment, commenting on this topic she cites a passage from Cicero's

Tusculanae disputationes (1.39–40) when he wrote "errare, mehercule malo cum Platone...quam cum istis (sc. Pythagoraeis) vera sentire"; a passage for which she gives the following translation: "I prefer before heaven to go astray with Plato rather than hold true views with his opponents."[50] Her comments on this sentence, which she defines as "a very bold, even an outrageously bold statement, especially because it concerns truth", explains in the best possible way what this proximity between Arendt and the rhetorical tradition is all about:

> What Cicero in fact says is that for the true humanist neither the verities of the scientist nor the truth of the philosopher nor the beauty of the artist can be absolutes; the humanist, because he is not a specialist, exerts a faculty of judgment and taste which is beyond the coercion which each speciality imposes upon us. This Roman *humanitas* applied to men who were free in every respect, for whom the question of freedom, of not being coerced, was the decisive one even in philosophy, even in science, even in the arts.[51]

It is clear then on this very important question among Cicero, the rhetor and the humanist, rather than with Plato, the philosopher, Arendt takes side with the former. If, as I said, for her politics also has a fundamental, transcending dimension, such a dimension cannot be understood as a striving for some eternal truths. Nonetheless, Arendt's position cannot be equated to the relativist stance of the radical defenders of rhetoric such as the sophists. On the contrary, in "Truth and Politics"—one of the texts where she clearly warns of the risk truth poses to political freedom—she also clarifies that truth has a crucial function, which she describes metaphorically as that of "the ground on which we stand and the sky that stretches above us."[52] In a sense, thus, this demonstrates that Arendt, as Cicero, forges a middle ground between the philosophical absolutism of Plato and the radical relativism of the sophists. If for Cicero the pursuit of truth through philosophy has a fundamental value in orienting and expanding the limits of political action, by a constant dialectical interaction between theory and practice under the guide of rhetoric, for Arendt it is truth that sets the limits within which political action can develop and that must therefore be respected in order to preserve it.

It is in that same essay furthermore that Arendt introduces another very important distinction, which is indispensable for a full account of her views on the value of truth in politics and which confirms, I think, the proximity with the rhetorical view of Aristotle and Cicero. This is the distinction she establishes between 'factual' and 'rational' or 'philosophical' truth. Differently from the latter, the former is for Arendt "political by nature" as it "always related to other people; it concerns events and circumstances in which many are involved; it is established by witnesses and depends upon testimony; it exists only to the extent that it is spoken about."[53] That is, factual truths, being related to social events—events produced through human interaction—are for her not only compatible with a plurality of opinions and dialogue but, rather, their very condition.[54] Indeed, without a certain level of agreement on some factual truths—however contestable and provisional they may be—it is impossible to establish that 'common world' which creates the ontological conditions for the development of politics. The loss of such a common, intersubjective world and the consequent world alienation was for Arendt the most important precondition for the advent of totalitarian movements and at the same time one of their most pernicious effects.[55] Arendt's trenchant position on the despotic character of truth, then, has to be qualified in some key aspects. Without denying the force of her rebuke against the employment of the category of absolute truth in the public sphere, she realizes that philosophical and factual truths cannot be dispensed with. Nevertheless such distinctions and nuances don't dispel all the doubts. Just to mention one problem: there is the obvious fact that to distinguish between facts and interpretations is very complicated. Arendt indeed concludes her essay by remarking that "a commitment even to factual truth" may represent "an anti-political attitude."[56]

A further important element in clarifying her position is another distinction she makes and whose value in her thought, as Dana Villa has pointed out, is difficult to overestimate.[57] I am talking about the distinction she takes from Kant, between truth and meaning, to which corresponds that between the intellect and knowing (*Verstand*), on the one hand, and reason and thinking (*Vernunft*), on the other. The faculty of knowing belongs to the intellect and is the one that pursues truth, asking about the 'evidence' of what our senses perceive, or about the logical conclusions our rationality produces. Once it has reached that 'evidence', a 'truth', it stops. The faculty of thinking, instead, belongs to reason and is what brings the individual to keep questioning the meaning of the world without being ever able to give final conclusions; it is what poses those 'unanswerable questions' that it is in the very essence of human being to pose.[58] This distinction recalls that between the natural sciences and the human sciences (*Geisteswissenschaft* and *Naturwissenschaft*), of which Vico is one of the forefathers.[59] In Arendt the distinction is fundamental because through it she can sustain her idea of politics as a very substantial activity—indeed, the noblest human activity—even if not subjected to absolute truths. Politics is one of those fundamental activities (along with philosophy and art) through which human beings try to escape to the blind automatisms of nature and give sense to the world. Its peculiarity (and its strength) consists in the fact that in politics this search for meaning becomes in the most evident sense a collective effort, that is, it becomes public.[60]

In this sense then, if Arendt rejects submitting politics to the coercion of absolute Truth and of any kind of teleological logic, we cannot conclude that for her politics is completely unprincipled. On the contrary, political principles play a crucial role for her in inspiring and leading political activity. But in defending the role of principles in politics she is very careful to make compatible such a leading and inspiring role with the preservation of political freedom. She refers to Montesquieu's idea of 'principles of action', as fundamental beliefs that don't "operate from within the self as motives do", but that "inspire...from without." These are principles that dwell outside the political realm and transcend its concrete manifestations.[61] Their value is universal, so that they can be "repeated again and again". Their concrete meaning becomes "fully manifest only in the performing act itself," to the extent that similar to rhetorical *topoi*, they are "much too general to prescribe particular goals."[62] This is how for Arendt political principles can lead and inspire action but without fully pre-determining it: on the one hand, their presence avoids making of politics an utterly unprincipled and unethical form of action,[63] and on the other, their nature allow us to preserve politics as one of those fundamental activities through which humans are freed to endow meaning to the world. Their political character is determined furthermore by the fact that the endeavour to give meaning to the world through them is a collective one. As suggested by Montesquieu, to different regimes correspond different political principles: virtue for republics, moderation in aristocracies, freedom for the *polis* (or also in corrupted regimes: fear and suspicion in tyrannies, etc.). These are political principles because they are standards shared by a collectivity and used to regulate its common affairs.[64]

At this general level, we can see that the Arendtian account of politics resembles quite precisely the description we get from the rhetorical humanistic tradition. In both cases, politics is approached not from the point of view of absolute standards and theoretical knowledge, but rather from its interior, we can say, that is, from the way in which it is commonly and contingently experienced. In both cases, nonetheless, this doesn't entail renouncing altogether the idea of politics as a normative endeavour. Principles do have a role, but their role has to be understood always in relation to a concrete manifestation through action. The transcending dimension of politics then manifests itself through a performative search for excellence. This is why Arendt's approach to politics has been often labelled by her scholars as phenomenological, or poetic. It is an approach "guided by a desire to recover not concepts, but a certain way of being-in-the-world" and to protect its existential, political, and ethical value by the constant threat of "the philosophical/human-all-too-human desire to escape its contingency and groundlessness and find a more stable alternative."[65] Something similar could certainly be said about the rhetorical humanistic tradition. In both cases, politics is seen as a communicative interaction among a plurality over some of the most important things of the community, which is conducted by appealing not to indisputable truths, but rather to a multiplicity of relative and contingent (even though sometimes very deep rooted) opinions and beliefs. This is why in both cases the practice of dialogue and the exercise of judgment acquire such an important role. They are, indeed, the only possible ways we have to deal with contingency and the striving for transcendence, without resorting to authoritarian solutions.

The Arendtian view of the difference between truth and meaning, the importance of opinions and beliefs, is in effect in line with the understanding of rhetoric by Aristotle or Cicero. According to this tradition there is a clear link between the plurality of opinions, persuasion, and freedom. This results not only from the obvious fact that the art of persuasion can thrive only under the condition that political affairs are conducted through dialogue and consent rather than violence[66]; but also because the persuasion endorsed by them is of a kind considered authentic only if the argument proposed by the speaker can find the assent of the listeners, through the active participation of their judgment. Because of the prevalence of the verisimilar in the public sphere, for Arendt and the tradition of rhetoric, the practice of common deliberation and persuasion is crucial to guaranteeing political freedom. In this respect, it is telling that Arendt cites as a paradigmatic example of a deliberative body the Senate of the United States as conceived by the Founding Fathers,[67] that is, an institution deeply inspired by the example of the Roman Republic, probably the epoch where the art of rhetoric reached its climax. This deliberative body for

Arendt produces the kind of dialogical reason that—differently from the divinely informed reason or the reason of the philosophers—is compatible with the exercise of politics because, as she writes: "[s]ince opinions are formed and tested in a process of exchange of opinion against opinion, their differences can be mediated only by passing them through the medium of a body of men, chosen for the purpose."[68]

6.4 Politics as Judgment and Persuasion

This understanding of politics—as a transcending endeavour to endow meaning which occurs in the contingent domain of plurality—highlights two fundamental dimensions of judgment. The first one has to do with the question of how to manage such contingency: that is, how to take decisions in every circumstance. The second, instead, has to do with the creation and interpretation of those transcending meanings, or principles, that politics tries to embody, and with the discernment of particular events as a manifestation of them. Both dimensions appear clearly in Arendt and rhetoric.

As we know, the question of judgment in Arendt has attracted increasing attention among Arendt scholars in recent years.[69] This is not surprising, because judgment is a faculty that operates at the crossroad of the two domains which interested her most—thinking and acting—and whose combination makes politics possible. As the capacity to link the general with the particular, judgment is crucial in establishing a connection between thinking and acting. For Arendt it is "one of the fundamental abilities of man as a political being insofar as it enables him to orient himself in the public realm, in the common world."[70] The event of totalitarianism, and in particular the trial of Eichmann, were crucial for Arendt to realize the importance of this faculty. In her analysis, the deep crisis of modernity that prepared the conditions to make this event possible has two main dimensions: on the one hand, it was a cultural crisis. It was the crisis caused by the fact that, in a formulation by Tocqueville that Arendt cites, "the past has ceased to throw its light upon the future and the mind of man wanders in obscurity."[71] On the other hand, it was a political crisis, the crisis caused by the disappearance of the common world and thus of the conditions to act politically, which for Arendt means also taking responsibility for this common world.[72]

Arendt's reflections on this topic in effect develops on two levels: that of the history of ideas and that of actual politics. In regard to the latter aspect, the case of Eichmann is emblematic as it shows what dire consequences could come from a failure in judging.[73] In regard to the former, for Arendt a very telling aspect is the prolonged reserve of western philosophy in regard to this faculty, which she considers not only the most distinctive and mysterious human capacity, but also the most political one.[74] These two levels are of course connected, because judgment is the link between thinking and acting. Or better, it is, as Arendt argues, what realizes thinking to the extent that it is the faculty that makes the invisible things and general ideas, which thought engenders, appear in the external world as concrete and particular elements. Now, in light of the chasm that according to Arendt political philosophy has created between these two poles, it is not very strange that a faculty like judgment, which dwells in-between them, didn't receive much attention. She describes judgment as the faculty through which we endow action with meaning, by defining it in terms of general principles of action, such as goodness and badness, beauty and ugliness, rather than truth and falsehood. Judgment therefore must appeal to some kinds of general ideas, but not in the same way as logic does, subsuming the particular under well-defined universal laws. In the long process of figuring out the essence of the mysterious faculty of judgment, Arendt has come to realize that all real judgment is a 'reflective judgment': that is, an operation in which from a given particular, a universal, which is not given beforehand, is generated.[75] Judgment then is in her account a faculty that evaluates particular things, relying on some sort of rules, which however cannot be straightforwardly universalized and thus transformed into absolute rules to follow. Only this understanding could in effect explain the political nature of judgment, by making it compatible with the plurality and freedom of the domain of human affairs. The somehow "elusive" and puzzling character of Arendt's conception of judgment, many scholars have noted, is the consequence of a difficult compromise she was trying to make, by explaining how through this faculty we can find an orientation in the world but at the same time without becoming enslaved to the standards it produces.[76] In other words, we can say that what she has attempted to explain is that judging is a normative act, but one compatible with political freedom: first, because it does not exempt the individual from responsibility to take a position in every particular event (as would happen instead, if judgment operated through a mere subsumption of the particular under the universal); and, second, because it is able to orientate political action, but without compromising its freedom by producing generalizations that escape from the domain of what is debatable.[77]

The tension in judgment between the particular and the general, or also between the contingent and the transcendent, can also be seen from another perspective. As is well known, Arendt's account of judgment emphasizes at the same time two apparent dimensions: on the one hand, a practical dimension connected to the perspective of the acting individual; on the other, a contemplative aspect of judging, which can be seen at work in the judging spectator. The first dimension can be associated with Aristotle's idea of *phronesis*. Here the aim is to act, to take a decision, and the judgment cannot be understood without taking into consideration also the specific interest of the actor. The second dimension, instead, can be associated with Kant's aesthetic theory. It has to do with the spectator who tries to understand the meaning of events that occur in front of her. This twofold dimension of judgment has been underlined by many scholars, talking with different accents of an unresolved tension, or of a productive dichotomy.[78] But according to the reading I am proposing here, these two dimensions are better understood as complementary components of judgment, their relationship being a manifestation of the necessary connection between thinking and acting.

The case of Eichmann helps to understand the reasons for this. For Arendt, the case of Eichmann is emblematic of the incapacity to think and judge for oneself and of the consequences that such an incapacity can have. What she considers more shocking about this individual was his apparent normality: the fact that according to the standards of his society he could be considered a respected and law-abiding citizen. But such a normality didn't prevent him from participating in tremendous crimes. Even more, in line with his apparent normality, Eichmann came to sustain during the trial the view that he lived his life according to the Kantian conception of duty.[79] Here the connection between thinking and acting, between the general and the concrete, emerges clearly. For Arendt, Eichmann was applying a distorted version of the categorical imperative that, nonetheless, maintains something essential in the spirit of that principle: not only the obedience to the law, but the complete coincidence with the will that stands behind the law: in Kant, practical reason, and in Eichmann's mind, the will of the Führer.[80] This for Arendt is a problem of being unable to think and judge autonomously. Thinking can in some cases be paralysing, as it questions the bases upon which we act. But, on the other hand, thinking also serves a crucial role in action, as its questioning capacity puts in suspension the unquestioned conventions handed down by tradition and therefore opens once again the possibility of judging anew. Furthermore, thinking, through an internal dialogue with oneself, creates as a by-product conscience: the necessary internal coherence that is, for Arendt, the necessary condition for acting rightfully.[81] It is in this respect that the necessary connection between theory and practice emerges. Because according to Arendt the great problem of those philosophies, which separate the theoretical from the practical through a distinction between general principles and their application, is that they end up making irrelevant the necessity to think and judge autonomously, as they reduce politics to a mechanical application of universal laws.[82] The difficulty of understanding judgment lies precisely in that it is a capacity that operates according to some general rules, but without getting enslaved to them, because otherwise this would excuse the individual's responsibility to think autonomously.

This is of course a problem that concerns directly practical reason. All the history of practical thinking, indeed, is concerned with the question of how to act rightly without mechanically applying universal laws. Ancient rhetoric, as a part of that tradition, was very much concerned with it. But Arendt has tried to make sense of the problem by looking to Kant's aesthetic theory. In Kant's *Critique of Judgment* indeed she has found not only one of the few philosophic treatments of judgment as an independent faculty, but above all an understanding of it in harmony with her general conception of politics. First of all, it is because for Kant aesthetic judgment is a faculty that operates at the level of appearance, of perceptions, even if it implies a certain level of conceptualization. Second, and more crucially for Arendt, it is because it is a faculty that according to Kant can be fully developed only in the midst of plurality. For these reasons Arendt considers that Kant's *Critique of Judgment* provides an understanding of judgment that does justice to its quintessentially political nature, to the fact of being "one, if not the most, important activity in which this sharing-the-world-with-others comes to pass."[83] Differently from the Critique of Practical Reason, indeed, the emphasis in the Third Critique is not on how to engender general laws as universal and absolute principles for action, but rather on how to express a normative stance on the particular, without denying the fact of plurality and excusing the capacity to think and judge autonomously.[84] What is interesting from the perspective of this book, is that in explaining why the Third Critique could be used as a source to think judgment as a really political faculty, Arendt brings to the fore all the rhetorical dimensions of that work.

Once again, the case of Eichmann provides important clues. For Arendt, the fact that Eichmann was unable to think and judge means also that within him the internal dialogue that produces conscience didn't work properly. What is particular striking in this individual, furthermore, is the great indifference for the positions of others that he revealed. It is an incapacity to take into consideration their points of view, which as Arendt notes, corresponded to an incapacity to express himself.[85] This correspondence is, of course, very telling if analysed from a rhetorical point of view. Because according to this perspective there is always a link between ethos and eloquence. It is here that we reach the most political part of judgment. To judge properly, internal coherence (which for Arendt is the pillar on which ethics rests) is not enough. What judgment also requires is to consider "the presence of others 'in whose place' it must think, whose perspectives it must take into consideration, and without whom it never has the opportunity to operate at all."[86] It is precisely in regard to this politically crucial passage from the internal solitude of thinking to the external company of judgment, that Arendt has found many important suggestions in her rhetorical interpretation of Kant's *Critique of Judgment*. It is there that she has discovered the resources to explain how judgment operates politically by transforming a subjective stance into something general, public, based only on the incomplete and undefined generalities that are possible in the political realm.

A significant part of Kant's investigation about taste can be explained by bearing in mind the maxim *de gustibus non disputandum est*. Taste (like smell) is a completely subjective, private sense. But if we consider the aesthetic meaning of taste—a judgment about beauty, for instance—then we can see its public nature: 'beauty' is a category that for Kant is meaningful only in society, as it is demonstrated by the fact that this kind of judgment always strives for a general acceptance.[87] As Arendt writes, "the chief problem of the Critique of Judgment...became the question of how propositions of judgment could possibly claim, as they indeed do, general agreement."[88] How something that is experienced as a subjective feeling of pleasure can, at the same time, reclaim a universal acceptance? This is the problem Kant tried to resolve in the Third Critique. And here lies the gist of the political meaning of aesthetic judgment and its rhetorical dimension. In aesthetic judgments, the passage from the subjective to the general cannot be made by appealing to well-defined universal concepts, but on a general idea that lacks this kind of completeness. In rhetorical terms this passage cannot be based on indisputable truths, but only on good arguments. To convince someone about our aesthetic judgment—precisely as it happens in politics—requires an effort of (rhetorical) persuasion. Understood in these terms, then, judgment is a faculty that inevitably calls for dialogue and persuasion: it "finds itself always and primarily...in an anticipated communication with others with whom I know I must finally come to some agreement."[89] It is a faculty that calls for an effort of communicability that, lacking the basis of determinate and definite concepts, needs to rely on what we share in the common world of appearance. First, on common sense: understood in Arendt's way as what is common to everyone; and second, on the capacity of imagination to "enlarge our mentality", that is, to detach ourselves from ourselves in order to assume a disinterested standpoint and make room in our thinking for the representations of the perspectives of the others.[90] Moreover and crucially, it is an effort of communication that for Arendt cannot but rest on the conviction that the capacity to judge is diffuse among the people. Indeed, for Kant, to have an aesthetic judgment is not necessary a matter of technical expertise. The same is true, for Arendt, in relation to political opinions. Judgment is a capacity that is present in everyone, even if certainly in different degrees, because it is natural to the human being. In this respect, it is interesting to see that, to support this point, Arendt refers precisely to a passage of a classic text of rhetoric—Cicero's *De oratore*—where he noted "how little difference there is between the learned and the ignorant in judging" and that when someone is less equipped with this capacity, it is very important to rely on common sense.[91]

The link between aesthetics and politics thus has a lot to do with rhetorical persuasion.[92] In commenting on this aspect of Kant's aesthetic theory, Arendt underlines how important, following the tradition of critical thinking started by Socrates, was the question of the public use of reason and its communicability for him. For Kant, she writes, "it is a natural vocation of mankind to communicate and speak one's mind, especially in all matters concerning man as such."[93] So, even if Kant was aware that thinking needs solitude, at the same time it was, for him, fundamental to give a public justification, to "give an account...to be able to say how one came to an opinion, and for what reasons one formed it."[94] But it is only in the field of aesthetics that he was forced to imagine a kind of universal communication that, without the support of universal concepts, has to rely on something intrinsically political as 'common sense' and an extra-rational faculty such as 'imagination'.[95] It is on these rhetorical elements then that Arendt's political reading of the Kantian version of judgment is based. Indeed it is on this basis, that she establishes a connection between this capacity and the Greek concept of *peithein*: convincing and persuading by speech in the *polis*, which the Greeks regarded as the typically political intercourse where not only physical violence but also the coercion of truth were banned.[96]

6.5 Conclusion: Politics Between Distinction and Deliberation, Agonism and Persuasion

I started this chapter by suggesting that, viewed in the context of the tradition of philosophy, Arendt may appear as a quite idiosyncratic figure. Such idiosyncrasy is confirmed by the strong affinity between her vision of politics and that of another tradition that has always been in a certain tension with philosophy: rhetoric. What I have tried to make clear is that at the bottom of this proximity there is a particular kind of humanism that connects Arendt with the spirit of ancient rhetoric, and in particular with Cicero's political and philosophical conception. It is a humanism that emphasizes the relativeness and finitude of human beings, on the one hand, but also their freedom and capacity to transcend their contingent condition, on the other. It is a humanism that considers that these two dimensions are best expressed in politics, and finally, that invites us to understand this realm from within rather than from some external point of view.

In Cicero, as I have argued, the interrelation between the contingent and transcendent dimensions of politics can be seen in the way he tries to combine in his figure of the perfect orator an existential ideal of self-improvement and a political (and ethical) one. Because of this combination the perfect orator gives expression to two contrasting aims: the urge to distinction and the necessity of agreement and compromise. Something very similar can be said about Arendt's political theory. The insuperable value of politics resides for her in that, through it, human beings exercise their freedom and disclose their unique identity in the public realm, leaving behind something memorable and thereby resisting their alienation from the world. This disclosure occurs mainly through the pronunciation of "great words" and the doing of "great deeds" and is stirred by what Arendt calls, quoting John Adams, the "passion for distinction." It is a passion, she writes, that pervades the public realm with a "fiercely agonal spirit, where every body has constantly to distinguish himself from all others."[97] But if disclosure in the public realm concerns the individual, the crucial fact for her is that it has to be manifest in the midst of a plurality, since politics cannot but be a plural phenomenon. This implies that the basic stimulus for acting needs to be regulated, to avoid becoming a threat for political life: first, by making political speech assume above all the form of persuasion[98]; and second, by counterbalancing the passion for distinction with moderation, "one of the political virtues par excellence."[99] Prudence, or moderation, indeed is for Arendt necessary in politics not only because the passion for distinction can always run the risk of transforming itself into its opposite—ambition or *hubris*—but also because, acting in the midst of a plurality of individuals—everyone with a particular point of view and with a potential to start a new course of actions—implies that political actions are inevitably unpredictable and unbounded.[100]

This is why for Arendt the passion for distinction cannot be dissociated from judgment and persuasion. The latter are not only a means to allow this passion to express itself without threating plurality, but also the best means for disclosing our individual personality in the *agon* of the public sphere. It is also by way of judging and trying to persuade others that for Arendt we reveal our specific place in the world and our perspective on it.[101] In that way, similarly to Cicero's conception of eloquence, her political theory combines these two dimensions: existential and political, agonist and deliberative. In the same way as Cicero attempts to merge the existential-ethical endeavour of self-cultivation with the political pursuit of justice and the good, through the creation of the 'communicative' ideal of the perfect orator, for Arendt individual striving for excellence in the public sphere should be undertaken through modalities which are essentially relational and democratic: persuading and judging.[102]

Notes

1. Hannah Arendt and Jerome Kohn, *Essays in Understanding, 1930–1954* (New York: Schocken, 1994), 1–2; Hannah Arendt, *The Life of the Mind* (New York: Harcourt, 1978), 3.
2. Hannah Arendt, *On Revolution* (New York: Viking Press, 1971), 281. In the same text, some pages earlier, Arendt declares quite unequivocally that "that no one could be called either happy or free without participating, and having a share, in public power." Ibid., 255.

3. Hannah Arendt, "Karl Jaspers: A Laudatio," in *Men in Dark Times* (New York: Harcourt, Brace, 1970), 73–4.
4. Hannah Arendt, "What Is Freedom?," in *Between Past and Future* (New York: The Viking Press, 1968), 166; Hannah Arendt, "What Is Authority?," in *Between Past and Future* (New York: The Viking Press, 1968), 126.
5. On the other hand, however, Arendt credits Cicero with some brilliant philosophic intuitions and recognizes the deep influence of Roman thought on the same Hegel. Arendt, *The Life of the Mind*, 84. On this see: Silvia Giorcelli Bersani, *L'auctoritas degli antichi. Hannah Arendt tra Grecia e Roma* (Florence: Le Monnier, 2010), 2, 128; Dean Hammer, "Hannah Arendt and Roman Political Thought: The Practice of Theory," *Political Theory* 30 (2002).
6. Hannah Arendt, *The Human Condition* (Chicago: Chicago University Press, 1958), 7, 195.
7. On Arendt and Roman thought, see: Kirstie M. McClure, "The Odor of Judgment: Exemplarity, Propriety, and Politics in the Company of Hannah Arendt," in *Hannah Arendt and the Meaning of Politics*, ed. Craig J. Calhoun and John McGowan (Minneapolis: University of Minnesota Press, 1997); Hammer, "Hannah Arendt and Roman Political Thought: The Practice of Theory;" Jacques Taminiaux, "Athens and Rome," in *The Cambridge Companion to Hannah Arendt*, ed. Dana Villa (Cambridge: Cambridge University Press, 2000); Giorcelli Bersani, *L'auctoritas degli antichi*, 2, 128. On Arendt's republicanism see e.g., Margaret Canovan, *Hannah Arendt: A Reinterpretation of Her Political Thought* (Cambridge and New York: Cambridge University Press, 1992), esp. Ch. 6; Jürgen Habermas, "Hannah Arendt: On the Concept of Power," in *Philosophical-Political Profiles* (Cambridge, MA: MIT Press, 1985); Iseult Honohan, *Civic Republicanism* (London and New York: Routledge, 2002); Fernando Vallespín, "Hannah Arendt y el Republicanismo," in *El siglo de Hannah Arendt*, ed. Manuel Cruz (Barcelona: Paidós, 2006).
8. For instance: Arendt, "Preface: The Gap between Past and Future," 14; Arendt, "What Is Freedom?," 154.
9. Dana Villa, *Arendt and Heidegger: The Fate of the Political* (Princeton: Princeton University Press, 1996), xi. Even if deeply inspired by Heidegger, the deconstructive gesture against the tradition promoted by Arendt does not exempt him. According to Arendt, indeed, also Heidegger's philosophy is tainted by the typical prejudice of philosophy against politics. Taminiaux has argued that Arendt's *The Human Condition* can be read as a sort of retort and reply to Heidegger in order to expose the centrality of political dimension in the human condition.

Jacques Taminiaux, *La fille de Thrace et le penseur professionnel, Arendt et Heidegger* (Paris: Payot, 1992).
10. David L. Marshall, "The Origin and Character of Hannah Arendt's Theory of Judgment," *Political Theory* 38 (2010): 376.
11. For instance: Ronald Beiner, "Hannah Arendt on Judging," in *Lectures on Kant's Political Philosophy*, ed. Ronald Beiner (Chicago: University of Chicago Press, 1982), 135, 38; Theodore Kisiel, "Rhetorical Protopolitics in Heidegger and Arendt," in *Heidegger and Rhetoric*, ed. Daniel M. Gross and Ansgar Kemmann (Albany, NY: SUNY Press, 2005); Bryan Garsten, *Saving Persuasion: A Defense of Rhetoric and Judgment* (Cambridge, MA: Harvard University Press, 2006), 84–5; Linda M. G. Zerilli, "'WeFeel Our Freedom': Imagination and Judgment in the Thought of Hannah Arendt," *Political Theory* 33 (2005); David L. Marshall, "The Origin and Character of Hannah Arendt's Theory of Judgment," 376–80.
12. Marshall has analysed some Arendt's unpublished manuscripts and her *Denktagebuch* and come to the conclusion that Arendt studied Aristotle's *Rhetoric* in 1953 and that this text was an important source to develop her idea of judgment. Marshall emphasizes the proximity between Arendt's conception of politics and that of the tradition of rhetoric, but observes that the *Rhetoric* was not a text she referred back to often. Marshall, "The Origin and Character of Hannah Arendt's Theory of Judgment," 379.
13. Hannah Arendt, "Philosophy and Politics," *Social Research* 57 (1990): 79.
14. We can have a hint of how deeply Arendt is aware of the tension between thought and action considering the fact that her two masterpieces—*The Human Condition* (originally to be titled *Vita activa*) and *The Life of the Mind*—are devoted respectively to action and to the life of the mind.
15. Arendt, *The Life of the Mind*, 74–6; Arendt, *On Revolution*, 6, 14. Cf. Hannah Arendt, *The Origins of Totalitarianism* (New York: Meridian Books, 1958), 476; Hannah Arendt, "Action and the Pursuit of Happiness" (paper presented at the American Political Science Association, 1960).
16. Arendt, "Tradition and the Modern Age," 25.
17. See for instance: Ronald Beiner, "Rereading 'Truth and Politics'," *Philosophy Social Criticism* 34 (2008): 128.
18. Arendt, *On Revolution*, 177. Cf. Hannah Arendt, *Lectures on Kant's Political Philosophy*, ed. Ronald Beiner (Chicago: University of Chicago Press, 1982), 22.
19. As Arendt writes: "In the entire tradition of philosophical, and particularly of political thought, there has perhaps been no single factor of such

overwhelming importance and influence on everything that was to follow than the fact that Plato and Aristotle wrote in the fourth century, under the full impact of a politically decaying society, and under conditions where philosophy quite consciously either deserted the political realm altogether or claimed to rule it like a tyrant." Hannah Arendt, "Karl Marx and the Tradition of Western Political Thought," *Social Research* 69 (2002): 297.
20. Arendt, "What Is Authority?," 107. Arendt, "Philosophy and Politics," 73–4.
21. Arendt, "What Is Authority?," 108. Cf. Arendt, "Philosophy and Politics," 75.
22. Arendt, *The Human Condition*, 189–90, 95, 220–8. Arendt, "What Is Authority?," 109–15; Arendt, "Karl Marx and the Tradition of Western Political Thought," 296–8. Dana Villa has synthesized Arendt's assessment of western philosophy writing that: "The bottom line is that the (philosophic) constitution of the 'political' in the West coincides with the erection of a teleocratic concept of action, a concept that submits action to the rule of a goal-representing reason and a commanding, sovereign will." Villa, *Arendt and Heidegger*, 244.
23. Judgment is for Arendt "one, if not the most, important activity in which this sharing-the-world-with-others comes to pass" Arendt, "The Crisis in Culture," 221.
24. Arendt, *The Human Condition*, 222.
25. Cf. Marshall, "The Origin and Character of Hannah Arendt's Theory of Judgment," 379.
26. This polemical scope is made quite explicit in *The Life of the Mind* where Arendt tries to offer arguments in favour of an upturn of the hierarchy between essence and appearance traditionally established by metaphysics. Arendt, *The Life of the Mind*, 23–30.
27. Arendt, *On Revolution*, 98.
28. Arendt, *The Human Condition*, 50; Arendt, *The Life of the Mind*, 19–30.
29. On the necessary public—in the sense of visible to all who act in them—character of the political domain, Arendt writes: "This space does not always exist, and although all men are capable of deed and word, most of them—like the slave, the foreigner, and the barbarian in antiquity, like the laborer or craftsman prior to the modern age, the jobholder or businessman in our world—do not live in it. No man, moreover, can live in it all the time. To be deprived of it means to be deprived of reality, which, humanly and politically speaking, is the same as appearance. To men the reality of the world is guaranteed by the presence of others, by its appearing to all 'for what appears to all, this we call Being,' [Aristotle *Nicomachean Ethics*, 1172b36ff.] and whatever lacks this appearance

comes and passes away like a dream, intimately and exclusively our own but without reality." Arendt, *The Human Condition*, 199.
30. Quintilian, *Institutio Oratoria*, trans. Harold Edgeworth Butler (Cambridge, MA: Harvard Univsity Press, 1963), 4.2.34–5, cf. 12.1.2.
31. Giambattista Vico, "Il metodo degli studi del tempo nostro," in *Opere*, ed. Fausto Nicolini (Milan and Naples: Riccardo Ricciardi Editore, 1953). Cf., Giambattista Vico, "Prinicipi di Scienza Nuova," in *Opere*, ed. Fausto Nicolini (Milan and Naples: Riccardo Ricciardi Editore, 1953), par. 137, 140.
32. Villa, *Arendt and Heidegger*, 266.
33. Arendt, *The Human Condition*, 245–7, see also 6–7, 178, etc.
34. Ibid., 190–2.
35. Ibid., 24–7, 175–81.
36. Arendt, "Philosophy and Politics," 80.
37. Ibid., 74, 81.
38. Arendt, *The Human Condition*, 57.
39. Hannah Arendt, "Truth and Politics," in *The Portable Hannah Arendt*, ed. Peter Baehr (New York: Penguin Books, 2000), 557.
40. Ibid., 560–1.
41. Hannah Arendt, "On Humanity in Dark Times: Thoughts About Lessing," in *Men in Dark Times* (New York: Harcourt, Brace, 1970), 27.
42. Arendt, *On Revolution*, 227.
43. Arendt, "Philosophy and Politics," 73–4. Cf. Arendt, *The Human Condition*, 57; Hannah Arendt, "Introduction into Politics," in *The Promise of Politics*, ed. Jerome Kohn (New York: Schocken Books, 2005), 134–5.
44. Arendt, "The Crisis in Culture," 222–3.
45. Arendt, "Philosophy and Politics," 79. Arendt quotes the first line of Aristotle's *Rhetoric* (1354a1), where rhetoric is defined as the counterpart of the dialectic, to sustain her claim that for Aristotle such distinction was a matter of course. In this respect is interesting that, as David Marshall has reported, in her notes on the *Rhetoric* she glosses this line writing that "public speaking is the counterpart of philosophical speech." The translation/interpretation of this passage shows that Arendt accentuates the contrast between rhetoric and dialectic in Aristotle. Marshall, "The Origin and Character of Hannah Arendt's Theory of Judgment," 378–9.
46. Arendt, "The Crisis in Culture," 222–3. See also Arendt, "Philosophy and Politics," 79–80; Arendt, "Truth and Politics," 549–50.
47. Arendt, "Truth and Politics," 554.
48. Ibid., 556.
49. Arendt, "Philosophy and Politics," 84–5.
50. Arendt, "The Crisis in Culture," 224.

51. Ibid., 224–5.
52. Arendt, "Truth and Politics," 574.
53. Ibid., 553–4.
54. "Freedom of opinion is a farce unless factual information is guaranteed and the facts themselves are not in dispute" and thus, Arendt concludes, "factual truth informs political thought just as truth informs philosophical speculations." Ibid.
55. Arendt, *The Origins of Totalitarianism*, 341–64. Differently from other theorists, such as Rousseau and Marx, for Arendt modern alienation is political, rather than existential. It has to do with the loss of the common world and the possibility to inter-act, not much with the loss of oneself. In her account this loss is the consequence of the turning inward promoted, among other things, by the philosophical revolution sparkled by Descartes's methodical doubt and by what she calls "the rise of the social." Arendt also differentiates between two kinds of alienation: alienation from 'the world' (understood as the conjoint of objects constructed by *labour*), which is caused mainly by the accumulation of wealth, and alienation from the 'earth', a deeper state of alienation, caused by a number of scientific and technological discoveries (including that of America, the invention of aeroplanes and telescopes, the conquest of space), which have made us relativize the concept of the earth. Arendt, *The Human Condition*, pp. 6, 254–84, 298; Arendt, "The Concept of History," 53–6; Arendt, "The Crisis in Education," 191, 199. On this see: Maurizio Passerin d'Entrèves, *The Political Philosophy of Hannah Arendt* (London and New York: Routledge, 1994), 37–42.
56. Arendt, "Truth and Politics," 553–4, 568–9.
57. Villa, *Arendt and Heidegger*, 50.
58. Arendt, *The Life of the Mind*, 15, 57–62; Hannah Arendt, "Thinking and Moral Considerations," in *Responsibility and Judgment*, ed. Jerome Kohn (New York: Schocken, 2003), 163; Hannah Arendt, "Understanding and Politics," in *Essays in Understanding, 1930–1954*, ed. Jerome Kohn (New York: Schocken, 1994), 317; Arendt, *The Human Condition*, 171–2.
59. For instance: Isaiah Berlin, *Three Critics of the Enlightenment: Vico, Hamann, Herder*, ed. Henry Hardy (Princeton, NJ: Princeton University Press, 2000), 44, 88.
60. For Arendt indeed opinions such as "all men are created equal", even if they lack the coercive power of philosophical or religious truths (since they are neither self-evident nor provable), are "politically of the greatest importance." Differently from philosophical or religious truths, their significance derives precisely from the fact of being formed through the experience of participation in the realm of human affairs. Indeed they are precisely what gives the "human quality" to this intercourse and what influences more its quality. Arendt, "Truth and Politics," 561.

61. Arendt, "What Is Freedom?," 152; Arendt, "Introduction into Politics," 193–4.
62. Arendt, "What Is Freedom?," 152.
63. In *On Revolution* Arendt writes: "What saves the act of beginning from its own arbitrariness is that it carries its own principles within itself…The absolute from which the beginning is to derive its own validity and which must stave it, as it were, from its inherent arbitrariness is the principles which, together with it, makes appearance in the world." Arendt, *On Revolution*, 212.
64. Arendt, "What Is Freedom?," 152; Arendt, *The Origins of Totalitarianism*, 467. Cf. Arendt, *The Life of the Mind*, 201–2; Hannah Arendt, "On the Nature of Totalitarianism: An Essay in Understanding," in *Essays in Understanding, 1930–1954*, ed. Jerome Kohn (New York: Schocken, 1994), 329–30.
65. Villa, *Arendt and Heidegger*, 11.
66. The connection between rhetoric and political freedom is evoked by Cicero in the introduction to his dialogue *Brutus*, where he tells the history of Roman oratory. In there Cicero writes bitter words on the decline of this art in his period, marked by the turbulences and violence unleashed by Caesar's dictatorship: "For were Hoertensius alive today he would doubtless have occasion, along with other good and loyal men, to mourn the loss of many things; but one pang he would feel beyond the rest, or with few to share it: the spectacle of the Roman forum, the scene and stage of his talents, robbed and bereft of that finished eloquence worthy of the ears of Rome or even of Greece. For me too it is a source of deep pain that the state feels no need of those weapons of counsel, of insight, and of authority, which I learned to handle and to rely upon,—weapons which are the peculiar and proper resource of a leader in the commonwealth and of a civilized and law-abiding state. Indeed if there ever was a time in the history of the state when the authority and eloquence of a good citizen might have wrested arms from the hands of angry partisans, it was exactly then when through blindness or fear the door was abruptly closed upon the cause of peace", Cicero, "Brutus," in *Brutus, Orator*, trans. G. L. Hendrickson and H. M. Hubbell (Cambridge, MA: Harvard University Press, 1934), 6–7, cf. 45. See also: Tacitus, "A Dialogue on Oratory," in *Tacitus: Dialogus, Agricola, Germania*, trans. W. Peterson and M. Winterbottom (Cambridge, MA: Harvard University Press, 1958), 36–40. Garsten has remarked that Cicero's defence of rhetoric was accompanied by a concomitant defence of the republican institutions and virtues, which for Cicero constitutes its indispensable pre-conditions. Garsten, *Saving Persuasion*, 166–9.
67. Arendt, *On Revolution*, 226–7.
68. Ibid., 227.

69. The literature on the question of judgment in Arendt is extensive. Beyond the works cited in note 11, see also: George Kateb, *Hannah Arendt: Politics, Conscience, Evil* (Oxford: Robertson, 1984), 8–14; Richard J. Bernstein, *Philosophical Profiles: Essays in a Pragmatic Mode* (Philadelphia: University of Pennsylvania Press, 1986), 231, 237; Seyla Benhabib, "Judgment and the Moral Foundations of Politics in Arendt's Thought," *Political Theory* 16 (1988); Villa, *Arendt and Heidegger*, 35; Taminiaux, *La fille de Thrace et le penseur professionnel*, 105–14; Andrew Norris, "Arendt, Kant, and the Politics of Common Sense," *Polity* 29 (1996); Majid Yar, "From Actor to Spectator: Hannah Arendt's 'Two Theories' of Political Judgment," *Philosophy and Social Criticism* 26 (2000).
70. Arendt, "The Crisis in Culture," 221. See also: Arendt, "Introduction into Politics," 167–8; Arendt, *The Life of the Mind*, 192; Arendt, "Philosophy and Politics," 83–4; Arendt, "Truth and Politics," 556.
71. Arendt, "Preface: The Gap between Past and Future," 7.
72. For instance: Arendt, "Tradition and the Modern Age," 26; Arendt, "Understanding and Politics," 308.
73. Cf., Beiner, "Hannah Arendt on Judging," 99–101.
74. Arendt, "The Crisis in Culture," 221; Arendt, *The Life of the Mind*, 215; Arendt, *Lectures on Kant's Political Philosophy*, 4; Arendt, "Philosophy and Politics," 84; Arendt, "Thinking and Moral Considerations," 188.
75. Marshall, "The Origin and Character of Hannah Arendt's Theory of Judgment," 8–9. In this article Marshall reconstructs all the process through which Arendt came to develop her idea of judgment. Beyond the Kant's *Critique of Judgment*, which is a well-known source for Arendt in this respect, he individuates as crucial inspiration for Arendt Hegel's *Science of Logic* and Aristotle's *Rhetoric*. See also supra note 12.
76. Cf., Bryan Garsten, "The Elusiveness of Arendtian Judgment," *Social Research* 74 (2007); Passerin d'Entrèves, *The Political Philosophy of Hannah Arendt*, 102; Alessandro Ferrara, *The Force of the Example: Explorations in the Paradigm of Judgment* (New York: Columbia University Press, 2008), 43.
77. See e.g., Arendt, *The Life of the Mind*, 192–3, 213–15; Arendt, "Thinking and Moral Considerations," 189.
78. Ronald Beiner is the first to have called the attention on a shifting of the focus in Arendt's account of judgment from the role of the actor (in her writings until 1971, among which above all *The Human Condition*) to that of the spectator (in her writings after 1971, starting with 'Thinking and Moral Considerations'). Beiner, "Hannah Arendt on Judging," 101. Such a shift would demonstrate, according to Beiner, that Arendt came progressively to lose faith in the possibility to act politically and thus came

to be concerned more with judging politics from a spectatorial perspective. Ronald Beiner, "Rereading Hannah Arendt's Kant Lectures," *Philosophy and Social Criticism* 23 (1997). However Garsten has remarked the importance of the role of the judging spectator in contemporary politics through Arendt's account. Garsten, "The Elusiveness of Arendtian Judgment," 1097–8. For Bernstein, instead, such double accounts of judgment reflects a major tension in Arendt's theory about the relation between acting and thinking. Bernstein, *Philosophical Profiles*, 230–7. David Marshall, instead, has argued that judging to decide and judging to discern—actor and spectator—are not only compatible according to Arendt but mutually dependent. Marshall, "The Origin and Character of Hannah Arendt's Theory of Judgment." On this see also: Yar, "From Actor to Spectator: Hannah Arendt's 'Two Theories' of Political Judgment"; Ferrara, *The Force of the Example*, Ch. 2.

79. Hannah Arendt, *Eichmann in Jerusalem: A Report on the Banality of Evil* (New York: Penguin Books, 1994), 135. Cf., Arendt, "Thinking and Moral Considerations," 159–60.
80. Arendt, *Eichmann in Jerusalem*, 136–7.
81. Arendt, "The Crisis in Culture," 220–1; Arendt, *The Life of the Mind*, 170–8; Arendt, "Thinking and Moral Considerations," 188–9.
82. Arendt, *The Human Condition*, 185, 225.
83. Arendt, "The Crisis in Culture," 221.
84. Arendt, *Lectures on Kant's Political Philosophy*, 19.
85. Arendt, *Eichmann in Jerusalem*, 47–9.
86. Arendt, "The Crisis in Culture," 221.
87. Immanuel Kant, *The Critique of Judgement*, trans. James C. Meredith (Oxford: Oxford University Press, 2007), par. 41.
88. Arendt, *The Life of the Mind*, 111.
89. Arendt, "The Crisis in Culture," 221.
90. Ibid., 221–2; Arendt, *Lectures on Kant's Political Philosophy*, 42–4, 63–8. Cf. Arendt, *The Origins of Totalitarianism*, 475–6. It is important to underline, however, that, differently from the rhetorical tradition, for Arendt the capacity to enlarge our mentality has nothing to do with empathy. Empathy is for her a slippery concept, if applied to the political ream, because it can imply accepting passively the prejudgments of the others, rather than actively include their points of view. Arendt, *The Life of the Mind*, 92–4. The rejection of the idea of empathy in politics is connected to Arendt's critique of modern subjectivism, which she considers one of the great flaws of modern culture. On this see: Shiraz Dossa, *The Public Realm and the Public Self: The Political Theory of Hannah Arendt* (Waterloo: Wilfrid Laurier University Press, 1989).
91. Cicero cited in: Arendt, *Lectures on Kant's Political Philosophy*, 63.

92. Also Zerilli develops her parallelism between Arendt, aesthetic, and rhetoric starting from here. Zerilli, "'We Feel Our Freedom': Imagination and Judgment in the Thought of Hannah Arendt," 172–6.
93. Kant cited in: Arendt, *Lectures on Kant's Political Philosophy*, 40.
94. Ibid., 41.
95. Kant, *The Critique of Judgement*, par. 17, 22, 40–1, 45, etc. Kant however had a quite negative conception of oratory, understood as the art of persuasion, which he defines as an art "of deceiving by means of a beautiful illusion" and an "art of using people's weakness for one's own aims." He had a positive view only on rhetoric understood as "excellence of speech." Ibid., par. 53. For a critique from a rhetorical perspective of Kant's notion of 'universal communicability' and 'sociability' and of Arendt's recovery of it, see: Garsten, *Saving Persuasion*, 85–6, 102–3.
96. Arendt, "The Crisis in Culture," 221.
97. Arendt, *The Human Condition*, 25; Arendt, *On Revolution*, 69.
98. Arendt, *The Human Condition*, 25–6; Arendt, *On Revolution*, 86, 91; Arendt, "Truth and Politics," 554, 560–1.
99. Arendt, *The Human Condition*, 191.
100. Ibid., 175, 190–2; Arendt, *On Revolution*, 119.
101. See e.g., Arendt, *Lectures on Kant's Political Philosophy*, 43.
102. On the combination of agonism and deliberation in Arendt's political theory, see: Shmuel Lederman, "Agonism and Deliberation in Arendt," *Constellations* 21 (2014); Dana Villa, "Beyond Good and Evil: Arendt, Nietzsche, and the Aestheticization of Political Action," *Political Theory* 2 (1992).

CHAPTER 7

Afterword

I have argued in this book that three distinctive, but similarly influential, theorists—Leo Strauss, Richard Rorty, and Hannah Arendt—offer visions of politics that converge in one crucial respect: they describe this activity as one characterized by an interplay between the basic dimensions of transcendence and contingency. Transcendence in politics acquires a different meaning for each of them: according to Strauss it entails a normative search through reason for the principles of communal life, as part of a more general search for the principles of the cosmos; for Rorty it involves a continuous reinvention of oneself and one's own community through the expansion and transformation of conventional vocabularies; and for Arendt it is an endeavour to leave something immortal in the world, which at the same time reveals one's own identity. For all these thinkers, it is because of this transcendent dimension that politics has a paramount normative value. It is normative, however, not in the sense of authoritatively prescribing a set of fixed rules, but rather in expressing a supreme vision of the human good that directs and inspires action. On the other hand, they also believe that the transcendent dimension of politics takes place in a realm deeply marked by contingency. As the striving for transcendence informs the contingent and practical happening of politics, so in turn the latter cannot but crucially modify the process of the former. Finally and crucially, we have seen that each of these thinkers considers that a form of communicative mastery—or in other words, of rhetoric—plays a

© The Author(s) 2018
G. Ballacci, *Political Theory between Philosophy and Rhetoric*, Rhetoric, Politics and Society, https://doi.org/10.1057/978-1-349-95293-9_7

183

fundamental role in mediating between the two dimensions: as the art of writing between the lines for Strauss; or the art of redescription for Rorty; or, finally, as the ability to judge and persuade in public for Arendt.

How to interpret the crucial interplay in politics between transcendence and contingency, according to the argument proposed in the first part of the book, is one of the most important issues at stake in the ancient quarrel between philosophy and rhetoric. From this perspective, the Platonic attack against rhetoric can be understood as the reclamation of a transcending dimension against rhetoric's devotion to the specificities of the context and the audience. On the other hand, Aristotle's articulation of rhetoric as a civic art of discourse is based on the idea that contingency is an unavoidable feat of political life, with which we have to deal rather than attempt to eradicate once and for all. Finally, Cicero's ideal of a union between wisdom and eloquence—one of the founding elements of humanism—represents perhaps the most compelling attempts in the history of political thought to combine these two fundamental dimensions of politics, making of eloquence the privileged locus and medium for such a combination. It is because of this that I have focused particularly on Cicero's conception to develop my reading of Strauss, Rorty, and Arendt.

Clearly, the argument presented in this book could only unfold at a general level of analysis. In line with the rhetorical humanistic ideal of Cicero, Vico, or also of Rorty, in writing it I have relied more on an associative and inclusive kind of logic than on a dissociative and analytical one. My aim has been to create a broad narrative that brings together a number of important thinkers, rather than a more detailed analysis, in order to make a general argument about the meaning of politics. Of course, I think this method has its advantages. But at the same time I am aware that it also has downsides: first of all, it makes it difficult to dwell sufficiently on themes that could be deepened and, second, it cannot address closely some potential objections. In these concluding lines I want, just briefly, to say something about one of these potential objections that I consider particularly significant.

There are a number of critical points that could be made against the reproposition today of the old fashioned rhetorical humanistic ideal and its related notion of *phronesis*. For instance, it could be argued that this reproposition would require us to take into consideration the hyper-specialization that characterizes our societies, or on a different level, to discuss current anti-humanist, or post-humanist attacks on humanism. It could be remarked, as well, that the classical and humanistic notion of rhetoric centred on persuasion (even if with persuasion being understood as incomplete, biased, and unstable) is outdated and that I should have engaged also with contemporary approaches on rhetoric, which stress much more the context over the agent and question the same possibilities of a real communication. These are certainly important points. But the objection that I think more directly affects what I have defended in this book is another one and has to do with elitism. Indeed it is undeniable that behind such a lofty ideal as the Ciceronian figure of the perfect orator (and behind Cicero's political views in general) lies an indisputable degree of elitism. More generally, we can say that the pedagogic model based on the liberal arts has habitually been considered aristocratic: a model that conceals a haughty disrespect for more ordinary and practical problems. And not unrelatedly, we can also remind ourselves that the crisis of rhetoric in the modern epoch, with the consolidation of more democratic forms of government, has among its causes the fact that it came to be associated with a form of linguistic manipulation used by elites against the masses.[1] Finally, there is also the fact that not only Cicero, but all the thinkers considered in the second part of the book can be said to endorse a form of elitism: not only Strauss, but arguably Arendt and Rorty as well.

Now, the problem is that elitism not only jars with the egalitarianism of democracy, but also more specifically with an important premise of the book: namely, that a capacity to judge and act politically is diffuse among the citizens. I don't want to deny that a tension between elitism and this democratic and egalitarian presupposition exists. I think a lofty conception of politics inevitably invokes a certain elitism, since it implies distinction and thus a separation between the few and the many. Every politics of distinction is exclusive in this way to some extent. In that respect, however, we don't have to forget that the kind of proficiency defended by our thinkers is essentially of a political kind: political in the sense of, as I have argued, being related above all to 'relational' and 'communicative' capacities. It is these sort of 'political' capacities that my rhetorical reading of Cicero, Arendt, or Rorty, has stressed. In the case of Cicero, for instance, the philosophical search for truth and the process of self-cultivation through education should always be combined with an engagement in politics. Otherwise it would be considered incomplete, or even worthless. This is why the rhetorical humanistic ideal can be said to be an ideal both for the individual and for the community. Such communicative and relational capacities can, undoubtedly, be developed at different levels by different individuals, thus generating a hierarchy. But they remain in reach of everyone and thus they can be judged by everyone.

In this sense, I think the kinds of agonism and the politics of distinction endorsed by Cicero and Arendt (and, even if more problematically, by Rorty as well) are particularly interesting in that they promote distinction mainly through dialogue and interaction. Eloquence in effect is an art that can be brought to perfection, but which is not limited to the specialists. Thus the image of the ideal orator may yet offer a clue as to how we may continue to renew democratic politics.

Notes

1. Terry Eagleton, "A Short History of Rhetoric," in *Rhetoric in an Antifoundational World*, ed. Michael Bernard-Donals and Richard R. Glejzer (New Haven and London: Yale University Press, 1998), 90.

BIBLIOGRAPHY

Abizadeh, Arash. 2002. The Passions of the Wise: 'Phronêsis', Rhetoric, and Aristotle's Passionate Practical Deliberation. *The Review of Metaphysics* 56 (2): 267–296.

———. 2007. On the Philosophy/Rhetoric Binaries: Or, Is Habermasian Discourse Motivationally Impotent? *Philosophy and Social Criticism* 33 (4): 445–472.

Adams, John. 2001. *The Political Writings of John Adams*. Washington, DC: Regnery Publishing.

Allen, Danielle S. 2004. *Talking to Strangers: Anxieties of Citizenship since Brown V. Board of Education*. Chicago: University of Chicago Press.

———. 2010. *Why Plato Wrote*. Malden: Wiley-Blackwell.

Altman, William H.F. 2015. Introduction. In *Brill Companion to the Reception of Cicero*, ed. William H.F. Altman. Leiden/Boston: Brill.

Arendt, Hannah. 1958a. *The Human Condition*. Chicago: Chicago University Press.

———. 1958b. *The Origins of Totalitarianism*. New York: Meridian Books.

———. 1960. Action and the Pursuit of Happiness. Paper presented at the American Political Science Association.

———. 1968a. The Concept of History. In *Between Past and Future*. New York: The Viking Press.

———. 1968b. The Crisis in Culture. In *Between Past and Future*. New York: The Viking Press.

———. 1968c. The Crisis in Education. In *Between Past and Future*. New York: The Viking Press.

© The Author(s) 2018
G. Ballacci, *Political Theory between Philosophy and Rhetoric*, Rhetoric, Politics and Society,
https://doi.org/10.1057/978-1-349-95293-9

———. 1968d. Preface: The Gap Between Past and Future. In *Between Past and Future*. New York: The Viking Press.

———. 1968e. Tradition and the Modern Age. In *Between Past and Future*. New York: The Viking Press.

———. 1968f. What Is Authority? In *Between Past and Future*. New York: The Viking Press.

———. 1968g. What Is Freedom? In *Between Past and Future*. New York: The Viking Press.

———. 1970a. Karl Jaspers: A Laudatio. In *Men in Dark Times*. New York: Harcourt, Brace.

———. 1970b. On Humanity in Dark Times: Thoughts About Lessing. In *Men in Dark Times*. New York: Harcourt, Brace.

———. 1971. *On Revolution*. New York: Viking Press.

———. 1978. *The Life of the Mind*. New York: Harcourt.

———. 1982. In *Lectures on Kant's Political Philosophy*, ed. Ronald Beiner. Chicago: University of Chicago Press.

———. 1990. Philosophy and Politics. *Social Research* 57 (1): 73–103.

———. 1994a. *Eichmann in Jerusalem: A Report on the Banality of Evil*. New York: Penguin Books.

———. 1994b. On the Nature of Totalitarianism: An Essay in Understanding. In *Essays in Understanding, 1930–1954*, ed. Jerome Kohn. New York: Schocken.

———. 1994c. Understanding and Politics. In *Essays in Understanding, 1930–1954*, ed. Jerome Kohn. New York: Schocken.

———. 1994d. What Remains? The Language Remains: A Conversation with Gunter Gaus. In *Essays in Understanding*, ed. Jerome Kohn. New York: Schocken.

———. 2000. Truth and Politics. In *The Portable Hannah Arendt*, ed. Peter Baehr. New York: Penguin Books.

———. 2002. Karl Marx and the Tradition of Western Political Thought. *Social Research* 69 (2): 273–319.

———. 2003. Thinking and Moral Considerations. In *Responsibility and Judgment*, ed. Jerome Kohn. New York: Schocken.

———. 2005. Introduction into Politics. In *The Promise of Politics*, ed. Jerome Kohn. New York: Schocken.

Aristotle. 1980. *The Nicomachean Ethics*. Trans. Hippocrates G. Apostle. Dordrecht/Boston: Reidel.

———. 1991. *On Rhetoric: A Theory of Civic Discourse*. Trans. George Kennedy. New York/Oxford: Oxford University Press.

———. 1998. *Politics*. Trans. C.D.C. Reeve (With Introduction and Notes). Indianapolis: Hackett.

———. 2011. *The Eudemian Ethics*. Trans. Anthony Kenny. Oxford: Oxford University Press.

Armada, Pawel. 2011. Leo Strauss as Erzieher: The Defense of the Philosophical Life or the Defense of Life against Philosophy. In *Modernity and What Has Been Lost: Considerations on the Legacy of Leo Strauss*, ed. Pawel Armada and Arkadiusz Górnisiewicz. Indiana/Kracow: Jagiellonian University Press and St. Augustine's Press.

Arnhart, Larry. 1981. *Aristotle on Political Reasoning: A Commentary on the Rhetoric*. DeKalb: Northern Illinois University Press.

Aubenque, Pierre. 1963. *La prudence chez Aristote*. Paris: Presses universitaires de France.

Aune, James Arnt. 2009. Coping with Modernity Strategies of 20th-Century Rhetorical Theory. In *The Sage Handbook of Rhetorical Studies*, ed. Rosa A. Eberly, Andrea Lunsford, and Kirt H. Wilson. London: SAGE.

Auxier, Randall. 2010. Preface. In *In the Philosophy of Richard Rorty*, ed. Randall E. Auxier and Lewis Edwin Hahn. Chicago: Open Court.

Ball, Terence, William Connolly, Peter Dews, and Alan Malachowski. 1990. Review Symposium on Richard Rorty. *History of the Human Sciences* 3 (1): 101–122.

Ballacci, Giuseppe. 2015. Reassessing the Rhetoric Revival in Political Theory: Cicero, Eloquence, and the Best Form of Life. *Redescriptions: Political Thought, Conceptual History and Feminist Theory* 18 (2): 158–180.

Baraz, Yelena. 2012. *A Written Republic: Cicero's Philosophical Politics*. Princeton: Princeton University Press.

Barilli, Renato. 1989. *Rhetoric*. Minneapolis: University of Minnesota Press.

Barthes, Roland. 1985. *L'aventure sémiologique*. Paris: Éd. du Seuil.

Batnitzky, Leora. 2009. Leo Strauss and the "Theological-Political Predicament". In *The Cambridge Companion to Leo Strauss*, ed. Steven B. Smith. New York: Cambridge University Press.

Battistini, Andrea. 1994. On the Encyclopedic Structure of the New Science. *New Vico Studies* 12: 16–32.

Baumlin, James S., and Joseph J. Hughes. 1996. Eloquence. In *Encyclopedia of Rhetoric and Composition: Communication from Ancient Times to the Information Age*, ed. Theresa Enos. New York/London: Garland.

Behnegar, Nasser. 1999. The Intellectual Legacy of Leo Strauss (1899–1973). *Annual Review of Political Science* 2: 95–116.

Beiner, Ronald. 1982. Hannah Arendt on Judging. In *Lectures on Kant's Political Philosophy*, ed. Ronald Beiner. Chicago: University of Chicago Press.

———. 1983. *Political Judgment*. Chicago: University of Chicago Press.

———. 1997. Rereading Hannah Arendt's Kant Lectures. *Philosophy and Social Criticism* 23 (1): 21–32.

———. 2008. Rereading 'Truth and Politics'. *Philosophy and Social Criticism* 34 (1–2): 123–136.

Benardete, Seth. 1991. *The Rhetoric of Morality and Philosophy: Plato's Gorgias and Phaedrus.* Chicago/London: University of Chicago.
Benhabib, Seyla. 1988. Judgment and the Moral Foundations of Politics in Arendt's Thought. *Political Theory* 16 (1): 29–51.
Berlin, Isaiah. 2000. In *Three Critics of the Enlightenment: Vico, Hamann, Herder*, ed. Henry Hardy. Princeton: Princeton University Press.
Bernstein, Richard J. 1986. *Philosophical Profiles: Essays in a Pragmatic Mode.* Philadelphia: University of Pennsylvania Press.
———. 1992. *The New Constellation: The Ethical-Political Horizons of Modernity/Postmodernity.* Cambridge, MA: MIT Press.
———. 2008. Richard Rorty's Deep Humanism. *New Literary History* 39 (1): 13–27.
Blair, Carole, Sander L. Gilman, and David J. Parent. 1989. Introduction. In *Friedrich Nietzsche on Rhetoric and Language*, ed. Carole Blair, Sander L. Gilman, and David J. Parent. New York/Oxford: Oxford University Press.
Bloom, Allan D. 1955. *The Political Philosophy of Isocrates.* PhD Dissertation, University of Chicago.
———. 1991. Interpretative Essay. In *The Republic of Plato.* Trans. and Ed. Allan D. Bloom. New York: Basic Books.
Bloomer, Martin. 1997. Schooling in Persona: Imagination and Subordination in Roman Education. *Classical Antiquity* 16 (1): 57–78.
Boesche, Roger. 1996. *Theories of Tyranny: From Plato to Arendt.* University Park: Pennsylvania State University Press.
Bullard, Paddy. 2011. *Edmund Burke and the Art of Rhetoric.* Cambridge: Cambridge University Press.
Camporeale, Salvatore. 1972. *Lorenzo Valla. Umanesimo e teologia.* Florence: Istituto Palazzo Strozzi.
Canovan, Margaret. 1992. *Hannah Arendt: A Reinterpretation of Her Political Thought.* Cambridge/New York: Cambridge University Press.
Cassin, Barbara. 1995. *L'effet sophistique.* Paris: Gallimard.
Cervantes, Miguel de. 1982. *El ingenioso hidalgo Don Quijote de la Mancha.* 2 vols. Vol. II, Madrid: Castalia.
Chambers, Simone. 2009. Rhetoric and the Public Sphere: Has Deliberative Democracy Abandoned Mass Democracy? *Political Theory* 37 (3): 323–350.
Cicero. 1923a. De Divinatione. Trans. W.A. Falconer. In *On Old Age. On Friendship. On Divination.* Cambridge, MA: Harvard University Press.
———. 1923b. Pro Archia. Trans. Nevile Hunter Watts. In *Pro Archia. Post Reditum in Senatu. Post Reditum Ad Quirites. De Domo Sua. De Haruspicum Responsis. Pro Plancio.* Cambridge, MA: Harvard University Press.
———. 1930. On the Agrarian Law. Trans. J.H. Freese. In *Pro Quinctio. Pro Roscio Amerino. Pro Roscio Comoedo. On the Agrarian Law.* Cambridge, MA: Harvard University Press.

———. 1933. De Natura Deorum. Trans. H. Rackham. In *On the Nature of the Gods. Academics*. Cambridge, MA: Harvard University Press.
———. 1934a. Brutus. Trans. G.L. Hendrickson and H.M. Hubbell. In *Brutus, Orator*. Loeb Classical Library. Cambridge, MA: Harvard University Press.
———. 1934b. Orator. Trans. G.L. Hendrickson and H.M. Hubbell. In *Brutus, Orator*. Loeb Classical Library. Cambridge, MA: Harvard University Press.
———. 1949. De Inventione. Trans. M. Hubbell. In *De Inventione, De Optimo Genere Oratorum, Topica*. Cambridge, MA: Harvard University Press.
———. 1960. *Tusculan Disputations*. Trans. J.E. King. Cambridge, MA: Harvard University Press.
———. 1968. Paradoxa Stoicorum. Trans. H. Rackham. In *De Oratore, Book Iii; De Fato; Paradoxa Stoicorum*. Cambridge, MA: Harvard University Press.
———. 1995. *Philippics*. Trans. Walter C.A. Ker. Cambridge, MA: Harvard University Press.
———. 1997. *De Officiis*. Trans. Walter Miller. Cambridge, MA: Harvard University Press.
———. 2000a. De Legibus. Trans. Clinton Walker Keyes. In *De Republica (on the Republic) & De Legibus (on the Laws)*. Cambridge, MA: Harvard University Press.
———. 2000b. De Re Publica. Trans. C.W. Keyes. In *De Re Publica (on the Republic) & De Legibus (on the Laws)*. Loeb Classical Library. Cambridge, MA: Harvard University Press.
———. 2001. *On the Ideal Orator (De Oratore)*. Trans. James M. May and Jakob Wisse. New York: Oxford University Press.
Clarke, Martin L. 1964. Non Hominis Nomen, Sed Eloquentiae. In *Cicero*, ed. T.A. Dorey. London: Routledge & Kegan Paul.
Cole, Thomas. 1999. *The Origins of Rhetoric in Ancient Greece*. Baltimore: Johns Hopkins University Press.
Connolly, Joy. 2007a. *The State of Speech: Rhetoric and Political Thought in Ancient Rome*. Princeton/Oxford: Princeton University Press.
———. 2007b. Virile Tongues: Rhetoric and Masculinity. In *A Companion to Roman Rhetoric*, ed. William Dominik and Jon Hall. Malden: Blackwell.
Cox, Virginia, and John O. Ward. 2006. *The Rhetoric of Cicero in Its Medieval and Early Renaissance Commentary Tradition*. Leiden/Boston: Brill.
Curtis, William M. 2015. *Defending Rorty: Pragmatism and Liberal Virtue*. Cambridge: Cambridge University Press.
Danisch, Robert. 2013. The Absence of Rhetorical Theory in Richard Rorty's Linguistic Pragmatism. *Philosophy and Rhetoric* 46 (2): 156–181.
Dossa, Shiraz. 1989. *The Public Realm and the Public Self: The Political Theory of Hannah Arendt*. Waterloo: Wilfrid Laurier University Press.
Dow, Jamie. 2015. *Passions and Persuasion in Aristotle's Rhetoric*. Oxford: Oxford University Press.

Dryzek, John S. 2010. Rhetoric in Democracy: A Systemic Appreciation. *Political Theory* 38 (3): 319–339.
Dugan, John. 2005. *Making a New Man: Ciceronian Self-Fashioning in the Rhetorical Works*. New York: Oxford University Press.
———. 2009. Rhetoric and the Roman Republic. In *The Cambridge Companion to Ancient Rhetoric*, ed. Erik Gunderson. Cambridge: Cambridge University Press.
Eagleton, Terry. 1998. A Short History of Rhetoric. In *Rhetoric in an Antifoundational World*, ed. Michael Bernard-Donals and Richard R. Glejzer. New Haven/London: Yale University Press.
Elshtain, Jean B. 1997. *Real Politics: At the Center of Everyday Life*. Baltimore: Johns Hopkins University Press.
Fantham, Elaine. 1995. The Concept of Nature and Human Nature in Quintilian's Psychology and Theory of Instruction. *Rhetorica* 13 (2): 125–136.
Ferrara, Alessandro. 1990. The Unbearable Seriousness of Irony. *Philosophy and Social Criticism* 16 (2): 81–107.
———. 2008. *The Force of the Example: Explorations in the Paradigm of Judgment*. New York: Columbia University Press.
Finlayson, Alan. 2012. Rhetoric and the Political Theory of Ideologies. *Political Studies* 60 (4): 751–767.
Finlayson, Alan, and James Martin. 2008. 'It Ain't What You Say…': British Political Studies and the Analysis of Speech and Rhetoric. *British Politics* 3 (4): 445–464.
Fish, Stanley. 1989. *Doing What Comes Naturally: Change, Rhetoric, and the Practice of Theory in Literary and Legal Studies*. Durham/London: Duke University Press.
Fontana, Benedetto. 2005. The Democratic Philosopher: Rhetoric as Hegemony in Gramsci. *Italian Culture* 23: 97–123.
———. 2006. Reason and Politics: Philosophy Confronts the People. *Boundary 2* 33 (1): 7–35.
Fontana, Benedetto, Cary J. Nederman, and Gary Remer, eds. 2004a. *Talking Democracy: Historical Perspectives on Rhetoric and Democracy*. University Park: Pennsylvania State University Press.
———. 2004b. Introduction: Deliberative Democracy and the Rhetorical Turn. In *Talking Democracy: Historical Perspectives on Rhetoric and Democracy*, ed. Benedetto Fontana, Cary J. Nederman, and Gary Remer. University Park: Pennsylvania State University Press.
Fortenbaugh, William W. 2002. *Aristotle on Emotion: A Contribution to Philosophical Psychology, Rhetoric, Poetics, Politics and Ethics*. London: Duckworth.
Fortenbaugh, William W., and David C. Mirhady, eds. 1994. *Peripatetic Rhetoric After Aristotle*. New Brunswick: Transaction Publishers.

Fradkin, Hillel. 1991. Philosophy and Law: Leo Strauss as a Student of Medieval Jewish Thought. *The Review of Politics* 53 (1): 40–52.
Fraser, Nancy. 1988. Solidarity or Singularity? Richard Rorty Between Romanticism and Technocracy. *Praxis International* 8 (3): 257–272.
———. 1991. From Irony to Prophecy to Politics: A Response to Richard Rorty. *Michigan Quarterly Review* 30: 259–266.
Frazer, Michael L. 2006. Esotericism Ancient and Modern. *Political Theory* 34 (1): 33–61.
Fumaroli, Marc. 1994. *L'âge de l'éloquence. Rhétorique et "res literaria" de la Renaissance au seuil de l'époque classique*. Paris: Albin Michel.
Fussi, Alessandra. 2000. Why Is the Gorgias So Bitter? *Philosophy and Rhetoric* 33 (1): 39–58.
Gadamer, Hans-Georg. 1980. *Dialogue and Dialectic: Eight Hermeneutical Studies on Plato*. New Haven: Yale University Press.
———. 1991. *Plato's Dialectical Ethics: Phenomenological Interpretations Relating to the "Philebus"*. New Haven: Yale University Press.
———. 1993. *Truth and Method*. 2nd rev ed. London/New York: Continuum.
Gadamer, Hans-Georg, and Riccardo Dottori. 2004. *A Century of Philosophy: Hans Georg Gadamer in Conversation with Riccardo Dottori*. New York: Continuum.
Gaines, Robert. 1995. Cicero's Response to the Philosophers in De Oratore, Book 1. In *Rhetoric and Pedagogy*, ed. Winifred Bryan Horner and Michael Leff. Mahwah: Lawrence Erlbaum Associates.
Gaonkar, Dilip P. 1993. The Revival of Rhetoric, the New Rhetoric, and the Rhetorical Turn: Some Distinctions. *Informal Logic* 15 (1): 53–64.
———. 1999. Rhetoric and Its Double: Reflections of the Rhetorical Turn in the Human Sciences. In *Contemporary Rhetorical Theory: A Reader*, ed. John Louis Lucaites, Celeste Michelle Condit, and Sally Caudill. New York/London: The Guilford Press.
Garin, Eugenio. 1965. *L'umanesimo italiano. Filosofia e vita civile nel Rinascimento*. Bari: Laterza.
Garsten, Bryan. 2006. *Saving Persuasion: A Defense of Rhetoric and Judgment*. Cambridge, MA: Harvard University Press.
———. 2007. The Elusiveness of Arendtian Judgment. *Social Research* 74 (4): 1071–1108.
———. 2011. The Rhetoric Revival in Political Theory. *Annual Review of Political Science* 14 (1): 159–180.
Garver, Eugene. 1994. *Aristotle's Rhetoric: An Art of Character*. Chicago/London: University of Chicago Press.
Gildenhard, Ingo. 2007. *Paideia Romana: Cicero's Tusculan Disputations*. Cambridge: Cambridge University Press.

———. 2010. *Creative Eloquence: The Construction of Reality in Cicero's Speeches.* Oxford/New York: Oxford University Press.
Giorcelli Bersani, Silvia. 2010. *L'auctoritas degli antichi. Hannah Arendt tra Grecia e Roma.* Florence: Le Monnier.
Gleason, Maud W. 2008. *Making Men: Sophists and Self-Presentation in Ancient Rome.* Princeton: Princeton University Press.
Gorgias. 1982. *Encomium of Helen.* Trans. D.M. Macdowell. Bristol: Bristol Classical Press.
Gowing, Alain M. 2013. Tully's Boat: Responses to Cicero in the Imperial Period. In *The Cambridge Companion to Cicero,* ed. Catherine Steel. Cambridge: Cambridge University Press.
Grassi, Ernesto. 1988. *La filosofia dell'umanesimo. Un problema epocale.* Naples: Tempi Moderni.
———. 1992. *Vico e l'umanesimo.* Milan: Guerini.
———. 1999. *Retorica come filosofia. La tradizione umanistica,* ed. Massimo Marassi. Naples: La città del sole.
Grilli, Alberto. 2002. Cicerone Tra Retorica E Filosofia. In *Interpretare Cicerone. Percorsi della critica contemporanea. Atti del II Symposium Ciceronianum Arpinas,* ed. Emanuele Narducci. Florence: Felice Le Monnier.
Grimaldi, William M.A. 1958. Rhetoric and the Philosophy of Aristotle. *The Classical Journal* 53 (8): 371–375.
———. 1972. *Studies in the Philosophy of Aristotle's Rhetoric.* Wiesbaden: Franz Steiner Verlag.
———. 1980. *Aristotle, Rhetoric I: A Commentary.* 2 vols. Vol. I, New York: Fordham University Press.
Gross, Alan G. 2001. The Conceptual Unity of Aristotle's Rhetoric. *Philosophy and Rhetoric* 34 (4): 275–291.
Gross, Daniel. 2005. Introduction. In *Heidegger and Rhetoric,* ed. Daniel M. Gross and Ansgar Kemmann. Albany: SUNY.
Gross, Daniel, and Ansgar Kemmann, eds. 2005. *Heidegger and Rhetoric.* Albany: SUNY.
Gross, Alan G., and Arthur E. Walzer. 2000. Preface. In *Rereading Aristotle's Rhetoric,* ed. Alan G. Gross and Arthur E. Walzer. Carbondale: Southern Illinois University Press.
Guignon, Charles B., and David R. Hiley. 2003. Introduction: Richard Rorty and Contemporary Philosophy. In *Richard Rorty,* ed. Charles B. Guignon and David R. Hiley. Cambridge/New York: Cambridge University Press.
Gunderson, Erik. 2000. *Staging Masculinity: The Rhetoric of Performance in the Roman World.* Ann Arbor: University of Michigan Press.
Habermas, Jürgen. 1985. Hannah Arendt: On the Concept of Power. In *Philosophical-Political Profiles.* Cambridge, MA: MIT Press.

———. 2000. Richard Rorty's Pragmatic Turn. In *Rorty and His Critics*, ed. Robert Brandom. Malden: Blackwell Publishers.
Halbertal, Moshe. 2007. *Concealment and Revelation: Esotericism in Jewish Thought and Its Philosophical Implications*. Princeton: Princeton University Press.
Halliwell, Stephen. 1994. Popular Morality, Philosophical Ethics, and the Rhetoric. In *Aristotle's Rhetoric: Philosophical Essays*, ed. David J. Furley and Alexander Nehamas. Princeton: Princeton University Press.
———. 1996. The Challenge of Rhetoric to Political and Ethical Theory in Aristotle. In *Essays on Aristotle's Rhetoric*, ed. Amâelie Rorty. Berkeley/London: University of California Press.
Hammer, Dean. 2002. Hannah Arendt and Roman Political Thought: The Practice of Theory. *Political Theory* 30 (1): 124–149.
Heidegger, Martin. 1997. *Plato's Sophist*. Bloomington: Indiana University Press.
———. 2009. *Basic Concepts of Aristotelian Philosophy*. Bloomington: Indiana University Press.
Honohan, Iseult. 2002. *Civic Republicanism*. London/New York: Routledge.
Ijsseling, Samuel. 1976. *Rhetoric and Philosophy in Conflict: An Historical Survey*. The Hague: Martinus Nijhoff.
Irwin, Terence H. 1992. Plato: The Intellectual Background. In *The Cambridge Companion to Plato*, ed. Richard Kraut. Cambridge: Cambridge University Press.
———. 1996. Ethics in the Rhetoric and in the Ethics. In *Essays on Aristotle's Rhetoric*, ed. Amâelie Rorty. Berkeley/London: University of California Press.
Isocrates. 1929a. Against the Sophists. Trans. George Norlin. In *Isocrates II*. London: William Heinemann.
———. 1929b. Antidosis. Trans. George Norlin. In *Isocrates II*. London: William Heinemann.
———. 1929c. Panathenaicus. Trans. George Norlin. In *Isocrates II*. London: William Heinemann.
———. 1945. Helen. Trans. Larue Van Hook. In *Isocrates III*. London: William Heinemann.
Jaeger, Werner. 1945. *Paideia: The Ideals of Greek Culture*. Vol. 3: *The Conflict of Cultural Ideas in the Age of Plato*. Oxford: Basil Blackwell.
Janssens, David. 2008. *Between Athens and Jerusalem: Philosophy, Prophecy, and Politics in Leo Strauss's Early Thought*. Albany: State University of New York Press.
Johnstone, Christopher Lyle. 2006. Sophistical Wisdom: Politikê Aretê and 'Logosophia'. *Philosophy and Rhetoric* 39 (4): 265–289.
Kant, Immanuel. 2007. *The Critique of Judgement*. Trans. James Creed Meredith. Oxford: Oxford University Press.

Kapust, Daniel. 2011a. Cicero on Decorum and the Morality of Rhetoric. *European Journal of Political Theory* 10 (1): 92–112.

———. 2011b. *Republicanism, Rhetoric, and Roman Political Thought: Sallust, Livy, and Tacitus*. New York: Cambridge University Press.

Kastely, James. 1991. In Defense of Plato's Gorgias. *PMLA* 106 (1): 96–109.

Kateb, George. 1984. *Hannah Arendt: Politics, Conscience, Evil*. Oxford: Robertson.

Katula, Richard A. 2003. Quintilian on the Art of Emotional Appeal. *Rhetoric Review* 22 (1): 5–15.

Kennedy, George. 1972. *The Art of Rhetoric in the Roman World, 300 B.C.–A.D. 300*. Princeton: Princeton University Press.

———. 1980. *Classical Rhetoric and Its Christian and Secular Tradition from Ancient to Modern Times*. Chapel Hill: University of North Carolina Press.

———. 1991. Prooemion. In *Aristotle: On Rhetoric: A Theory of Civic Discourse*, ed. George A. Kennedy. New York/Oxford: Oxford Universiy Press.

———. 1994. *A New History of Classical Rhetoric*. Princeton: Princeton University Press.

Kerferd, G.B. 1981. *The Sophistic Movement*. Cambridge: Cambridge University Press.

Kisiel, Theodore. 2005. Rhetorical Protopolitics in Heidegger and Arendt. In *Heidegger and Rhetoric*, ed. Daniel M. Gross and Ansgar Kemmann, 131–160. Albany: SUNY Press.

Kraus, Jiří. 2016. *Rhetoric in European Culture and Beyond*. Prague: Karolinum Press, Charles University.

Kristeller, Paul O. 1979. In *Renaissance Thought and Its Sources*, ed. Michael Mooney. New York: Columbia University Press.

———. 1988. Humanism. In *The Cambridge History of Renaissance Philosophy*, ed. Charles B. Schmitt, Quentin Skinner, Eckhard Kessler, and Jill Kraye. Cambridge: Cambridge University Press.

Laclau, Ernesto. 1996. Deconstruction, Pragmatism, Hegemony. In *Deconstruction and Pragmatism*, ed. Chantal Mouffe. London/New York: Routledge.

———. 2014. *The Rhetorical Foundations of Society*. London: Verso.

Lanham, Richard A. 1976. *The Motives of Eloquence: Literary Rhetoric in the Renaissance*. New Haven: Yale University Press.

Lederman, Shmuel. 2014. Agonism and Deliberation in Arendt. *Constellations* 21 (3): 327–337.

Leff, Michael. 1998. Cicero's Pro Murena and the Strong Case for Rhetoric. *Rhetoric & Public Affairs* 1 (1): 61–88.

Llanera, Tracy. 2016. Rethinking Nihilism: Rorty Vs. Taylor, Dreyfus and Kelly. *Philosophy and Social Criticism* 42 (9): 937–950.

Machiavelli, Niccolò. 2005. *The Prince*. Trans. Peter E. Bondanella. Oxford/New York: Oxford University Press.

Mahon, Áine. 2014. *The Ironist and the Romantic: Reading Richard Rorty and Stanley Cavell*. London: Bloomsbury.
Marshall, David L. 2010. The Origin and Character of Hannah Arendt's Theory of Judgment. *Political Theory* 38 (3): 367–393.
Martin, James. 2014. *Politics and Rhetoric: A Critical Introduction*. London: Routledge.
May, James M., and Jakob Wisse. 2001. Introduction. In *Cicero: On the Ideal Orator*. Trans. James M. May and Jakob Wisse. New York/Oxford: Oxford University Press.
McCarthy, Thomas. 1990. Private Irony and Public Decency: Richard Rorty's New Pragmatism. *Critical Inquiry* 16 (2): 355–370.
McClure, Kirstie M. 1997. The Odor of Judgment: Exemplarity, Propriety, and Politics in the Company of Hannah Arendt. In *Hannah Arendt and the Meaning of Politics*, ed. Craig J. Calhoun and John McGowan. Minneapolis: University of Minnesota Press.
McComiskey, Bruce. 1992. Disassembling Plato's Critique of Rhetoric in the Gorgias (447a–466a). *Rhetoric Review* 10 (2): 205–216.
McConnell, Sean. 2014. *Philosophical Life in Cicero's Letters*. Cambridge: Cambridge University Press.
McCoy, Marina. 2008. *Plato on the Rhetoric of Philosophers and Sophists*. Cambridge/New York: Cambridge University Press.
McGeer, Victoria, and Philip Pettit. 2009. Sticky Judgment and the Role of Rhetoric. In *Political Judgement: Essays for John Dunn*, ed. Richard Bourke and Raymond Geuss. Cambridge: Cambridge University Press.
Meier, Heinrich. 2006. *Leo Strauss and the Theologico-Political Problem*. Cambridge: Cambridge University Press.
———. 2014. How Strauss Became Strauss. In *Reorientation: Leo Strauss in the 1930s*, ed. Martin D. Yaffe and Richard S. Ruderman. New York: Palgrave Macmillan.
Melzer, Arthur. 2007. On the Pedagogical Motive for Esoteric Writing. *Journal of Politics* 69 (4): 1015–1031.
Meyer, Michel. 1999. *Histoire De la rhétorique des Grecs à nos jours*. Paris: Librairie générale française.
Michel, Alain. 2003. *Les rapports de la rhétorique et de la philosophie dans l'oeuvre de Cicéron. Recherches sur les fondements philosophiques de l'art de persuader*. Louvain/Paris: Peeters.
Mommsen, Theodor. 2010. *The History of Rome*. Vol. 4 – Part II. Cambridge: Cambridge University Press.
Mooney, Michael. 1985. *Vico in the Tradition of Rhetoric*. Princeton: Princeton University Press.
Morgan, Kathryn A. 2000. *Myth and Philosophy from the Pre-Socratics to Plato*. Cambridge/New York: Cambridge University Press.

Mouffe, Chantal. 1996. Deconstruction, Pragmatism and the Politics of Democracy. In *Deconstruction and Pragmatism*, ed. Chantal Mouffe. London: Routledge.

Murray, James S. 1988. Disputation, Deception, and Dialectic: Plato on the True Rhetoric (Phaedrus 261–266). *Philosophy and Rhetoric* 21 (4): 279–289.

Narducci, Emanuele. 1997. *Cicerone e l'eloquenza romana*. Bari: Laterza.

———. 2009. *Cicerone. La parola e la politica*. Rome: Laterza.

Nederman, Cary J. 1992. The Union of Wisdom and Eloquence Before the Renaissance: The Ciceronian Orator in Medieval Thought. *Journal of Medieval History* 18 (1): 75–95.

Nicgorski, Walter. 1984. Cicero's Paradoxes and His Idea of Utility. *Political Theory* 12 (4): 558–578.

———. 1991. Cicero's Focus: From the Best Regime to the Model Statesman. *Political Theory* 19 (2): 230–251.

———. 2012. *Cicero's Practical Philosophy*. Notre Dame: University of Notre Dame Press.

Nichols, Mary P. 1987. Aristotle's Defense of Rhetoric. *The Journal of Politics* 49 (3): 657–677.

Nietzsche, Friedrich. 1989. In *Friedrich Nietzsche on Rhetoric and Language*, ed. Carole Blair, Sander L. Gilman, and David J. Parent. Oxford: Oxford University Press.

Nightingale, Andrea W. 1995. *Genres in Dialogue: Plato and the Construct of Philosophy*. Cambridge: Cambridge University Press.

Norris, Andrew. 1996. Arendt, Kant, and the Politics of Common Sense. *Polity* 29 (2): 165–191.

Nussbaum, Martha. 1996. Aristotle on Emotions and Rational Persuasion. In *Essays on Aristotle's Rhetoric*, ed. Amâelie Rorty. Berkeley/London: University of California Press.

———. 2001. *The Fragility of Goodness: Luck and Ethics in Greek Tragedy and Philosophy*. Cambridge: Cambridge University Press.

Palonen, Kari. 1999. Contingency in Political Theory. *Redescriptions: Political Thought, Conceptual History and Feminist Theory* 3: 5–10.

———. 2003. *Quentin Skinner: History, Politics, Rhetoric*. Cambridge/Malden: Polity Press.

Pangle, Thomas. 1989. Introduction. In *The Rebirth of Classical Political Rationalism: An Introduction to the Thought of Leo Strauss*, ed. Thomas Pangle. Chicago: University of Chicago Press.

———. 2006. *Leo Strauss: An Introduction to His Thought and Intellectual Legacy*. Baltimore: Johns Hopkins University Press.

Passerin d'Entrèves, Maurizio. 1994. *The Political Philosophy of Hannah Arendt*. London/New York: Routledge.

Perelman, Chaïm, and Lucie Olbrechts-Tyteca. 1988. *Traité de l'argumentation. La nouvelle rhétorique.* Brussels: Editions de l'Université de Bruxelles.
Pippin, Robert. 2003. The Unavailability of the Ordinary: Strauss on the Philosophical Fate of Modernity. *Political Theory* 31 (3): 335–358.
Plato. 1985. *Euthydemus.* Trans. Rosamond Kent Sprague. Indianapolis: Bobbs-Merrill.
———. 1986. *Phaedrus.* Trans. Christopher Rowe. Warminster: Aris and Phillips.
———. 1987. *Gorgias.* Trans. Donald J. Zeyl. Indianapolis: Hackett.
———. 1990. *The Theaetetus of Plato.* Trans. Jane Levett. Indianapolis: Hackett.
———. 1991. *The Republic of Plato.* Trans. Allan D. Bloom. New York: Basic Books.
———. 1997. Apology. Trans. G.M.A. Grube. In *Plato: Complete Works*, ed. John M. Cooper. Indianapolis: Hackett.
Poulakos, John. 1995. *Sophistical Rhetoric in Classical Greece.* Columbia: University of South Carolina Press.
———. 2004. Rhetoric and Civic Education: From the Sophists to Isocrates. In *Isocrates and Civic Education*, ed. Takis Poulakos and David J. Depew. Austin: University of Texas Press.
Poulakos, Takis, and David J. Depew, eds. 2004. *Isocrates and Civic Education.* Austin: University of Texas Press.
Powell, Jonathan. 1994. The Rector Rei Publicae of Cicero's De Republica. *Scripta Classica Israelica* 13: 19–29.
Quintilian. 1963. *Institutio Oratoria.* Trans. Harold Edgeworth Butler. Cambridge, MA: Harvard University Press.
Remer, Gary. 1996. *Humanism and the Rhetoric of Toleration.* University Park: Pennsylvania State University Press.
Rice, Eugene F. 1958. *The Renaissance Idea of Wisdom.* Cambridge, MA: Harvard University Press.
Rogers, Melvin. 2004. Rorty's Straussianism; or, Irony against Democracy. *Contemporary Pragmatism* 1 (2): 95–121.
Roiz, Javier. 2003. *La recuperación del buen juicio.* Madrid: Foro Interno.
Rorty, Richard. 1979. *Philosophy and the Mirror of Nature.* Princeton: Princeton University Press.
———. 1982a. Philosophy as a Kind of Writing. In *Consequences of Pragmatism: Essays, 1972–1980.* Minneapolis: University of Minnesota Press.
———. 1982b. Pragmatism, Relativism, and Irrationalism. In *Consequences of Pragmatism: Essays, 1972–1980.* Minneapolis: University of Minnesota Press.
———. 1982c. Professionalized Philosophy and Transcendentalist Culture. In *Consequences of Pragmatism: Essays, 1972–1980.* Minneapolis: University of Minnesota Press.
———. 1991a. Introduction. In *Objectivity, Relativism, and Truth: Philosophical Papers, Volume 1.* Cambridge/New York: Cambridge University Press.

———. 1991b. Moral Identity and Private Autonomy: The Case of Foucault. In *Essays on Heidegger and Others: Philosophical Papers, Volume 2.* Cambridge/New York: Cambridge University Press.

———. 1991c. Philosophy as Science, as Metaphor, and as Politics. In *Objectivity, Relativism, and Truth: Philosophical Papers, Volume 1.* Cambridge/New York: Cambridge University Press.

———. 1991d. Postmodernist Bourgeois Liberalism. In *Objectivity, Relativism, and Truth: Philosophical Papers, Volume 1.* Cambridge/New York: Cambridge University Press.

———. 1991e. Priority of Democracy to Philosophy. In *Objectivity, Relativism, and Truth: Philosophical Papers, Volume 1.* Cambridge/New York: Cambridge University Press.

———. 1995. *Contingency, Irony, and Solidarity.* Cambridge/New York: Cambridge University Press.

Rorty, Amâelie, ed. 1996. *Essays on Aristotle's Rhetoric.* Berkeleyand/London: University of California Press.

Rorty, Richard. 1998a. Feminism and Pragmatism. In *Truth and Progress: Philosophical Papers, Volume 3.* Cambridge: Cambridge University Press.

———. 1998b. Human Rights, Rationality, and Sentimentality. In *Truth and Progress: Philosophical Papers, Volume 3.* Cambridge: Cambridge University Press.

———. 1999a. The Humanistic Intellectual: Eleven Theses. In *Philosophy and Social Hope.* London: Penguin Books.

———. 1999b. A Spectre Is Haunting the Intellectuals: Derrida on Marx. In *Philosophy and Social Hope.* London: Penguin Books.

———. 1999c. Trotsky and the Wild Orchids. In *Philosophy and Social Hope.* London: Penguin Books.

———. 1999d. Truth Without Correspondence to Reality. In *Philosophy and Social Hope.* London: Penguin Books.

———. 2000. Universality and Truth. In *Rorty and His Critics*, ed. Robert Brandom. Cambridge: Blackwell.

———. 2001. Response to Daniel Conway. In *Richard Rorty: Critical Dialogues*, ed. Matthew Festenstein and Simon Thompson. Cambridge/Malden: Polity Press.

———. 2007a. Cultural Politics and the Question of the Existence of God. In *Philosophy as Cultural Politics: Philosophical Papers, Volume 4.* Cambridge/New York: Cambridge University Press.

———. 2007b. Justice as a Larger Loyalty. In *Philosophy as Cultural Politics: Philosophical Papers, Volume 4.* Cambridge/New York: Cambridge University Press.

———. 2007c. Pragmatism as Romantic Polytheism. In *Philosophy as Cultural Politics: Philosophical Papers 4.* Cambridge/New York: Cambridge University Press.

———. 2010a. Intellectual Autobiography. In *The Philosophy of Richard Rorty*, ed. Randall E. Auxier and Lewis E. Hahn. Chicago: Open Court.
———. 2010b. Nineteenth-Century Idealism and Twentieth-Century Textualism. In *The Rorty Reader*, ed. Christopher J. Voparil and Richard J. Bernstein. Malden: Wiley-Blackwell.
———. 2010c. Philosophy as a Transitional Genre. In *The Rorty Reader*, ed. Christopher J. Voparil and Richard J. Bernstein. Malden: Wiley-Blackwell.
———. 2010d. Redemption from Egotism: James and Proust as Spiritual Exercises. In *The Rorty Reader*, ed. Christopher J. Voparil and Richard J. Bernstein. Malden: Wiley-Blackwell.
———. 2010e. Reply to J. B. Schneewind. In *The Philosophy of Richard Rorty*, ed. Randall E. Auxier and Lewis E. Hahn. Chicago: Open Court.
———. 2010f. Reply to Raymond D. Boisvert. In *The Philosophy of Richard Rorty*, ed. Randall E. Auxier and Lewis E. Hahn. Chicago: Open Court.
Rorty, Richard, and Eduardo Mendieta. 2006. *Take Care of Freedom and Truth Will Take Care of Itself: Interviews with Richard Rorty*. Stanford: Stanford University Press.
Rorty, Richard, Derek Nystrom, and Kent Puckett. 2002. *Against Bosses, Against Oligarchies: A Conversation with Richard Rorty*. Chicago: Prickly Paradigm.
Ross, William D. 1923. *Aristotle*. London: Methuen & Co.
Rubinelli, Sara. 2009. *Ars Topica: The Classical Technique of Constructing Arguments from Aristotle to Cicero*. New York: Springer.
Sachs, Joe. 2009. Introduction. In *Plato: Gorgias, and Aristotle: Rhetoric*. Trans. Joe Sachs. Newburyport: Focus.
Sallis, John. 1996. *Being and Logos: Reading the Platonic Dialogues*. Bloomington: Indiana University Press.
Scarano Ussani, Vincenzo. 2008. *Il retore e il potere*. Napoli: M. D'Auria.
Schiappa, Edward. 1999. *The Beginnings of Rhetorical Theory in Classical Greece*. New Haven/London: Yale University Press.
Seigel, Jerrold. 1968. *Rhetoric and Philosophy in Renaissance Humanism: The Union of Eloquence and Wisdom, Petrarch to Valla*. Princeton: Princeton University Press.
Shapiro, Ian, and Sonu Bedi. 2007. *Political Contingency: Studying the Unexpected, the Accidental, and the Unforeseen*. New York: New York University Press.
Skinner, Quentin. 1978. *The Foundations of Modern Political Thought: Vol. 1. The Renaissance*. Cambridge/New York: Cambridge University Press.
———. 1996. *Reason and Rhetoric in the Philosophy of Hobbes*. Cambridge: Cambridge University Press.
———. 2002. *Visions of Politics, Vol. 1: Regarding Method*. Cambridge: Cambridge University Press.
Skowronski, Krzysztof P. 2015. *Values, Valuations, and Axiological Norms in Richard Rorty's Neopragmatism*. Lanham: Lexington Books.

Smith, Steven B. 2006. *Reading Leo Strauss: Politics, Philosophy, Judaism.* Chicago: University of Chicago Press.

———. 2009. Philosophy as a Way of Life: The Case of Leo Strauss. *The Review of Politics* 71 (1): 37–53.

———. 2013. Leo Strauss's Discovery of the Theologico-Political Problem. *European Journal of Political Theory* 12 (4): 388–408.

Stauffer, Devin. 2006. *The Unity of Plato's Gorgias: Rhetoric, Justice, and the Philosophic Life.* Cambridge: Cambridge University Press.

Strauss, Leo. 1953. *Natural Right and History.* Chicago: University of Chicago Press.

———. 1963. Plato. In *History of Political Philosophy,* ed. Leo Strauss and Joseph Cropsey. Chicago: Rand McNally & Co.

———. 1964. *The City and Man.* Chicago: Rand McNally & Co.

———. 1975. *On Tyranny (Revised and Enlarged).* Ithaca: Cornell University Press.

———. 1978. *Thoughts on Machiavelli.* Chicago: University of Chicago Press.

———. 1982. *Spinoza's Critique of Religion.* New York: Schocken Books.

———. 1988a. How to Study Spinoza's Theologico-Political Treatise. In *Persecution and the Art of Writing.* Chicago: University of Chicago Press.

———. 1988b. Introduction. In *Persecution and the Art of Writing.* Chicago: University of Chicago Press.

———. 1988c. The Law of Reason in the Kuzari. In *Persecution and the Art of Writing.* Chicago: University of Chicago Press.

———. 1988d. The Literary Character of The Guide for the Perplexed. In *Persecution and the Art of Writing.* Chicago: University of Chicago Press.

———. 1988e. On the Basis of Hobbes's Political Philosophy. In *What Is Political Philosophy? And Other Studies.* Chicago: University of Chicago Press.

———. 1988f. On Classical Political Philosophy. In *What Is Political Philosophy? And Other Studies.* Chicago: University of Chicago Press.

———. 1988g. On a Forgotten Kind of Writing. In *What Is Political Philosophy? And Other Studies.* Chicago: University of Chicago Press.

———. 1988h. What Is Political Philosophy? In *What Is Political Philosophy? And Other Studies.* Chicago: University of Chicago Press.

———. 1989a. An Epilogue. In *Liberalism, Ancient and Modern.* Ithaca: Cornell University Press.

———. 1989b. Liberal Education and Responsibility. In *Liberalism, Ancient and Modern.* Ithaca: Cornell University Press.

———. 1989c. The Problem of Socrates: Five Lectures. In *The Rebirth of Classical Political Rationalism: An Introduction to the Thought of Leo Strauss,* ed. Thomas L. Pangle. Chicago: University of Chicago Press.

———. 1989d. Progress or Return? In *The Rebirth of Classical Political Rationalism,* ed. Thomas L. Pangle. Chicago: Chicago University Press.

———. 1989e. Social Social Science and Humanism. In *The Rebirth of Classical Political Rationalism: An Introduction to the Thought of Leo Strauss*, ed. Thomas Pangle. Chicago: University of Chicago Press.

———. 1989f. The Three Waves of Modernity. In *An Introduction to Political Philosophy: Ten Essays*, ed. Hilail Gildin. Detroit: Wayne State University Press.

———. 1995. *Philosophy and Law: Contributions to the Understanding of Maimonides and His Predecessors*. Albany: State University of New York.

———. 1996. The Origins of Political Science and the Problem of Socrates. *Interpretation: A Journal of Political Philosophy* 23 (2): 127–207.

———. 2001. La Crise De Notre Temps. In *Nihilisme Et Politique*. Paris: Payot & Rivages.

Stroup, Sarah C. 2007. Greek Rhetoric Meets Rome: Expansion, Resistance, and Acculturation. In *A Companion to Roman Rhetoric*, ed. William Dominik and Jon Hall. Malden: Blackwell.

Tacitus. 1958. A Dialogue on Oratory. Trans. W. Peterson and M. Winterbottom. In *Tacitus: Dialogus, Agricola, Germania*. Cambridge, MA: Harvard University Press.

Taminiaux, Jacques. 1992. *La fille de Thrace et le penseur professionnel, Arendt et Heidegger*. Paris: Payot.

———. 2000. Athens and Rome. In *The Cambridge Companion to Hannah Arendt*, ed. Dana Villa. Cambridge: Cambridge University Press.

Tanguay, Daniel. 2007. *Leo Strauss: An Intellectual Biography*. New Haven: Yale University Press.

Timmerman, David M., and Edward Schiappa. 2010. *Classical Greek Rhetorical Theory and the Disciplining of Discourse*. New York: Cambridge University Press.

Topper, Keith. 1995. Richard Rorty, Liberalism and the Politics of Redescription. *The American Political Science Review* 89 (4): 954–965.

Umphrey, Stuart. 1984. Why Politiké Philosophia? *Man and World* 17: 431–452.

Urbinati, Nadia. 2014. *Democracy Disfigured: Opinion, Truth, and the People*. Cambridge, MA: Harvard University Press.

Vallespín, Fernando. 2006. Hannah Arendt y el republicanismo. In *El siglo de Hannah Arendt*, ed. Manuel Cruz, 107–138. Barcelona: Paidós.

Velkley, Richard. 2008. On the Roots of Rationalism: Strauss' Natural Right and History as Response to Heidegger. *Review of Politics* 70: 245–259.

Vickers, Brian. 1988. *In Defence of Rhetoric*. Oxford: Clarendon Press.

Vico, Giambattista. 1948. *The New Science of Giambattista Vico*. Trans. Thomas Goddard Bergin and Max Harold Fisch. Ithaca: Cornell University Press.

———. 1953a. Autobiografia. In *Opere*, ed. Fausto Nicolini. Milan/Naples: Riccardo Ricciardi Editore.

———. 1953b. Il metodo degli studi del tempo nostro. In *Opere*, ed. Fausto Nicolini. Milan/Naples: Riccardo Ricciardi Editore.

———. 1953c. Prinicipi di Scienza Nuova. In *Opere*, ed. Fausto Nicolini. Milan/Naples: Riccardo Ricciardi Editore.

———. 1953d. Seconda Risposta. In *Opere*, ed. Fausto Nicolini. Milan/Naples: Riccardo Ricciardi.

———. 1990. *On the Study Methods of Our Time*. Trans. Elio Gianturco. Ithaca: Cornell University Press.

Villa, Dana. 1992. Beyond Good and Evil: Arendt, Nietzsche, and the Aestheticization of Political Action. *Political Theory* 2 (2): 274–308.

———. 1996. *Arendt and Heidegger: The Fate of the Political*. Princeton: Princeton University Press.

Viroli, Maurizio. 2002. *Republicanism*. New York: Hill and Wang.

Voegelin, Eric. 1990. Reason: The Classic Experience (1974). In *Pubblished Essays, 1966–1985*, ed. Ellis Sandoz. Baton Rouge/London: Louisiana State University Press.

———. 1998. In *History of Political Ideas, Vol. 6: Revolution and the New Science*, ed. Barry Cooper. Columbia: University of Missouri Press.

———. 2000a. The New Science of Politics (1952). In *Modernity without Restraint: The Political Religions, the New Science of Politics, and Science, Politics, and Gnosticism*, ed. Manfred Henningsen. Columbia/London: University of Missouri Press.

———. 2000b. In *Order and History, Volume III, Plato and Aristotle*, ed. Dante Germino. Columbia: University of Columbia Press.

Voparil, Christopher. 2006. *Richard Rorty: Politics and Vision*. Lanham: Rowman & Littlefield Publishers.

———. 2014. Taking Other Human Beings Seriously: Rorty's Ethics of Choice and Responsibility. *Contemporary Pragmatism* 11 (1): 83–102.

Wain, Kenneth. 1993. Strong Poets and Utopia: Rorty's Liberalism, Dewey and Democracy. *Political Studies* 41 (3): 394–407.

———. 1996. Might Is the Truth and It Shall Prevail? In *Essays on Aristotle's Rhetoric*, ed. Amâelie Rorty. Berkeley/London: University of California Press.

Wardy, Robert. 1996. *The Birth of Rhetoric: Gorgias, Plato, and Their Successors*. London/New York: Routledge.

Webb, Ruth. 1997. Imagination and the Arousal of Emotions in Greco-Roman Rhetoric. In *The Passions in Roman Thought and Literature*, ed. Susanna Morton Braund and Christopher Gill. Cambridge: Cambridge University Press.

White, Stephen K. 2009. *The Ethos of a Late-Modern Citizen*. Cambridge, MA: Harvard University Press.

Witt, Ronald G. 2000. *In the Footsteps of the Ancients: The Origins of Humanism from Lovato to Bruni*. Leiden/Boston: Brill.

Wolin, Sheldon S. 1990. Democracy in the Discourse of Postmodernism. *Social Research* 57 (1): 5–30.

Yack, Bernard. 1993. *The Problems of a Political Animal: Community, Justice, and Conflict in Aristotelian Political Thought*. Berkeley: University of California Press.

———. 2006. Rhetoric and Public Reasoning: An Aristotelian Understanding of Political Deliberation. *Political Theory* 34 (4): 417–438.

Yaffe, Martin D., and Richard S. Ruderman, eds. 2014. *Reorientation: Leo Strauss in the 1930s, Recovering Political Philosophy*. New York: Palgrave Macmillan.

Yar, Majid. 2000. From Actor to Spectator: Hannah Arendt's 'Two Theories' of Political Judgment. *Philosophy and Social Criticism* 26 (2): 1–27.

Young, Iris M. 2000. *Inclusion and Democracy*. Oxford/New York: Oxford University Press.

Yunis, Harvey. 1996. *Taming Democracy: Models of Political Rhetoric in Classical Athens*. Ithaca/London: Cornell University Press.

Zarecki, Jonathan. 2014. *Cicero's Ideal Statesman in Theory and Practice*. London/New York: Bloomsbury.

Zerilli, Linda M.G. 2005. 'We Feel Our Freedom': Imagination and Judgment in the Thought of Hannah Arendt. *Political Theory* 33 (2): 158–188.

Zuckert, Catherine, and Michael Zuckert. 2006. *The Truth About Leo Strauss*. Chicago/London: University of Chicago Press.

———. 2014. *Leo Strauss and the Problem of Political Philosophy*. Chicago: University of Chicago Press.

Index[1]

A
Action, *see* Practice, its relation with theory
Adams, John, 70n4, 117
Adeimantus, 23
Aesthetics, *see Critique of Judgment* (Kant, Immanuel)
Agonism
  Cicero and Arendt on politics, distinction and, 7, 152, 171–172, 186
Agreement, and disagreement, 157, 169–171
Alfarabi, 103
Alienation
  Arendt, Hannah on, 162, 171, 177n55
  Strauss, Leo on, 98
Antonius, 68, 79n62
Appearance
  as opposed to essence or reality, 20, 76n32, 128, 155–156
  See also Arendt, Hannah, on appearance and politics
Arendt, Hannah
  on appearance and politics, 118n29, 155–156, 168, 170
  compared with Cicero, 150, 160, 161, 171–172
  compared with the tradition of rhetoric, 151–152, 155–157
  and contingency, 157, 167
  on dialogue and persuasion, 154, 158, 164, 170–172
  on Eichmann, 165–169
  on the existential value of politics, 149–150, 162–163, 171–172
  on judgment, 153–154, 165–172
  on Kant's Critique of Judgment, 168–171
  on opinions and politics, 157–160, 164–165
  on Plato, 153–155, 157–161

---

[1] Note: Page numbers followed by "n" refers notes.

© The Author(s) 2018
G. Ballacci, *Political Theory between Philosophy and Rhetoric*, Rhetoric, Politics and Society,
https://doi.org/10.1057/978-1-349-95293-9

Arendt, Hannah (*cont.*)
  on politics, agonism, and distinction, 171–172
  on thinking and acting, 153, 165–167
  on the tradition of philosophy, 149–157, 166
  and transcendence, 164, 167, 171
  on truth and politics, 156–163
Aristotle
  compared with Plato, 28–31
  and contingency, 28–29
  on deliberation and rhetoric, 32–36
  on ethos and rhetoric, 30, 35–36
  on forensic rhetoric, 30
  on how to mediate the relation between the particular and the general through rhetoric, 32–38
  influence of his conception of rhetoric, 34
  on logos and rhetoric, 29–32, 36
  on pathos (passions and emotions) and rhetoric, 30, 32–37, 48n106, 48n109
  on practical reason and rhetoric, 31–38
  on rhetoric and demagoguery, 35, 36
  on rhetoric as an art, 29–31, 34–38
  on rhetoric as a virtue, 30, 36–38
Art
  Plato, on why rhetoric is not an, 21
  See also Aristotle, on rhetoric as an art
Athens, 14–17, 22, 79n62, 150
Aubenque, Pierre, 28
Audience, 15, 20–21, 25–37, 49n121, 50n123, 58–60, 67–68, 107, 108, 129, 184
Austin, John, L., 3
Autonomy, 7, 120, 132, 133, 137
Auxier, Randy, 124

B
Bacon, Francis, 90
Barthes, Roland, 7
Bernstein, Richard, 120, 124, 137
Best form of life, 22, 51, 63, 70n1
  philosophy as, 26, 100–101, 108–109
  rhetoric as, 5, 55, 64–65
  See also Vita activa and vita contemplativa
Biblical morality, 112n25
Bruni, Leonardo, 54, 62, 150
Brutus (Cicero), 178n66
Burke, Kenneth, 27

C
Caesar, Julius, 58, 76n34, 178n66
Callicles, 19–23, 42n43
Cato the Elder, 77n47
Cato the Younger, 59–60
Cicero
  on the combination between eloquence and wisdom (rhetoric and philosophy), 51–64
  compared with Arendt, 151, 160–161, 171–172
  on the domain of eloquence, 55–57
  on eloquence and self-cultivation, 52–55, 57, 63, 67–70
  his encyclopedic ideal of wisdom, 5, 52–56, 129
  his influence on the Renaissance humanists, 54
  on the ideal of the (perfect) orator, 4–5, 53, 57–58, 63, 131, 171–172, 185
  influence of Aristotle on, 55
  influence of Isocrates on, 55
  similarities with Plato, 55, 64
  on Socrates, 56
  and transcendence, 57
  on vita activa and vita contemplativa, 52–63

Common good, 31, 37, 63, 64, 88, 91, 95, 98, 107, 115n74, 117n93
Common sense, and commonsensical, 46n88, 60, 89, 98, 99, 106, 117n93, 122, 133–136, 170
Connolly, Joy, 68, 78n59, 83n99
Consensus, 123, 135, 145n85, 146n90
Consent, 132, 158, 164
Contingency, Irony, and Solidarity (Rorty, Richard), 120, 126, 131–133
Crassus, 56–63, 75n30, 79n60, 79n62
"Crisis in Culture, The" (Arendt, Hannah), 106
Critica, ars, 1
Critique of Judgment (Kant, Immanuel), 169, 179n75
Critique of religion
  enlightenment critique of religion, 93
Curtis, William, 123, 141n14

D
d'Alembert, Jean le Rond, 129
Decorum, 135–136
De inventione (Cicero), 55, 56, 74–75n28
De legibus (Cicero), 63
Deliberation
  Arendt on agonism, distinction and, 171–172
  See also Aristotle, on deliberation and rhetoric
Deliberative democracy
  rhetoric and the contemporary debate on, 1–3, 7, 27, 32–36
Demagoguery, *see* Aristotle, on rhetoric and demagoguery; Plato, his critique of rhetoric

De legibus (Cicero), 63
De officiis (Cicero), 56
De oratore (Cicero), 56–57, 60, 61, 63, 68, 71n6, 74n28, 78n55, 79n60, 79n62, 82n91, 136, 170
De re publica (Cicero), 63, 69, 78n55, 79n61
Descartes, René, 13
Dewey, John, 124, 132
Dialectic
  Aristotle on rhetoric and, 27–30, 32–34, 34n89, 159, 176n45
  Platonic and Socratic, 18
  Plato on rhetoric and, 24–26, 159
Diderot, Denis, 129
Dissimulation, 59
Distinction, *see* Arendt, Hannah, on politics, agonism, and distinction
Dogma, dogmatism, 21, 97, 103, 159
Doxa, *see* Opinion

E
Education, 5, 14–16, 29
  philosophical education (*paideia*), 65
  rhetorical and humanistic, 16, 54, 63–70, 75n32, 78n55, 80n67, 80n73, 82n88, 89, 129, 184
  Rorty's idea of sentimental education, 129
  Rorty on Bildung and education, 126, 130
Eichmann, Adolf, 165–169
Elitism
  in Arendt, 185
  in Cicero, 185
  in Rorty, 133–135, 141n13, 185
  in Strauss, 105, 107–109
  See also People, or the many as opposed to the few

Emancipation, 6, 39n10, 96–97
Emotions
  as opposed to reason, 5, 20, 34, 65
  Plato on, and persuasion, 20, 24–26
  Quintilian on, and persuasion, 66–68
  See also Aristotle, on pathos (passions and emotions) and rhetoric
Endoxa, 29
  See also Opinion
Enlightenment
  Strauss's critique of, 91–93
Enthymeme, 27–29, 34, 37
Esoteric/exoteric distinction, *see* Strauss, Leo, on the cause and functions of the esoteric/exoteric distinction and the 'art of writing'
Eternity
  Strauss on the 'modern oblivion of eternity,' 88, 90
  See also Immortality
Ethics, 95, 99, 169
  oratory and, in Cicero and Quintilian, 59, 62, 68, 72n13
  rhetoric and, in Aristotle, 27–30, 35
  See also Ethos
Ethos
  difference in the, between the philosopher and the sophist according to Plato, 19
  Quintilian on, 66–68, 131
  See also Aristotle, on ethos and rhetoric; Eunoia
Eunoia (goodwill)
  its relation to ethos and persuasion according to Aristotle, 35
Exempla
  in rhetoric, 61

F
Facts-values, distinction, 96
"Feminism and Pragmatism" (Rorty, Richard), 51, 146n90

Ferrara, Alessandro, 137
Fish, Stanley, 3–4
Flattery, *see* Aristotle, on rhetoric and demagoguery; Manipulation; Plato, his critique of rhetoric
Fontana, Benedetto, 108, 116n76
Forensic rhetoric, *see* Aristotle, on forensic rhetoric
Foucault, Michel, 122, 132
Fraser, Nancy, 121–122, 140n7
Freedom, 20, 28, 47n99, 92, 109, 125–126, 133, 157–164, 166, 167, 171, 117n54, 178n66
French Revolution, 127
Freud, Sigmund, 139

G
Gadamer, Hans-Georg, 9n5, 18, 27, 44n72, 45n86, 65, 126–127, 142n26
Garin, Eugenio, 143n40
Garsten, Bryan, 2, 7, 31–33, 75n31, 178n66
Garver, Eugene, 36, 47n98
Glaucon, 23
Goodwill, *see* Eunoia
Gorgias, 19–24, 39n10
Gorgias (Plato), 13, 19, 23–26, 41n39, 51, 57, 66, 156
Grassi, Ernesto, 62, 142n40
Greeks, 159, 171
  Roman prejudice against, 60–61

H
Habermas, Jürgen, 13, 132, 137
Hegel, Georg Wilhelm Friedrich, 13, 52, 70n4, 151, 173n5, 179n75
Heidegger, Martin, 8n5, 44n72, 52, 95–98, 114n49, 122, 132, 149–151, 173n9

Hermeneutics, 44n72, 108, 119, 124–127, 135, 142n26
Historicism
  in Rorty, 132
  Strauss's critique of, 95–100
Hobbes, Thomas, 13
  See also Strauss, Leo, on Machiavelli, Hobbes and the 'first wave' of modernity
Humanism
  and Arendt, 152, 155, 160, 171
  Cicero and the tradition of Renaissance humanism, 16–17, 55–56, 62, 72n12, 114n54, 87, 130, 152, 160, 184
  rhetorical-humanistic encyclopedic ideal of wisdom, 4–5, 52–57, 129
  See also Rorty, Richard, his humanism explained; his idea of literary culture and the humanistic intellectual

I
Imagination
  Arendt on, 170
  rhetoric and, 68, 79n60, 80n73, 129
  Rorty on, 123, 126–130, 135
Immortality
  Arendt on politics and immortality, 152
Institutio Oratoria (Quintilian), 4, 53–54, 61, 64–65, 80n72
Intellectual
  Strauss's view of, 108
  See also Rorty, Richard, his idea of literary culture and the humanistic intellectual
Interest
  general interest, 35
  particular, or self-interest, 13, 21, 31, 35–38, 59, 94, 107
  See also Aristotle, on how to mediate the relation between the particular and the general through rhetoric; Common good
In utramque partem, 157
Irony, see Rorty, Richard, on irony
Isocrates, 14–16, 39n13, 52–55, 156

J
Jaeger, Werner, 16
Judgment, see Arendt, Hannah, on judgment; Aristotle, on practical reason and rhetoric; Taste, Rorty on
Judicial rhetoric, see Forensic rhetoric

K
Kairos, 20
Kant, Immanuel, 13, 112n36, 149, 158, 162, 167–170
Knowledge, see Cicero, combination between eloquence and wisdom (rhetoric and philosophy); Opinion; Plato, his critique of rhetoric; Strauss, Leo, on the difference between ancient and modern philosophy/science; Wisdom

L
Laclau, Ernesto, 3, 137
Latini, Brunetto, 54, 150
Law
  Cicero's conception of, 59
  See also Nature (*physis*), in contrast to law (*nomos*)

Lessing, Gotthold, 158
Liberalism, 7, 95, 122–123, 131
Liberty, *see* Freedom
Lie, noble, 26, 89
Locke, John, 13
Logos, 14–18, 30, 32, 37, 55, 72n13

M
Machiavelli, Niccolò, 94, 112n30, 112n35, 150–151
Maimonides, Moses, 103
Manipulation, 89, 105, 128, 159, 185
  See also Aristotle, on rhetoric and demagoguery; Plato, his critique of rhetoric
Marx, Karl, 149, 177n55
Metaphor
  Quintilian on, 127
  Rorty on, 126
Mill, John S., 132
Modernity
  Arendt on the crisis of, 111
  rhetoric and, 5
  See also Strauss, Leo, on the difference between ancient and modern philosophy/science
Mommsen, Theodor, 70n4
Montesquieu, Baron Charles Louis de Secondat, 150–151, 163
Morality, 21, 31, 46n88, 46n89, 76n32, 95, 112n25
Music
  parallelism between rhetoric and, 41n38, 66, 80n72

N
Natality
  Arendt and the condition of, 7, 155–157
Natural Right and History (Strauss), 93, 113n40

Nature (*physis*), in contrast to law (*nomos*), 101
Nichomachean Ethics (Aristotle), 35–36
Nietzsche, Friedrich, 21–22, 52–54, 72n11, 95, 122, 132
Nihilism, 90–92, 96, 112n25

O
Olbrechts-Tyteca, Lucie, 47n99
On Revolution (Arendt), 150, 153
Opinion (or also doxa)
  rhetoric and its relation to knowledge, truth, and, 4, 20, 26–30, 46n88, 56–57
  See also Arendt, Hannah, on opinions and politics; Plato, his critique of rhetoric; Strauss, Leo, on the tension between philosophy and politics
Orator, *see* Cicero, on the ideal of the (perfect) orator
Orator (Cicero), 74n24, 74n28, 79n60

P
Paideia, *see* Education
Paradiastole, 67, 82n84, 127
Paradoxa Stoicorum (Cicero), 60
Passions, *see* Emotions
Pathos, *see* Aristotle, on pathos and rhetoric; Quintilian, on rhetoric and the emotions
People
  or the many as opposed to the few, 20, 29, 57, 89, 107, 133, 160
  See also Elitism
Perelman, Chaïm, 27, 45n86, 47n99
Pericles, 19, 79n62, 150
Petrarca, Francesco, 54, 62, 78n54
Phaedrus (Plato), 13, 19, 23–25, 42n43, 51, 68

"Philosophy and Politics" (Arendt), 157–159
Philosophy and the Mirror of Nature (Rorty), 125–126, 135, 142n26
Phronesis, 17, 35–37, 44n72, 46n91, 49n113, 68, 135–139, 167, 184
Pistis, 27
Plato
  Arendt's critique of, 153–160
  and Cicero, 47–49
  his critique of rhetoric, 17–24
  his version of rhetoric, 24–27
  parallelism between Rorty and, 133–134; and Strauss, 89, 107
  See also Dialectic, Platonic and Socratic; Quintilian, on Plato and rhetoric
Plurality
  Arendt and the condition of, 7, 155–157, 163–166, 171
Politics (Aristotle), 36
Polus, 19–23, 42n43, 42n45
Positivism, 2, 95, 98, 113n40
Practical reason, 3–4, 17, 28–32, 47n98, 59, 72n13, 131, 135–136, 146n92, 167–168
  See also Aristotle, on practical reason and rhetoric; Phronesis
Practice, its relation with theory
Strauss's account of the transformation in the understanding of this relation in modernity, 65–66
  See also Aristotle, on practical reason and rhetoric on practical reason and rhetoric; Cicero, on the combination between eloquence and wisdom; Practical reason; Phronesis
Pragmatism, 121–124
Praxis
  rhetoric as, 36n, 64
Pro Murena (Cicero), 59, 77n39

Prudence, 47n98, 80n68, 102–104, 116n76, 124, 172
Public-private relation, *see* Cicero, on eloquence and self-cultivation; on the ideal of the (perfect) orator; Rorty, Richard, his political liberalism; Rorty, Richard, on self-creation
Public realm, 150, 156, 158, 165, 171

Q
Quintilian
  Cicero's influence on, 53
  his critique of philosophy, 61
  on Plato and rhetoric, 61
  on rhetorical education and self-formation, 65–70
  on rhetoric and the emotions, 66–67

R
Reason
  as opposed to the emotions, 5, 20, 34, 66
  See also Revelation, Strauss's account of its relation to reason and philosophy
Redescription (*see* Paradiastole; Rorty, Richard, on the art of redescription)
Relativism, 96, 161
Religion
  Strauss's account of the modern critique of, 93
Renaissance, 16, 52, 56, 80n64, 87, 130
  See also Humanism
Republic (Plato), 21, 23, 41n29, 79n60

Republicanism, 2
  in Arendt, 151
  in Cicero, 17
  rhetoric as a republican art, 54
Res and verba, 62
Revelation
  Strauss's account of its relation to reason and philosophy, 89, 93, 103, 111n19
Rhetoric (Aristotle), 26–29, 32, 35, 44n70, 44n71, 45n83, 45n86, 47n98, 48n106, 68, 152, 174n12, 176n45, 179n75
Roman Republic, 53, 78n55, 150, 164
Romanticism
  Rorty and, 127
Rome, 59–62, 83n97, 151, 178n66
Rorty, Richard
  and contingency, 119, 132, 138
  criticisms of his distinction public/private, 120–122
  and Gadamer, 126–127
  his humanism explained, 124–130
  his idea of literary culture and of the humanistic intellectual, 128–129, 135
  his political liberalism, 122–123, 126, 131–132
  on human nature, 132, 137
  on irony, 121–123, 134–135
  and practical reason or *phronesis*, 135–139
  on redescription, 121, 125–130, 134–137
  and the rhetorical-humanistic tradition, 119, 128–129
  on self-creation (or self-fashioning), 124, 130–138
  on sentimental education, 129
  on truth and antifoundationalism, 125–128, 132, 137
  See also Elitism, in Rorty; Imagination, Rorty on; Plato, parallelism between Rorty and

S
Salutati, Coluccio, 52–54, 150
Scepticism, 7, 60, 80n64, 132, 157
Scientific Revolution, 90–91, 99
Self-creation, or also self-fashioning, self-cultivation, self-formation, *see* Cicero, on eloquence and self-cultivation; Quintilian, on rhetorical education and self-formation; Rorty, Richard, on self-creation
Skinner, Quentin, 2, 82n84
Socrates
  Arendt on, 149, 153, 157–158
  critique of, in Cicero's *De oratore*, 56
  Isocrates on, 16
  in Plato's *Gorgias*, 19–24
  in Plato's *Phaedrus*, 23–24
  Strauss on, 88, 91, 97, 100, 105–106
  See also Dialectic, Platonic and Socratic
Solidarity, 122, 124–137
Sophists, 4, 14–19, 39n10, 40n20, 125, 131, 161
Spinoza, Baruch, 93, 111n21
Stoicism, 60, 125
Strauss, Leo
  on the cause and functions of the esoteric/exoteric distinction and the 'art of writing', 103–104
  on classical political philosophy, 97–102, 107
  and contingency, 88–89, 101

on the difference between ancient and modern philosophy/science, 90–97
his conception of the 'art of writing' compared with Cicero, Quintilian, and Aristotle's understandings of rhetoric, 88, 105–107
on historicism and positivism, 95, 98
on Machiavelli, Hobbes and the 'first wave' of modernity, 91–93, 112n28, 112n30
on Maimonides and Alfarabi, 103
on Nietzsche, Heidegger and the 'third wave' of modernity, 95
on the tension between philosophy and politics, 87–88, 97, 100, 104–108
on the theological-political problem, 93
and transcendence, 88–90, 95–102
on Weber, 96–97, 113n40
Syllogism, rhetorical, *see* Enthymeme

T
Taste
  Rorty on, 161, 169
Techne, 24
  See also Art
Theological-political problem, *see* Strauss, Leo, on the theological-political problem
Theory, its relation with practice, *see* Practice, its relation with theory
Thrasymachus, 23
Topica, ars, 2–5, 7, 87, 129
Topoi, 1, 163
Topper, Keith, 131, 138
Totalitarianism, 165
"Trotsky and the Wild Orchids" (Rorty), 120, 125

Trust, 37, 49n121
Truth, *see* Arendt, Hannah, on truth and politics; Rorty, Richard, on truth and antifoundationalism
Tusculanae disputationes (Cicero), 74n24, 76n35, 161

V
Valla, Lorenzo, 54, 62, 78n54
Values-facts distinction, 96
Verba, and res, 62
Vico, Giambattista, 1, 2, 6, 52, 54, 62, 75n32, 80n72, 82n88, 87, 119, 123, 127, 129, 157, 162, 184
Violence, 32, 154, 159, 164, 171, 178n66
Viroli, Maurizio, 2
Vita activa and *vita contemplativa*, 5, 52–54, 57, 63, 70n1, 131, 150
Voegelin, Eric, 42n45, 92, 113n40

W
Weber, Max, 59, 96, 113n40
Wisdom, *see* Cicero, his encyclopedic ideal of wisdom; Cicero, on the combination between eloquence and wisdom (rhetoric and philosophy); Knowledge; Rorty, Richard, his idea of literary culture and the humanistic intellectual
Wittgenstein, Ludwig, 3
Wolin, Sheldon, 138

Y
Yeats, William Butler, 120

CPSIA information can be obtained
at www.ICGtesting.com
Printed in the USA
LVOW04*1343220118
563432LV00014BA/625/P

9 781349 952922